From Great Depression to Great Recession

The Elusive Quest for International Policy Cooperation

Editors
ATISH R. GHOSH and MAHVASH S. QURESHI

INTERNATIONAL MONETARY FUND

Cataloging-in-Publication Data
Joint Bank-Fund Library

Names: Ghosh, Atish R. | Qureshi, Mahvash Saeed. | International Monetary Fund.

Title: From great depression to great recession : the elusive quest for international cooperation / editors: Atish R. Ghosh and Mahvash S. Qureshi.

Description: Washington, DC : International Monetary Fund, 2017 | Includes bibliographical references and index.

Identifiers: ISBN 9781513514277 (paper)

Subjects: LCSH: Monetary policy--International cooperation | Economic policy--International cooperation | Recessions | Depressions—1929.

Classification: LCC HG230.3.F76 2017

ISBN 978-1-51351-427-7 (paper)
    978-1-47558-477-6 (PDF)
    978-1-47558-474-5 (ePub)
    978-1-47558-476-9 (Mobipocket)

Please send orders to:

International Monetary Fund, Publication Services
P.O. Box 92780, Washington, DC 20090, U.S.A.
Tel.: (202) 623-7430 Fax: (202) 623-7201
E-mail: publications@imf.org
Internet: www.elibrary.imf.org
www.imfbookstore.org

Contents

Foreword

In 2014, we celebrated the 70th anniversary of the Bretton Woods Conference; 2015 marked the 40th anniversary of the IMF's Second Amendment to the Articles of Agreement and the 30th anniversary of the Plaza Accord—one of the few instances of explicit international policy coordination. Against the backdrop of the world economy still limping out of the global financial crisis, these events provided the impetus for us to convene a symposium, *From Great Depression to Great Recession: The Elusive Quest for International Policy Cooperation*, at IMF headquarters in January 2015, with the aim of seeking insights from history about how to tackle present-day problems in international monetary relations.

The parallels with history are striking.

During the interwar period, for instance, deficit countries struggled to correct imbalances under the fixed exchange rates of the gold standard; there was an asymmetric burden of adjustment between deficit and surplus countries; and all countries, including those with surpluses, were reluctant to engage in fiscal expansion. The analogy may be inexact, but many of the same concerns are echoed in the European headlines of today. More disturbing is the parallel to the 1930s in the rise in populism, nationalism, and extremism—bred of unemployment, economic frustration, and social tension: the legacy of financial crisis.

The phrase "secular stagnation" was coined by Harvard economics professor Alvin Hansen in 1938; Larry Summers used it again in 2014 at the IMF's Fifteenth Jacques Polak Annual Research Conference. Nor are "currency wars," a coinage we hear all too often today, a new phenomenon—the interwar period was characterized by a disastrous combination of competitive devaluations, exchange restrictions, and trade barriers.

In addition, the 1930s saw a scramble for gold reserves, which imparted a huge deflationary bias to the world economy that was especially damaging to debtors. Today, the scramble may be less global, but emerging market economies have been relentless in accumulating reserves—partly to keep their currencies competitive in the face of current or capital account surpluses, partly as insurance against the volatility of private capital flows. Again, this trend may be imparting a deflationary bias at a time when the global economy can least afford it.

I believe these parallels—and there are plenty more—are not coincidental. They arise because the core challenges of the international monetary system are constant: (1) helping countries adjust without resorting to measures "destructive of national or international prosperity"; (2) promoting an equitable burden of adjustment between surplus and deficit countries; and (3) ensuring sufficient global liquidity—by which I mean the ability of solvent countries to finance deficits even during times of stress.

Though manifested in different ways, these challenges were present in the interwar period; they were present during the Bretton Woods years; they were present post–Bretton Woods; and they are surely with us today—indeed amplified by the growth in private capital flows, and rising global interconnectedness. That is why I believe that analyzing current issues through the prism of history can be instructive.

So what are the current issues with the international monetary system? Let me mention three—not necessarily with the expectation of getting immediate answers, but in the hope that they will foster discussion and debate.

The first, alluded to above, is the scramble for international reserves (and the underlying causes thereof). In 2007, emerging market economies held US$3.5 trillion reserves; as of the end of 2014, that has nearly doubled to US$6.6 trillion. There are various reasons to worry about this, but what is the solution? Should these countries be more symmetric in their foreign exchange intervention? Should they try to insulate themselves from volatile capital flows? Is this the time to fundamentally rethink the role of finance in national economies, and of cross-border banking flows in the world economy? How do we create credible alternatives to reserves accumulation for countries concerned about current or capital account shocks? What role can IMF contingent facilities such as the Flexible Credit Line (FCL) and Special Drawing Rights (SDRs) play? And do we need to revive ideas of sovereign bankruptcy mechanisms, and the interplay between official and private creditors?

The second issue is the risk of secular stagnation—a prolonged period of slow growth of the world economy because of low investment and deficient demand. Despite some positive signs in the US economy, and lower oil prices, the news from the rest of the world is far from reassuring. How can the global economy pull itself up by its bootstraps? Is this a time for paying down public debt? Or for embarking on much-needed public infrastructure investments? What role can emerging markets, including China, play in acting as a locomotive for the world economy without jeopardizing their own financial stability?

The third concern is that a world of secular stagnation will become a world of currency wars. With monetary policy at its limits, and fiscal policy hobbled by high debt and political constraints, it becomes very tempting to boost aggregate demand through currency depreciation. Personally, I do not believe the world is engaged in currency wars yet, but as a multilateral institution, we at the IMF need to consider very carefully how we think of foreign exchange intervention versus (conventional or unconventional) monetary policy when the impact on the exchange rate and capital flows—and hence on trading partners—may be much the same. Indeed, one may well ask whether, in a world of floating exchange rates, there is any meaningful distinction between monetary and exchange rate policies. Do we need to consider spillovers through the capital account as rigorously as those through the current account? More broadly, should we devise some mechanism for ensuring more equitable burdens of adjustment between surplus and deficit countries?

All this brings me to the issue of international policy coordination. The irony about coordination is the unanimity on the subject. Economists are unanimous that, provided there are fewer instruments than targets (which is surely the case these days), coordination will be beneficial; policymakers are equally unanimous that, whatever the merits of *others* coordinating, they themselves want no part of it. Why is this? Is it simply a lack of understanding that coordination is not about doing your neighbor a favor—it is about self-interested, but mutually beneficial, trades of policies? Or do the obstacles run deeper? And if so, what can be done about it?

Is there a useful role for some type of "neutral assessor" that can identify mutually beneficial coordinated packages and, most importantly, provide unbiased analysis of transmission effects? Without presuming to take on this role, the IMF has in recent years been increasing its analytical work on cross-border spillovers. An alternative, although potentially complementary, approach is to try to devise "rules of the road"—akin to those under Bretton Woods. Perhaps building on the IMF's Integrated Surveillance Decision, we can think of rules that circumscribe policies that have significant adverse spillovers through either the current account (currency manipulation; unfair trade practices) or the capital account (volatile capital flows). A related question is whether we need to devise some rules of the road concerning spillovers of what are usually termed domestic policies (monetary and fiscal policies) paralleling the Articles' strictures against exchange rate manipulation.

Whatever the approach, we need to find solutions. As Harry Dexter White, one of the principal architects of Bretton Woods, argued: "rich and powerful countries can safely and easily ignore the interests of poorer or weaker neighbors or competitors for long periods of time, but by doing so they imperil the future and reduce the potentiality of their own level of prosperity." The lesson, he concluded, is that "prosperous neighbors are the best neighbors; that a higher standard of living in one country begets higher standards in others; and that a high level of trade and business is most easily attained when generously and widely shared."

What has changed in the intervening 70 years is the composition of the "rich and powerful countries." At Bretton Woods, it was basically the United States and the United Kingdom; by Plaza, it was the G7; now with the rising importance of emerging market economies, we are talking G20. Today, more than ever, we need multilateralism. The IMF quota increase that a supermajority of the membership recently approved, and that recognizes the reality of the dynamics of the world economy, is a crucial accomplishment: we need to build on it with bold, innovative thinking to strengthen the international monetary system.

In closing the Bretton Woods Conference, US Secretary of the Treasury Henry Morgenthau remarked that, while the monetary agreement may seem mysterious and obscure to the general public, it lay at the most elementary "bread-and-butter realities" of their daily lives, and constituted a first step through which "the nations of the world will be able to help one another in economic development to their mutual advantage and for the enrichment of all."

The issues presented and discussed at the symposium by a distinguished group of historians, academics, and former policymakers lie at the very heart of the IMF's mandate. Perhaps more importantly, they also define the bread-and-butter realities of the lives of billions around the world. This collection of papers from that symposium extends the exchange of insights and perspectives—including on some of the issues I have raised here—and provides new grist for analysis and debate. I would like to extend my thanks to the contributors to this volume for sharing their expertise and views in drawing lessons from history for today's problems confronting the international monetary system.

David Lipton
First Deputy Managing Director, IMF

Preface

This volume is a collection of papers presented at a symposium on the history, functioning, and challenges of the international monetary system, organized by the IMF at its headquarters in Washington, DC, on January 23, 2015. The symposium, titled *From Great Depression to Great Recession: The Elusive Quest for International Policy Cooperation*, brought together eminent scholars and policymakers who provided in valuable insights into the origins and evolution of the present-day international monetary system, debated its performance, and exchanged views on the need for reform, and the prospects for international policy cooperation going forward.

The volume is divided into four parts—each corresponding to a session of the symposium, and including chapters that are based on the presentations made in that particular session. In addition, the first chapter provides a broad overview of the international monetary system over the past century, discussing the major events and challenges that shaped it, while the final chapter summarizes the key takeaways from the discussions during the symposium on fostering international policy cooperation. It must be reiterated, however, that the views expressed in this volume are those of the individual authors and do not necessarily represent those of the institutions with which they are affiliated.

Both the symposium and this volume were made possible because of the hard work of many people to whom we owe a debt of gratitude. Our special thanks to Chifundo Moya for his relentless and invaluable assistance in organizing the symposium, as well as in the publication of this volume; to Eun Sun Jang and colleagues in the IMF's Multimedia Services and Corporate Services and Facilities Department for assistance with the symposium logistics; to Joanne Creary, Michael Harrup, Patricia Loo, and Rumit Pancholi for their diligent and skillful assistance in the publication of this volume; and to all the contributors for enthusiastically participating in the symposium and enriching the discussions, and for patiently cooperating in the production of this volume.

Atish R. Ghosh
Mahvash S. Qureshi

Abbreviations

BIS	Bank for International Settlements
BRICS	Brazil, Russia, India, China, and South Africa
CAC	collective action clause
CRA	Contingent Reserve Arrangement
ECB	European Central Bank
EEC	European Economic Community
EMS	European Monetary System
ERM	Exchange Rate Mechanism
EU	European Union
FCL	Flexible Credit Line
G5	Group of Five
G7	Group of Seven
G10	Group of Ten
G20	Group of Twenty
IBRD	International Bank for Reconstruction and Development
LSAP	large-scale asset purchase
OCA	optimum currency area
OECD	Organisation for Economic Co-operation and Development
OPEC	Organization of the Petroleum Exporting Countries
QE	quantitative easing
SDR	Special Drawing Right
WTO	World Trade Organization

Contributors

Michael D. Bordo is a Board of Governors Professor of Economics and Director of the Center for Monetary and Financial History at Rutgers University. Previously, he held academic positions at the University of South Carolina and Carleton University. He has also been a visiting professor at the University of California, Los Angeles; Carnegie Mellon University; Princeton University; Harvard University; and Cambridge University. He is currently a Distinguished Visiting Fellow at the Hoover Institution at Stanford University and a Research Associate at the National Bureau of Economic Research. He has also been a visiting scholar at the IMF; the Federal Reserve Banks of St. Louis, Cleveland, and Dallas; the Federal Reserve Board of Governors; the Bank of Canada; the Bank of England; and the Bank for International Settlements. He holds a BA from McGill University, an MSc from the London School of Economics, and a PhD from the University of Chicago. His publications include many articles in leading journals and 15 books on monetary economics and monetary history. He is the editor of a book series, Studies in Macroeconomic History, for Cambridge University Press.

James M. Boughton is a Senior Fellow at the Centre for International Governance Innovation. From 1992 to 2012, he was Historian of the IMF, where during 2001–10, he also served as Assistant Director in the Strategy, Policy, and Review Department. From 1981 until he was named Historian, he held various positions in the IMF Research Department. Dr. Boughton holds a PhD in Economics from Duke University, and before joining the IMF staff, he was Professor of Economics at Indiana University and had served as an Economist at the Organisation for Economic Co-operation and Development. He has written two volumes of IMF history: *Silent Revolution: The International Monetary Fund 1979–1989* (2001) and *Tearing Down Walls: The International Monetary Fund 1990–1999* (2012). His publications also include a textbook on money and banking, a book on the US federal funds market, several books that he edited or coedited, and articles in professional journals on international finance, monetary theory and policy, international policy coordination, and the history of economic thought.

Richard N. Cooper is Maurits C. Boas Professor of International Economics at Harvard University. He is a member of the Trilateral Commission, the Council on Foreign Relations, and the Brookings Panel on Economic Activity. Educated at the London School of Economics and Harvard University, he has served in the US federal government as Chairman of the National Intelligence Council; Under Secretary of State for Economic Affairs; Deputy Assistant Secretary of State for International Monetary Affairs; and Senior Staff Economist at the Council of Economic Advisers. He was also Chairman of the Federal Reserve Bank of Boston and Vice Chairman of the Global Development Network (2001–07). His most recent books include *Boom, Crisis, and Adjustment* (1993); *Macroeconomic*

Management in Korea, 1970–1990 (1994); *Environment and Resource Policies for the World Economy* (1994); *What the Future Holds* (2002); and *Rebalancing the Global Economy* (2010).

Atish R. Ghosh is the Historian of the IMF. Before his current position, he was the Assistant Director, and Chief, Systemic Issues Division, in the Research Department of the IMF. Before joining the IMF, he was an Assistant Professor of Economics and International Affairs at Princeton University. He holds a BA, MA, and PhD in Economics from Harvard University. He also holds an MSc in Development Economics from Oxford University. He has published numerous articles on international economics, finance, and public policy in leading academic journals, as well as four books: *Economic Cooperation in an Uncertain World* (1994); *Exchange Rate Regimes: Choices and Consequences* (2003); *Currency Boards in Retrospect and Prospect* (2008); and *Nineteenth Street, NW* (2010), a novel about a global financial crash.

Eric Helleiner is Faculty of Arts Chair of International Political Economy at the University of Waterloo. Since receiving a PhD from the London School of Economics, he has won the Trudeau Foundation Fellows Prize, the Donner Book Prize, and the Canadian Political Science Association Prize in International Relations, and he is currently coeditor of the book series Cornell Studies in Money. Among his numerous books are *Forgotten Foundations of Bretton Woods* (2014); *The Status Quo Crisis: Global Financial Governance after the 2008 Meltdown* (2014); and (as coeditor) *The Great Wall of Money: Power and Politics in China's International Monetary Relations* (2014).

Harold James is Professor of History and International Affairs and the Claude and Lore Kelly Professor of European Studies at Princeton University, and Historian of the IMF. Educated at Cambridge University, he has written numerous books, including *International Monetary Cooperation since Bretton Woods* (1996) and, more recently, *The End of Globalization: Lessons from the Great Depression* (2001); *Europe Reborn: A History 1914–2000* (2003); and *Making the European Monetary Union* (2012). In 2004 he was awarded the Helmut Schmidt Prize for Economic History, and in 2005 the Ludwig Erhard Prize for writing about economics. He received an honorary PhD from the University of Lucerne.

Robert N. McCauley is a Senior Advisor in the Monetary and Economic Department of the Bank for International Settlements (BIS). Before October 2008 he served as BIS Chief Representative for Asia and the Pacific in Hong Kong Special Administrative Region. Before joining BIS, he was with the Federal Reserve Bank of New York for 13 years, leaving as head of the International Finance Department. He taught at the University of Chicago's Graduate School of Business in 1992. He is a member of the Scientific Council of the Fondation Banque de France.

Emmanuel Mourlon-Druol is a Lecturer in the Adam Smith Business School, University of Glasgow, a Non-Resident Fellow at Bruegel, and a Visiting Professor at the Université Libre de Bruxelles. Educated at the European University Institute, he was previously a Pinto Postdoctoral Fellow at London School of Economics. He is the author of *A Europe Made of Money: The Emergence of the*

European Monetary System (2012), and coeditor of *International Summitry and Global Governance: The Rise of the European Council and the G7, 1974–1991* (2014) with Federico Romero. He has published in journals including *Business History, Journal of Common Market Studies*, and *West European Politics*.

Maurice Obstfeld is the Economic Counsellor and Director of the Research Department at the IMF. He is on leave from the University of California, Berkeley, where he is the Class of 1958 Professor of Economics and a former Chair of the Department of Economics. He joined Berkeley's faculty in 1989, following appointments at Columbia University (1979–86) and the University of Pennsylvania (1986–89). From July 2014 to August 2015, he served as a member of President Obama's Council of Economic Advisers. He has previously served as an honorary advisor to the Bank of Japan's Institute of Monetary and Economic Studies. He is a Fellow of the Econometric Society and the American Academy of Arts and Sciences. He has served on the Executive Committee and as Vice President of the American Economic Association. He is the author of *International Economics: Theory and Policy* (with Paul Krugman and Marc Melitz, 2011); *Foundations of International Macroeconomics* (with Kenneth Rogoff, 1996); *Global Capital Markets: Integration, Crisis, and Growth* (with Alan Taylor, 2004); and of numerous articles in leading academic journals. He holds a PhD in economics from the Massachusetts Institute of Technology.

José Antonio Ocampo is a Professor at Columbia University and Chair of the UN Economic and Social Council Committee for Development Policy. He has been UN Under-Secretary-General for Economic and Social Affairs; Executive Secretary of the Economic Commission for Latin America and the Caribbean; and Minister of Finance, Minister of Agriculture, and Director of the National Planning Office of Colombia. His most recent books include *Global Governance and Development* (2016); *The Economic Development of Latin America since Independence*, with Luis Bértola (2012); *Development Cooperation in Times of Crisis*, edited with José Antonio Alonso (2012); and the *Oxford Handbook of Latin American Economics*, edited with Jaime Ros (2011).

Mahvash S. Qureshi is the Deputy Chief of the Systemic Issues Division in the Research Department of the IMF. Before joining the IMF, she held assignments at the Overseas Development Institute, United Nations University— World Institute for Development Economics Research, University of Cambridge, and the Sustainable Development Policy Institute. She has published extensively on international macroeconomic policy issues in scholarly journals and has coauthored and coedited several books, including *Taming the Tide: A Policy Maker's Vademecum for Managing Capital Flows* (forthcoming); *Capital Controls* (2015); and *Working Smart and Small: The Role of Knowledge-Based and Service Industries in Growth Strategies for Small States* (2008). She holds a PhD and MPhil in economics from University of Cambridge, Trinity College.

Catherine R. Schenk is a Professor of International Economic History at the University of Glasgow. She holds a PhD from the London School of Economics and has held numerous academic posts, including at Royal Holloway, University of London, Victoria University of Wellington, and visiting positions at the IMF and the Hong Kong Monetary Authority, as well as the University of Hong Kong and Nottingham Business School campus in Seminyeh, Malaysia. She is an Associate Fellow in the international economics department at Chatham House in London, and the author of several books, including *International Economic Relations since 1945* (2011) and *The Decline of Sterling: Managing the Retreat of an International Currency* (2010). She is coeditor of the *Oxford Handbook of Banking and Financial History* (2016). Her current research interests include the development of international banking regulation since the 1960s and the causes of the sovereign debt crisis of the 1980s.

Benn Steil is a Senior Fellow and the Director of International Economics at the Council on Foreign Relations in New York. He is also the Founding Editor of *International Finance* and lead writer of the Council's *Geo-Graphics* economics blog. His latest book, *The Battle of Bretton Woods: John Maynard Keynes, Harry Dexter White, and the Making of a New World Order*, won the 2013 Spear's Book Award in Financial History, took third prize in the Council on Foreign Relations' 2014 Arthur Ross Book Award competition, was shortlisted for the 2014 Lionel Gelber Prize, and was listed in Bloomberg's Best Books of 2013, a poll of global policymakers and chief executive officers.

Alexander K. Swoboda is a Professor of International Economics Emeritus and former Director of the Graduate Institute of International and Development Studies, Geneva. The Founding Director of the International Center for Monetary and Banking Studies, his academic appointments have included the University of Geneva, the University of Chicago's Graduate School of Business, the London School of Economics, the University of Lausanne, and Harvard University. He was a Senior Policy Advisor in the Research Department of the IMF (1998–2000) and member of the Council of the Swiss National Bank (1997–2009). He has published widely on international monetary, macroeconomic, and financial issues and holds a PhD from Yale University.

Edwin M. Truman is a nonresident Senior Fellow at the Peterson Institute for International Economics. He served as Assistant Secretary of the US Treasury for International Affairs from 1998 to 2001 and as Counselor to the Secretary in 2009. He directed the Division of International Finance of the Board of Governors of the Federal Reserve System from 1977 to 1998. He has taught at Yale University, Amherst College, and Williams College. He is the author, coauthor, and editor of numerous books and articles, including *Sovereign Wealth Funds: Threat or Salvation?* (2010); *Reforming the IMF for the 21st Century* (2006); *A Strategy for IMF Reform* (2006); *Chasing Dirty Money: The Fight against Money Laundering* (2004); and *Inflation Targeting in the World Economy* (2003).

Paul A. Volcker worked in the US federal government for nearly 30 years, culminating in two terms as Chairman of the Board of Governors of the Federal Reserve System from 1979 to 1987. For 10 years, he served as Chairman of Wolfensohn & Co. and as Professor Emeritus of International Economic Policy at Princeton University. He has chaired a committee to determine existing assets in Swiss banks of victims of Nazi persecution, served as Chairman of the Board of Trustees of the International Accounting Standards Committee, chaired an inquiry into the United Nations Oil-for-Food Programme, and chaired a panel of experts to review the operations of the Department of Institutional Integrity of the World Bank. From 2008 to 2011 he served as Chairman of the President's Economic Recovery Advisory Board. Educated at Princeton University, Harvard University, and the London School of Economics, he launched the Volcker Alliance in 2013 to address the challenge of effective execution of public policies and to help rebuild trust in government.

CHAPTER 1

From Great Depression to Great Recession: An Overview

ATISH R. GHOSH AND MAHVASH S. QURESHI

The global financial crisis and the ensuing Great Recession raised concerns about adjustment fatigue, deflation, currency wars, and secular stagnation that presented a sense of déjà vu: similar concerns had been raised at the time of the Great Depression and at the end of World War II. As with earlier crises, these concerns prompted calls for greater international policy cooperation and "rules of the game"—both to achieve a sustainable recovery from the crisis and to prevent future crisis as well. Against this background, in early 2015 the IMF convened a symposium of eminent scholars to discuss how history can inform current debates about the functioning and challenges of the international monetary system. Accordingly, the papers presented at the symposium—compiled in this volume—brought together historical and present-day perspectives on the problems of the international monetary system, insights on the origin and evolution of the current international monetary system, and views on the prospects for a more cooperative system in the future.

This introductory chapter sets the stage for the other chapters in this volume by giving a broad overview of the performance of the international monetary system over the past century, highlighting the key events and challenges that shaped it. The underlying premise of this chapter—indeed, of the entire volume—is that, although the world has experienced profound economic, social, and technological changes during this period, the core challenges to the international monetary system remain largely the same. What are these challenges? First, allowing countries with current account deficits to adjust to payments imbalances without—to put it in the parlance of the IMF's Articles of Agreement—"resorting to measures destructive of national or international prosperity"; second, ensuring an equitable burden of adjustment between surplus and deficit countries; and third, regulating global liquidity to promote the (noninflationary) growth of world trade and incomes. Although the context in which these challenges have manifested has obviously evolved—not least with the rise of private cross-border capital flows—they retain sufficient commonality over time to allow us to look into the experience of the past to get valuable insights for the problems of the present.[1]

The remainder of this chapter is organized into three sections: the next section provides a historical overview that recalls the performance of the world economy during the late nineteenth century and describes the main events during the interwar period and how these shaped the discussions at Bretton Woods that gave rise to the IMF. It also examines the challenges to the international monetary system in the Bretton Woods era, the advent of floating exchange rates, and the experiments in international policy coordination, before finally turning to the years before the global financial crisis, when the world economy was booming and the IMF seemed to be in the doldrums. The following section draws some parallels between the challenges of the past and issues of the present. The final section presents a brief summary of the chapters that follow.

A SNAPSHOT OF HISTORY

The Gold Standard

The latter part of the nineteenth century and the first decades of the twentieth are often called the golden era of globalization—and with good reason. During these years, world trade grew at an average rate of 6 percent per year, and the major capital exporters—France, Germany, and Great Britain—lent as much as 5 percent to 10 percent of their GDP each year, mainly in the form of long-term capital, to the developing and emerging market economies of the day (Figure 1.1). Expansion of international trade and investment, in turn, helped fuel historically unprecedented increases in output and living standards (Figure 1.2, panel 1).

Underpinning these cross-border movements were major technological advances in transport (railways, shipping, refrigeration) and communications (telegraph, telephone)—together with the gold standard, which provided long-term exchange rate stability and eliminated currency risk. According to Hume's price-specie flow mechanism, payments imbalances under a gold standard are self-adjusting: in surplus countries, unsterilized inflows (from the current or capital account) expand the money supply, raising prices and eroding competitiveness, thus serving to narrow

---

[1]The rise of cross-border capital flows has transformed the challenges facing the international monetary system in two key ways. First, although net capital flows contribute to global liquidity—financing countries with current account deficits—they also increase the need for country insurance and the public provision of liquidity because, in times of stress, far from being a source of financing, capital flows force deficit countries to run even larger surpluses. In this respect, gross flows (more precisely, the gross stock of liabilities into which they accumulate) may result in balance sheet vulnerabilities whose unwinding generally precipitates net capital outflows. This implies an intersection between the international monetary system, which is mainly concerned with net flows, and the global financial system, which is predominantly concerned with gross positions. Second, gross flows break the link between surplus and capital-source countries, and deficit and capital-recipient countries (for example, the United States is a deficit country but has been a source of large capital flows in recent years, whereas the converse has been true for China). For this reason, it is perhaps now more appropriate to view the challenges of the international monetary system in terms of deficit and capital-recipient (and surplus and capital-source) countries separately.

Figure 1.1. Net Capital Flows, 1880–1913
(Percent of GDP)

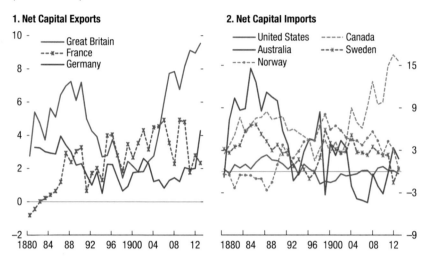

Sources: Authors' estimates based on Bloomfield 1968 and International Historical Statistics.

Figure 1.2. G7: Macroeconomic Performance, 1880–1913

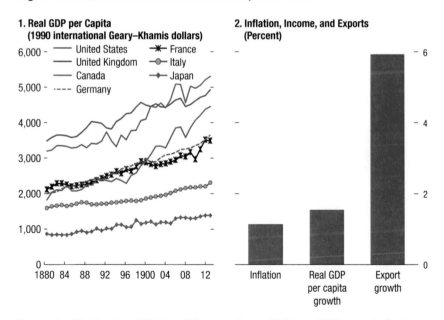

Sources: New Maddison Project Database (Bolt and van Zanden 2014) for real GDP per capita; Bordo 1993 for inflation and real GDP per capita growth; and UNSTATS for nominal export growth.
Note: Mean growth rate for inflation and real GDP per capita in panel 2 is calculated as the time coefficient from a regression of the natural logarithm of the variable on a constant and a time trend. Export growth is computed over 1900–13.

the surplus; in deficit countries, the opposite happens. Although it is doubtful that the gold standard of that time functioned exactly like this in practice, there is evidence that at least the core central banks (most notably, the Bank of England) generally played by the "rules of the game" instead of trying to vitiate the adjustment process by sterilizing inflows and outflows.[2] Moreover, with central banks mostly focused on maintaining the exchange rate parity, the system enjoyed a high degree of credibility that, in turn, resulted in largely stabilizing short-term capital flows.[3] This is not to imply that capital flows were not volatile: as shown in Figure 1.1, amid various panics and crises (together with developments in source countries), there were large fluctuations even in long-term capital flows. Nevertheless, it seems plausible that the stability of the international monetary system—in the form of the gold standard—contributed both to the resilience of the world economy and to its impressive performance over this period (Figure 1.2, panel 2).

The Interwar Period

During World War I, normal trade and capital flows among the major world economies largely ceased, and the gold standard was suspended de facto.[4] Following the cessation of hostilities, it was natural that private and central bankers of the leading nations (with the notable exception of the Soviet Union) should seek to restore the liberal—and for the great banking houses, highly profitable—pre–World War I international monetary order. As the 1922 Genoa Economic and Monetary Conference, held to discuss and resolve the problems in the postwar economic and financial reconstruction of Europe, resolved, "all artificial control of exchange … is futile and mischievous and should be abolished at the earliest possible date."[5]

Wartime dislocation, currency misalignments, and deficit financing of reparations and reconstruction costs delayed this process, especially in Europe.[6] But

---

[2]See, for example, Bordo 2007.

[3]In effect, central banks had only one target (maintaining the gold value of the currency), so with one instrument (the discount rate), they could achieve that target perfectly. As Eichengreen (1992) observes, under a gold standard, the gold points (deviations from the parity at which it becomes profitable to import or export gold) define a target zone, and in a fully credible target zone, speculative capital flows will be stabilizing.

[4]The United States maintained the gold standard almost throughout World War I, suspending convertibility only twice (once in July 1914 at the onset of the war, and then in 1917 as it entered the war; Crabbe 1989).

[5]Resolution 14 of the Financial Commission of the Genoa Economic and Monetary Conference; see Mills (1922, 366). To conserve scarce monetary gold, the Conference also recommended that most central banks be on a gold *exchange* standard (backing their currencies with gold and foreign exchange), while only the major reserve currencies would be on a gold coin or gold bullion standard (that is, payable in gold upon demand).

[6]The 1921 London Conference put Germany's responsibility for the war at 132 billion gold marks (the equivalent of $32 billion, or more than 1.5 times Britain's prewar stock of net foreign assets). The actual schedule of reparations was 50 billion gold marks, or $12 billion. During 1920–24, world output grew at 16 percent, whereas European output grew at only 2 percent (League of Nations 1932).

starting with the 1924 Dawes Plan and associated Dawes Loan (publicly endorsed but privately funded), Germany managed to stabilize its economy and put its new currency, the Reichsmark, on the gold standard. Britain returned to gold in 1925 at its prewar parity. France also de facto returned to gold in 1926 (de jure in 1928), albeit at a much depreciated exchange rate. By the late 1920s, most of the world's major economies were back on the gold standard.

Buoyed by the success of the Dawes Loan, and with the gold (exchange) standard reestablished, American banks entered a period of massive private international lending, averaging a billion dollars a year over 1924–29, half of which was destined for Europe, partly intermediated by British banks. Town halls in Germany were said to be inundated by representatives of international banks offering aggressively priced credits, spurring a huge economic and financial boom.[7]

This stability, however, proved short-lived. To effect the real transfer of resources required by its war reparations, Germany needed to generate a current account surplus, whereas the recipients of the reparations needed to generate a corresponding deficit (this phenomenon was termed the "transfer problem" by John Maynard Keynes). But surplus countries—most notably France and the United States—did not want to run current account deficits, and there was no mechanism to prevent them vitiating the adjustment process by sterilizing the inflows of reserves.[8] The Dawes Loan and other credits to Europe had not thus solved the underlying adjustment problem, whereby creditor nations were unwilling to increase imports to allow debtor countries to service their debts, it had merely postponed it.

When a boom in the New York Stock Exchange (which ultimately ended spectacularly in the October 1929 crash) drew both domestic and foreign capital to the United States, Europe suffered an equally massive sudden stop.[9] Unable to obtain fresh credits to meet her short-term obligations, in July 1931, Germany declared a standstill on foreign payments and imposed exchange restrictions. With London banks known to be heavily exposed to Germany and central Europe, this triggered a run on the pound sterling, which was forced off gold in September 1931. Because the pound sterling had been considered a reserve currency, the immediate impact of its devaluation was a loss of confidence in the gold exchange standard: central banks that had been holding reserves in the form of US dollar assets rushed to convert them into gold, in turn putting pressure on the dollar (which eventually devalued in July 1933).

---

[7]See Brown 1987 and Eichengreen 1992 for a detailed account of that period. During 1925–29, European output grew at 31 percent (compared with 20 percent of world output growth), while the demand for US machine tools rose by 87 percent (League of Nations 1932).

[8]The combination of having pegged at an undervalued exchange rate and insistence that the foreign currencies it received be converted into gold meant that the Banque de France's gold stock rose from 7 percent of central banks' total in 1926 to 27 percent by 1932.

[9]In Chapter 2, Harold James recounts how this cessation of credits revealed the precarious state of overleveraged central and eastern European banks, resulting in a cascade of financial crises.

What ensued was a decade of almost dizzying capital flight and hot money flows. As each country scrambled to build up its gold reserves, the world trade and payments system imploded in a morass of competitive devaluations, exchange restrictions, capital controls, and trade barriers. Exacerbating the decline in world output was that surplus countries responded to the downturn by fiscal tightening—as "prudent" budgetary policy of the time dictated—which not only made the external adjustment of deficit countries more difficult (requiring them to pursue even more contractionary policies than otherwise would have been necessary), it also dealt a deflationary blow to the world economy. Falling prices led to a higher real value of all nominal debts, further exacerbating the decline in aggregate demand, and transmitting the shock to the emerging market and developing countries through collapsing commodity prices (Figure 1.3, panel 1). Unemployment soared (reaching 25 percent in the United States; Figure 1.3, panel 2), and in many countries, the decline in output during the Great Depression was greater than it had been during World War I (Figure 1.4, panel 1).

Although it is difficult to disentangle the contribution of the resulting collapse of world trade (Figure 1.4, panel 2)—and hence of the failures of the international monetary system—to the collapse of world output during the Great Depression, it is noteworthy that as early as 1928, Gustav Cassel warned:

> The absolute necessity of international cooperation on broad lines for the stabilization of the value of gold is most clearly seen if we reflect on the alternative to such cooperation. This would obviously be a general and ruthless competition for gold, a consequent continual rise in the value of gold [and a decline in the price of all other goods], and a corresponding, world-wide economic depression for an unlimited future. A very disagreeable consequence…would be a general aggravation of all debts contracted in a gold standard, doubtless in many cases followed by an incapacity to pay debts or a refusal to do so (Cassel 1928, 98–99, cited in Irwin 2014).

Accordingly, it seems likely that failures of the international monetary system played no small role in turning a financial panic into a global Great Depression.

Bretton Woods

The interwar period amply demonstrated the three core challenges of the international monetary system: deficit countries, unable to obtain financing, resorted to a plethora of restrictive practices; surplus countries, unwilling to share the burden of adjustment, forced deficit countries to pursue even more contractionary policies; and the scramble for reserves against a limited supply of gold imparted a deflationary bias to the world economy.

Recognizing this, Keynes—who represented Great Britain at Bretton Woods in 1944—proposed to construct a new international monetary order that included substantial financing for countries with temporary balance of payments deficits, symmetric penalties on deficit and surplus countries alike, and a mechanism for controlling global liquidity with the creation (and revaluation) of a global currency, bancor. By contrast, the other main protagonist at Bretton Woods,

Figure 1.3. Great Depression: US Macroeconomic Performance

1. Interest Rates and Inflation
(Percent, left scale; US dollars per barrel, right scale)

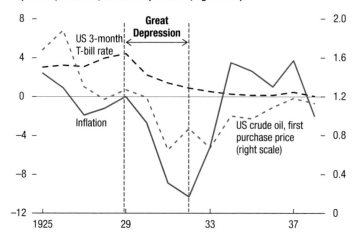

2. Unemployment Rate
(Percent)

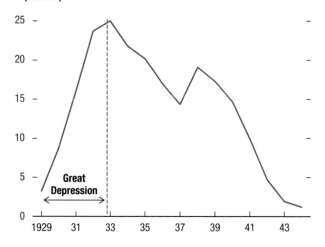

Sources: Federal Reserve Bank of Minneapolis; US Census Bureau; and US Energy Information Administration.

Harry Dexter White of the US Treasury, proposed a much smaller IMF that would allocate resources selectively to member countries on demand. He opposed Keynes's ideas for an equitable burden of adjustment between surplus and deficit countries and the creation of bancor (instead, White favored lending national currencies; Boughton 2002).

Figure 1.4. Great Depression: G7 Macroeconomic Performance

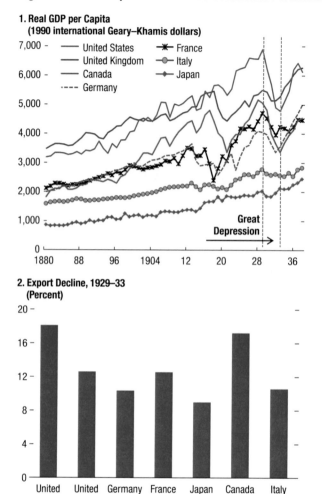

1. Real GDP per Capita
(1990 international Geary–Khamis dollars)

2. Export Decline, 1929–33
(Percent)

Sources: New Maddison Project Database (Bolt and van Zanden 2014) for real GDP per capita; and UNSTATS for exports.
Note: Average annual export decline for countries computed over 1929–33 (panel 2).

Much has been made of the differences between Keynes and White, but in reality, these were probably less intellectual debates than the prosaic fact that one was representing a major debtor country, which expected to run continued deficits, and the other represented the world's largest creditor country, which expected to run surpluses for the foreseeable future. In the event, White prevailed: the IMF had significantly fewer resources than Keynes wanted, surplus countries would face no penalty for failing to adjust, and there would be no bancor—the US dollar would be the sole substitute for gold.[10]

One issue that the two men did agree on was the need for structural capital controls (preferably enforced at both the source and recipient ends). This would allow governments to pursue the full employment policies increasingly expected by the electorate, while maintaining fixed exchange rates and avoiding competitive devaluations (in essence, capital account restrictions would resolve the "trilemma" of fixed exchange rates, an independent monetary policy, and free capital mobility). More generally, the experience of the interwar period had convinced both Keynes and White that free capital mobility and free trade were incompatible: destabilizing capital flows would spur protectionist measures—and given the choice, they preferred current account over capital account convertibility.[11]

During its initial years, the IMF lent little. Most developing countries, having supplied vital primary products during the war, had emerged from it with plentiful foreign exchange reserves, and as a matter of policy, the IMF did not lend to European countries that were recipients of Marshall Aid. But by the mid-1950s, as the membership expanded (Figure 1.5), so did the calls for financial support, and the IMF began fulfilling one of its core functions of assisting members facing balance of payments difficulties. More than 30 advanced and developing economies received IMF support during the 1950s, including programs with France and the United Kingdom in the aftermath of the Suez Crisis; in the following decade, the number of arrangements jumped to 220.

Already, however, stresses had begun to appear in the system. These were related to the failure of Bretton Woods to address the two other challenges of the international monetary system: asymmetry in the burden of adjustment and regulation of the supply of global liquidity. By the early 1960s, continued US balance of payments deficits were turning the postwar "dollar shortage" into a "dollar glut" as US corporations invested heavily in Europe and elsewhere. Unwilling to tighten monetary policy (Figure 1.6), the United States resorted to controls on capital outflows in the form of the Interest Equalization Tax, though this was insufficient to stem capital outflows completely. Moreover, as the decade proceeded, expenditure on the Great Society programs and the Vietnam War worsened the US current account, further contributing to the country's balance of payments deficit. But having scuppered Keynes's plan of symmetric penalties, the United States now found it difficult to force Germany, Japan, and other surplus countries to revalue their currencies or to undertake expansionary policies that would narrow their current account surpluses.

---

[10]Steil (2013) provides a fascinating account of the battle between Keynes and White. Although the final outcome at Bretton Woods was dominated by White's plan, and not that of Keynes, ironically among White's papers, a doggerel apparently scribbled by a member of the British delegation was found: In Washington Lord Halifax / Once whispered to Lord Keynes, / It's true they have all the money-bags / But we have all the brains (Gardner 1980, cited in Boughton 2002).

[11]As Helleiner (1994) recounts, powerful New York banking interests succeeded in watering down the provisions in the IMF's Articles of Agreement for restricting capital mobility; nevertheless, the Articles favor current account convertibility over capital account convertibility.

Figure 1.5. IMF Membership
(Number of countries)

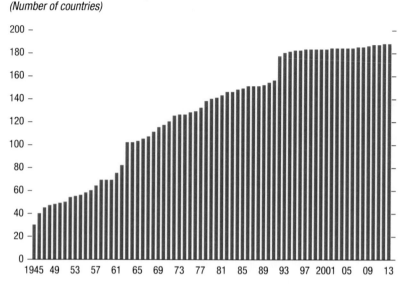

Source: IMF staff calculations (https://www.imf.org/external/np/sec/memdir/memdate.htm).

The second shortcoming of Bretton Woods—the lack of a mechanism to regulate global liquidity—gave rise to what became known as the Triffin dilemma. Global liquidity, in the context of the international monetary system, refers to the ability of (solvent) countries to finance current account deficits, especially in times of stress. The most obvious source of such liquidity is owned foreign exchange reserves, but there are others, such as central bank swap lines or IMF financing. In principle, private capital flows could be another source of global liquidity because they finance current account deficits—but in times of stress (a financial crisis in the country concerned, regional contagion, or disruptions in international capital markets more generally), such financing is likely to dry up, and borrowing countries may face a sudden stop. Worse, as foreign investors (sometimes joined by domestic residents) rush for the exit, they *increase* the country's financing needs—requiring it to use more of its reserves or to generate a larger current account surplus. On net, therefore, rising private capital flows—and growing international trade—tend to increase the need for global liquidity.[12]

---

[12]A simple numerical example illustrates why growth of world trade requires increased global liquidity. Suppose a country's imports and exports are $100 million so that its trade is balanced, but there is the risk that a shock would reduce exports by 10 percent to $90 million. In order not to have to adjust by reducing imports, the country would need to hold $10 million of foreign exchange reserves. Now suppose trade increases to $1 billion; a 10 percent decline in exports would lead to a $900 million trade deficit, and to cushion against such a shock, the country would need to hold $100 million of reserves.

Figure 1.6. US Reserve Money, 1950–73
(US$ billions)

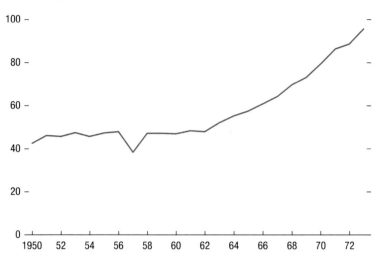

Source: IMF, International Financial Statistics database.

The Triffin dilemma was that, on the one hand, increasing world trade and capital flows meant that countries—and thus the system as a whole—needed the United States to run balance of payments deficits in order to create reserves, but on the other hand, larger deficits meant a shrinking stock of gold with which to redeem the dollars accumulating in the coffers of foreign central banks (Figure 1.7, panel 1). Bretton Woods was predicated on the dollar being "as good as gold" (that is, an immutable value of the dollar in terms of gold), and thus the generation of reserves by the United States meant that its stock of external liabilities increased, which undermined confidence in the system (Figure 1.7, panel 2). To solve this dilemma, the IMF in 1969 created the Special Drawing Right (SDR), an artificial reserve asset that harkened back to Keynes's bancor.[13] By allocating SDRs to member countries (in proportion to quota), the IMF could create additional global liquidity independently of US

---

[13]The SDR is both an asset and liability to participants in the SDR Department. It is an asset because ownership rights can be enforced (economic benefits are derived by the owners by holding them or using them over a period of time), and it is a store of value. But it also has attributes of a liability because countries are required to pay interest on it, and a country would be required to repay any allocation of SDRs if it left IMF membership (Galicia-Escotto 2005). Because an SDR has the nature of both an asset and a liability, Otmar Emminger (the vice president of the Bundesbank) in the late 1960s likened it to a zebra that might be considered as a black horse with white stripes or a white horse with black stripes (Solomon 1982, 142).

Figure 1.7. US Gold Holdings and External Assets and Liabilities

1. Official Gold Holdings
(Million ounces)

2. External Assets and Liabilities
(Billions of US dollars)

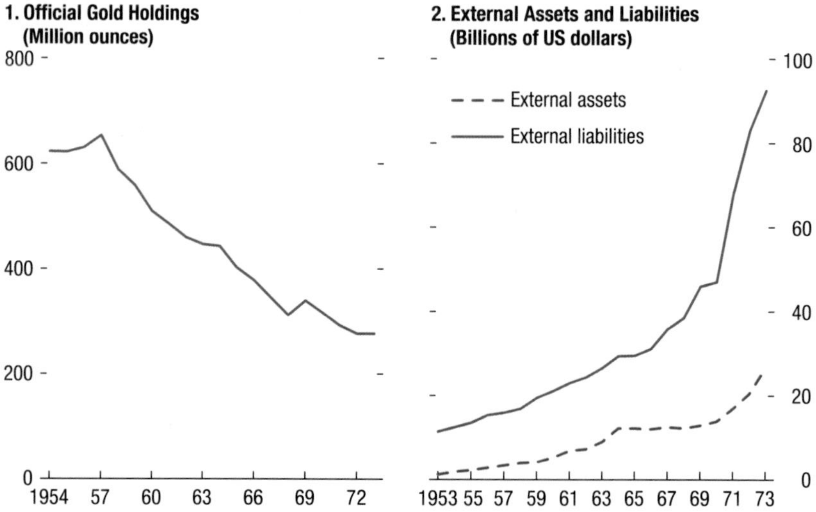

Source: IMF, International Financial Statistics database.

(or any other country's) deficits.[14] To date, however, there have been only three general allocations: SDR 9.3 billion in 1970–72; SDR 12.1 billion in 1979–81; and SDR 161.2 billion (together with a special allocation of SDR 21.5 billion) in 2009 in the aftermath of the global financial crisis. One reason for the long gap between the 1970s and the 2009 SDR allocations was the belief that the rise in private capital flows, especially to developing and emerging market economies, had obviated the need for additional global liquidity in the form of SDRs.

The SDR solved the Triffin dilemma, but continued US monetary and fiscal expansion in the late 1960s and early 1970s, and its worsening balance of payments, eventually resulted in the collapse of Bretton Woods—despite the deployment of an array of increasingly desperate measures to prop up the system, which included capital controls, swap lines, and moral suasion of key US trading partners.[15] As the US trade balance deteriorated (Figure 1.8, panel 1), anticipation of a devaluation of the dollar led to huge capital outflows, which reached $30 billion by 1971 (Figure 1.8, panel 2). On August 15, 1971, unable to stop this hemorrhage of capital, and frustrated that it could not persuade key surplus countries to revalue their currencies, President Nixon's administration suspended gold

---

[14]The IMF can also force countries to hold SDRs as reserves rather than employ them as long-term financing. By canceling SDRs, the IMF can also regulate global liquidity when it is deemed excessive.

[15]For detailed discussions, see Coombs 1976, Solomon 1982, and Volcker and Gyohten 1992.

Figure 1.8. US Balance of Payments, 1950–73

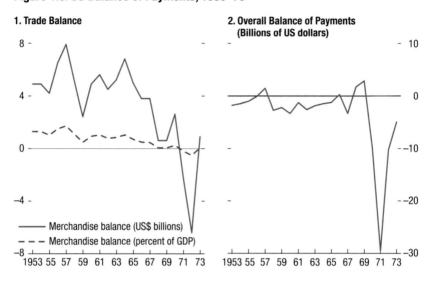

1. Trade Balance

2. Overall Balance of Payments
(Billions of US dollars)

Source: IMF, International Financial Statistics database.

convertibility of the dollar, imposed an across-the-board 10 percent import sur-charge, and instituted wage-price controls.

Following the "Nixon shock," a new set of parities was negotiated at the Smithsonian Agreement in December of that year, entailing a devaluation of the dollar of about 10 percent and a new official price of gold of $38 an ounce (though official dollar convertibility into gold was not restored). But this new agreement (which Nixon hailed "the most significant monetary arrangement in the history of the world") proved short-lived.[16] In February 1973, the dollar was devalued by a further 10 percent—but even that did not suffice. After massive foreign exchange intervention failed to stabilize exchange rates, the price of gold was allowed to reach its free market value (Figure 1.9, panel 1), and the major industrialized economies moved to generalized floating (Figure 1.9, panel 2).

After the collapse of Bretton Woods, in July 1972, the Committee of Twenty—a ministerial body composed of the constituencies represented at the IMF Board—identified two key goals for the reformed international monetary system: "achievement of symmetry in the obligations of all countries debtors and creditors alike," and "the better management of global liquidity"—precisely the same goals as had occupied Keynes and White at the time of Bretton Woods! Yet, as at Bretton Woods, agreement proved elusive. The 1974 oil price shock, which affected countries differently according to their oil dependence, also made it

---

[16]Nixon quote cited in Eichengreen 2008, 131.

Figure 1.9. Price of Gold and Exchange Rates

1. Price of Gold, 1935–75
(US dollars per ounce)

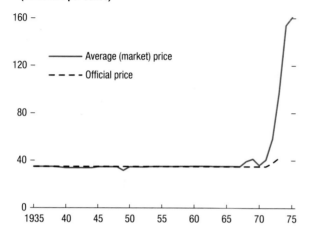

2. G7: Nominal Exchange Rates, 1957–75
(Local currency / US$)

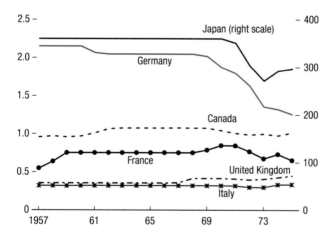

Sources: Gold price from National Mining Association; and nominal exchange rates from IMF, Information Notice System database.

difficult to reestablish fixed parities across the major industrialized countries. Instead, the IMF's Articles of Agreement were amended to legitimize floating exchange rates. To prevent competitive devaluations or depreciations, the new Article IV called on the IMF to "oversee the international monetary system to ensure its effective operation … [and to] exercise firm surveillance over the exchange rate policies of members." Thus, the term "surveillance" entered into the IMF's lexicon.[17]

At one level, Bretton Woods had been characterized by an extraordinary degree of international cooperation. Beyond the system itself, which was designed to avoid the competitive devaluations and beggar-thy-neighbor policies of the interwar period, key officials had cooperated closely—crafting the Gold Pool, central bank swap lines, and both implicit and explicit agreements not to convert dollars into gold—to safeguard and sustain that system. (Of course, the fundamental coordination—surplus countries agreeing to revalue their currencies and the United States pursuing tighter monetary and fiscal policies—was lacking, which is what ultimately led to the demise of the system.) Nevertheless, the system lurched from one crisis to the next, until it finally collapsed—ushering in a period of floating exchange rates that promised smoother adjustment to payments imbalances, and thus fewer crises, both in individual countries and in the system as a whole. Yet, the performance of the world economy—trade expansion, output growth, moderate inflation, and financial (notably, banking) stability—during Bretton Woods not only surpassed that of the gold standard era (Figure 1.10), it has been unparalleled ever since (see Figures 1.11 and 1.13).

Advent of Floating

For the IMF, the collapse of Bretton Woods presented an existential crisis: it seemed hard to justify an institution whose very raison d'être—the Bretton Woods system—had ceased to exist. But the 1974 oil price shock, petrodollar recycling, the buildup of developing country debt, and the subsequent debt crisis meant that, by the 1980s, the IMF was very much back in business, with demand for the use of IMF resources at an all-time high (Figure 1.12).

---

[17]Under Article IV, the IMF conducts bilateral surveillance in the form of consultations with each member country, typically once each year. The origin of these "Article IV consultations" is actually Article XIV, which requires annual consultations (starting five years after the establishment of the IMF) with all countries availing themselves of the transitional arrangements under Article XIV to maintain exchange restrictions. Because, in the early days of the IMF, countries often requested IMF support in the context of removing these restrictions, these consultations formed the basis of, or even substituted for, program discussions. In 1958 the United Kingdom gained Article VIII status (that is, removed exchange restrictions on the making of payments and transfers for current international transactions), but because the authorities were considering seeking IMF support, they voluntarily agreed to continue their annual consultations. When Article IV was amended in 1978, it introduced the obligation of members to consult with the IMF on exchange rate policies "when requested by the Fund," without specifying an annual cycle. The purpose of this consultation is to check compliance with members' obligations, in particular not to manipulate its exchange rate. The practice of annual consultations between the IMF and its members thus has a dual-track history—Article XIV via Article V (on conditions for the use of IMF resources), and the amended Article IV. In turn, surveillance serves two—quite distinct—functions: assessing macroeconomic or financial vulnerabilities, especially those that might spill onto the balance of payments and require the IMF's financial support; and assessing exchange rate policies to ensure that countries are not manipulating their exchange rates or gaining unfair competitive advantage.

Figure 1.10. Macroeconomic Performance and Crisis Prevalence, 1881–1970

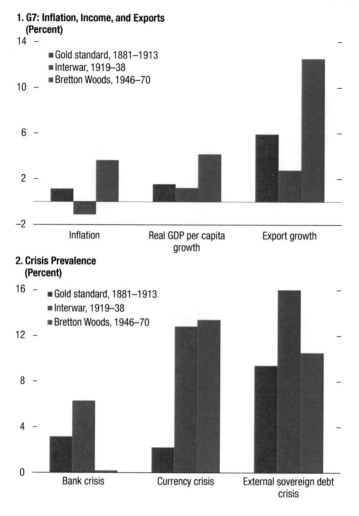

1. G7: Inflation, Income, and Exports
(Percent)

- Gold standard, 1881–1913
- Interwar, 1919–38
- Bretton Woods, 1946–70

2. Crisis Prevalence
(Percent)

- Gold standard, 1881–1913
- Interwar, 1919–38
- Bretton Woods, 1946–70

Sources: Bordo 1993 for inflation and real per capita growth data; Reinhart and Rogoff 2009 for crisis data; and UNSTATS for nominal export growth data (available for 1900–60).
Note: For the gold standard and interwar periods in panel 1, inflation and real GDP per capita mean growth are calculated as the time coefficient from a regression of the natural logarithm of the variable on a constant and a time trend. Crisis prevalence in panel 2 is computed as the percentage of all countries (for which information is available) in a crisis. All values are period averages.

On the surveillance side, and in terms of international policy coordination, however, the IMF's role was limited. Very quickly, it became apparent that floating exchange rates were not a panacea and that the system could still produce large current account imbalances. In particular, as before, there was no means of forcing surplus countries to reflate their economies, and although the loss of

Figure 1.11. Exchange Rate Volatility and Macroeconomic Performance

1. Nominal Exchange Rates, 1970–89
(Local currency / US$)

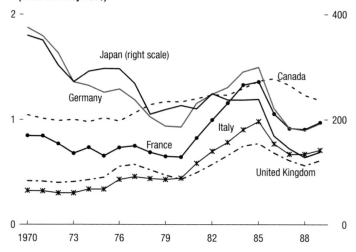

2. Inflation, Income, and Exports, 1881–2013
(Percent)

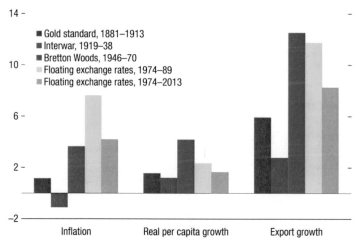

■ Gold standard, 1881–1913
■ Interwar, 1919–38
■ Bretton Woods, 1946–70
☐ Floating exchange rates, 1974–89
■ Floating exchange rates, 1974–2013

Sources: Bordo 1993 for inflation and real per capita growth up to the Bretton Woods period; IMF, World Economic Outlook database, for inflation and nominal export growth over 1974–2013; Reinhart and Rogoff 2009 for crisis data; UNSTATS for nominal export growth up to the Bretton Woods period (data available for 1900–60); and World Bank, World Development Indicators database, for real per capita growth over 1974–2013.

Note: For the gold standard and interwar periods (panel 2), inflation and real per capita mean growth are calculated as the time coefficient from a regression of the natural logarithm of the variable on a constant and a time trend.

Figure 1.12. IMF Arrangements, 1952–85

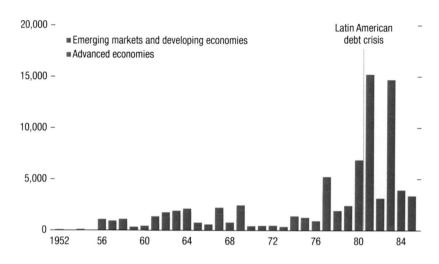

Source: IMF, Monitoring of Fund Arrangements database.
Note: Approved amount in US$ millions, 1952–71, and in SDR millions, 1972–2013.

financing typically forced adjustment on deficit countries, this did not apply to the United States, for whose assets there was a voracious global demand. The London and Bonn economic summits in 1977 and 1978, respectively, were attempts at addressing these imbalances through explicit policy coordination. In exchange for the United States undertaking to reduce its budget deficit, rein in inflation, and (subsequently) strive for the stability of the US dollar (including through coordinated intervention and the issuance of foreign currency–denominated Carter bonds), Japan and Germany agreed to implement expansionary policies—thus acting as a "locomotive" to the world economy.

The experiment turned out badly: just as Germany and Japan were implementing their fiscal expansion, the 1979 oil price shock dealt the world economy a fresh inflationary blow, and although these countries carried through their commitments, the experience gave policy coordination a bad name.[18] Meanwhile, in the United States, continued dollar weakness and high inflation prompted the Federal Reserve under the chairmanship of Paul Volcker to institute extremely tight monetary policies, while the Reagan administration's tax cuts and defense expenditures provided a significant fiscal impulse. The result was a sharp appreciation of the dollar and a steep rise in world interest rates—both of which increased the debt burden of developing countries. Together with the United States, several other major industrialized countries tightened monetary policy to

---

[18]For a detailed discussion, see for example, Putnam and Bayne 1984, 99.

lower inflation—in part by appreciating their currencies. Because exchange rates cannot simultaneously appreciate against each other, these uncoordinated attempts to disinflate likely resulted in excessively tight monetary policies, when the welfare gains to these countries of greater policy coordination would have been modest, yet measurable (Oudiz and Sachs 1984).

It was not until 1985, when the dollar had clearly reached an unsustainable peak, that the Group of Five (G5) returned to explicit policy cooperation—mainly in the form of the September 1985 Plaza Agreement on foreign exchange intervention. How much effect the Plaza Agreement had on the dollar has been much debated: the turning point of the dollar was some months earlier, but the signaling effect of the agreement that the nondollar currencies among the G5 had to appreciate may have had some impact on the markets. Indeed, the opposite view is that the Plaza Agreement succeeded only too well—necessitating the 1987 Louvre Accord to slow the depreciation of the dollar, and later prompting the October 1987 stock market crash (the response to which is one of the few examples of monetary policy coordination among the G7; Ghosh and Masson 1994).

Overall, the first 20 years of floating exchange rates were disappointing. Far from adjusting smoothly to trade imbalances—as Friedman (1953) had argued—both nominal and real exchange rates had been highly volatile (prompting renewed impetus toward a monetary union in Europe, in the form of the European Monetary System). Large imbalances had emerged among the major industrialized economies, and developing countries had struggled with external adjustment in the aftermath of the debt crisis. In addition, stagflation had beset many economies in the wake of the oil price shocks, and experiments at policy coordination had proven far from satisfactory. Trade growth remained robust (despite the high degree of exchange rate volatility; Figure 1.12, panel 1), but output growth was barely one-half of that attained during Bretton Woods, and inflation was considerably higher (Figure 1.12, panel 2).

As the 1980s drew to a close, and developing countries (most notably in Latin America) emerged from the "lost decade" of the debt crisis years, the role of the IMF was again in question—but not for long. The collapse of the Soviet Union and the fall of the Iron Curtain gave the IMF a fresh mandate: helping these centrally planned economies first to stabilize following price liberalization and then to transform into more market-oriented structures. Not surprisingly, there was an increase in the IMF's technical assistance and financing. An even greater call on IMF resources came from the "capital account crises" in emerging markets—as these countries pursued rapid capital account liberalization in the 1980s and early 1990s—starting with Mexico in 1994, and soon followed by the east Asian economies in 1996/97, Russia in 1998, Brazil in 1999, Turkey in 2001, Argentina in 2002, and Uruguay in 2003. Although the specifics differed across these cases, what they all amply demonstrated was that the rise of private cross-border capital flows, far from obviating the need for global liquidity (in the form of foreign exchange reserves or IMF financing), had increased that need by orders of magnitude (Figure 1.13).

Figure 1.13. Crisis Prevalence and IMF Arrangements

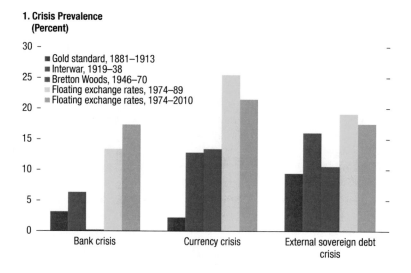

1. Crisis Prevalence
(Percent)

- Gold standard, 1881–1913
- Interwar, 1919–38
- Bretton Woods, 1946–70
- Floating exchange rates, 1974–89
- Floating exchange rates, 1974–2010

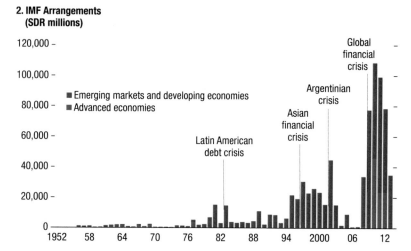

2. IMF Arrangements
(SDR millions)

- Emerging markets and developing economies
- Advanced economies

Latin American debt crisis

Asian financial crisis

Argentinian crisis

Global financial crisis

Sources: IMF, Monitoring of Fund Arrangements database; and Reinhart and Rogoff 2009.

The IMF in the Doldrums

By the early 2000s, as emerging markets recovered from these financial crises, capital flows resumed (Figure 1.14), and the need for IMF financing fell correspondingly. Meanwhile, among the world's most important economies (which by now included China), large current account imbalances began to emerge in the

Figure 1.14. Net Financial Flows to Emerging Market Economies, 1980–2013
(Billions of US dollars, left scale; percent of GDP, right scale)

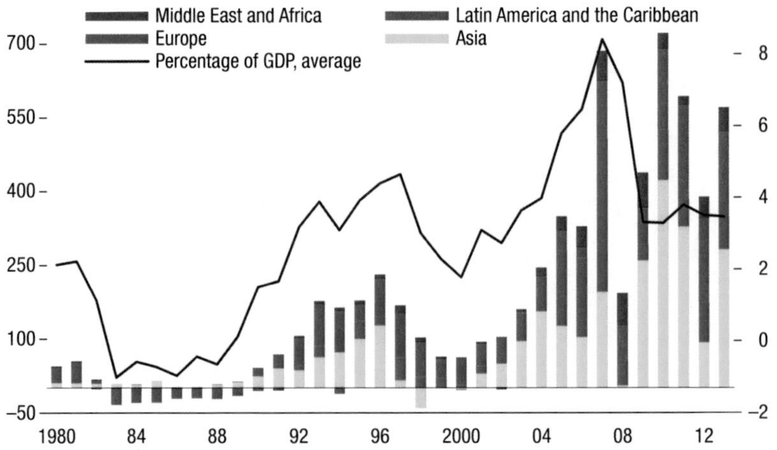

Source: IMF, International Financial Statistics database.
Note: Net financial flows excludes reserves and other investment liabilities of the general government. Flows for 2013 are provisional. Net financial flows in percentage of GDP is the average computed over all countries in the sample.

mid-2000s (Figure 1.15). On the deficit side, the United States was the major deficit country, while the largest surplus countries were China and other Asian emerging market economies, oil producers, and Germany. It was recognized that the current account surpluses of oil producers represented the transfer of their wealth from below the ground to above it, whereas Germany's surplus largely escaped unnoticed because the euro area as a whole was roughly in balance. It was therefore the Asian surplus economies that came under particular scrutiny, with the charge that they were deliberately undervaluing their currencies to gain competitive advantage as part of export-led growth strategies. These countries countered that the Asian (and other emerging market) financial crises had taught them the importance of ensuring that currencies not become overvalued, and of holding sufficient international reserves to buffer against capital account shocks (especially given the political stigma of having to seek the IMF's financial support).

Beyond the issue of possible unfair trade practices, the concern with the global imbalances was that, eventually, there could be a loss of confidence in the US dollar, which would force the Federal Reserve to raise interest rates sharply, with global repercussions. Such concerns about an abrupt unwinding of the global imbalances prompted the IMF to convene a "multilateral consultation" in 2006. This was a form of international policy coordination—albeit informal and outside the usual G5 or G7 setting—whereby surplus and deficit countries would undertake policies that, the IMF argued, would both be in their own interests and contribute to systemic stability.

Figure 1.15. Global Current Account Imbalances, 1980–2013
(Percent of world GDP)

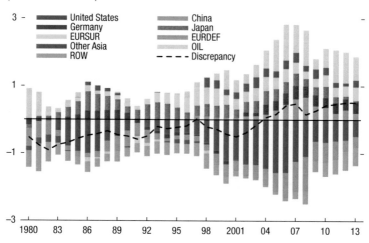

Source: IMF, World Economic Outlook database.
Note: EURSUR = euro area surplus countries; EURDEF = euro area deficit countries; OIL = oil exporters;
ROW = rest of the world.

The multilateral consultation, however, had very little impact. As before, nothing forced the surplus countries to adjust, while the main deficit country, the United States, continued to receive plentiful financing—and indeed was confident that, even if there were to be a crisis, the resulting "flight to safety" would be toward the dollar rather than away from it. Neither side, therefore, had much urgency to act. The IMF itself was very much in the doldrums: except for concessional loans to low-income countries, it was doing virtually no lending, and its surveillance activities had little traction in altering policies—especially those of its largest and most important members.

Things took a sharp turn as the global financial crisis erupted in September 2008; the IMF was back in business and very much on the front lines (shown in Figure 1.13, panel 2).

CHALLENGES OF TODAY

The main worry about global imbalances in the mid-2000s was the possibility that a sudden unwinding would lead to a sharp depreciation of the dollar. That did not happen: on the contrary, the immediate response was safe haven flows to the United States (notably Treasuries), strengthening the dollar against most currencies. But the global financial crisis did happen, and while the proximate trigger was the implosion of the US subprime mortgage market, the underlying cause has variously been attributed to the global savings glut (Bernanke 2005)—which resulted in excessive risk taking as investors searched for yield—or a global "banking glut" (Shin 2012), with overleveraged financial institutions that have cross-border assets (both explanations are reminiscent of the interwar period, prior to the 1931 sudden stop).

Yet, outcomes in the Great Recession have been significantly better than during the Great Depression (Figure 1.16)—partly because of vigorous monetary and fiscal measures (including coordinated G20 fiscal stimulus in the immediate aftermath of the crisis), and partly because countries did not succumb (nearly as much) to trade protectionism. The contraction in world trade has therefore been much shorter-lived than during the interwar period (Figure 1.17).

Nevertheless, there are some eerie similarities between the Great Depression and the Great Recession: highly volatile capital flows, a scramble for reserves, asymmetry in the burden of adjustment between deficit and surplus countries, secular stagnation, and currency wars.

Volatile Capital Flows

As in the interwar period, capital flows to the emerging markets have been highly volatile (shown in Figure 1.14). The immediate impact of the global financial crisis was large outflows from emerging markets to safe havens, notably the United States. With record monetary expansion, low returns, and diminished growth prospects in advanced economies, however, capital surged toward emerging markets in mid-2009 and early 2010. But the US sovereign debt rating downgrade at the end of 2011 sent capital scuttling back to the United States— ironically, into Treasuries. Thereafter, flows returned to emerging markets—until the "taper tantrum" in the second half of 2013, when the Federal Reserve announced its intention to wrap up the unconventional monetary policy measures (quantitative easing) that it had introduced in the aftermath of the crisis to boost economic recovery.

This volatility raises questions of how emerging market countries should respond. Should they simply allow capital to flow in and out of the country without regard to the macroeconomic and financial vulnerabilities that large flows may engender? Should they intervene in the foreign exchange market, incurring sterilization costs? Should they impose capital controls and risk financial deglobalization? Finally, what should be the responsibility of source countries when cross-border capital movements (especially banking flows) are destabilizing?

Scramble for Reserves

One way that emerging markets have been protecting themselves is by stockpiling reserves, with the average reserves-to-GDP ratio rising from about 12 percent of GDP before the Asian crisis to over 22 percent of GDP in 2013 (Figure 1.18). The global financial crisis made only a slight dent in the series, with the trend of accumulation accelerating after the crisis. But such reserve accumulation may also have downsides. First, it is an inefficient form of country insurance. Second, unless financed by long-term, stable capital flows, the buildup of net reserves requires emerging markets to run current account

Figure 1.16. Macroeconomic Performance: Great Depression vs. Great Recession

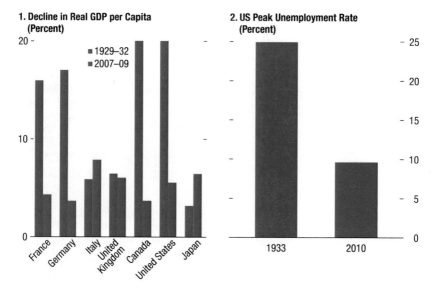

1. Decline in Real GDP per Capita
   (Percent)

   ■ 1929–32
   ■ 2007–09

2. US Peak Unemployment Rate
   (Percent)

   1933   2010

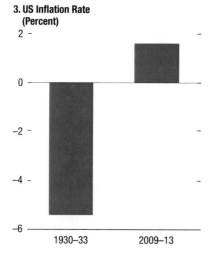

3. US Inflation Rate
   (Percent)

   1930–33   2009–13

Sources: Based on New Maddison Project (Bolt and van Zanden 2014); Federal Reserve Bank of Minneapolis; US Bureau of Labor Statistics; and US Census Bureau.
Note: Decline in real GDP per capita is computed over peak to trough (panel 1); unemployment rate is for individuals 14 years of age or older in 1933 and for individuals 16 years of age or older in 2010 (panel 2); inflation rate is mean for period average (panel 3).

Figure 1.17. World Trade Collapse: Great Depression vs. Great Recession

1. Great Depression

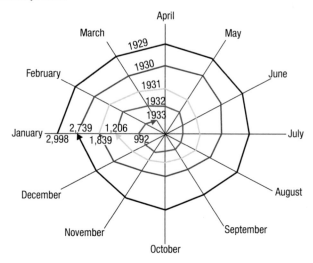

2. Great Recession

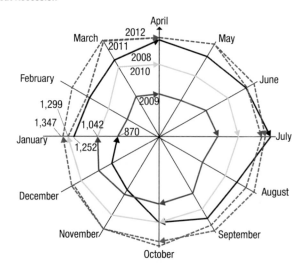

Sources: Kindleberger 1973 (panel 1); and World Trade Organization data (panel 2).
Note: Panel 1 is based on total imports of 75 countries (monthly values in terms of old US gold dollars in millions). Panel 2 is based on monthly merchandise imports of 70 countries.

Figure 1.18. Stock of Foreign Exchange Reserves in Emerging Markets, 1980–2013
(Billions of US dollars)

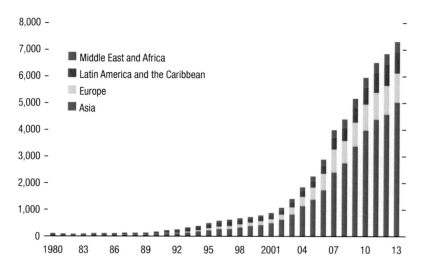

Source: IMF, International Financial Statistics database.

surpluses. Third, reserve accumulation raises the global demand for safe assets, depressing their rate of return—thus worsening the zero-lower-bound problem for advanced economy monetary policy.

Asymmetric Burden of Adjustment

The euro area crisis has again highlighted the difficulties that deficit countries face in undertaking external adjustment, especially when the nominal exchange rate is not available as an adjustment tool. Although intra–euro area imbalances were not the focus during the multilateral consultations on global imbalances in the mid-2000s, current account adjustments of the hardest hit euro area countries (and, earlier, in some eastern and central European countries) has been associated with severe output declines (Figure 1.19). At the same time, Germany—the largest surplus country within the euro area—has done little rebalancing toward domestic demand; indeed, its overall fiscal position has turned to surplus.

Secular Stagnation

Beyond the immediate crisis, the largely anemic recovery even in advanced economies where growth has resumed has led to worries of "secular stagnation" (Summers 2013). The term was originally coined during the Depression era by

Figure 1.19. Current Account and Real GDP Growth, 2008–13
(Percent)

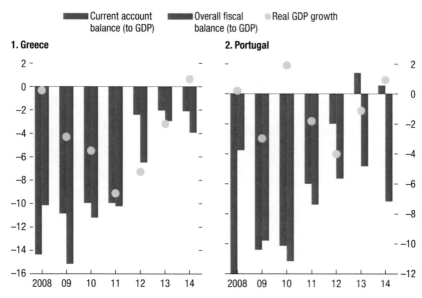

■ Current account
balance (to GDP)   ■ Overall fiscal
balance (to GDP)   ● Real GDP growth

1. Greece

2. Portugal

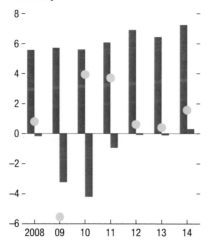

3. Germany

Source: IMF, World Economic Outlook database.

Alvin Hansen (1939), who noted that "a full recovery calls for something more than mere expenditure of depreciation allowances. It requires a large outlay on new investment, and this awaits the development of great new industries and new techniques. But such new developments are not currently available in adequate volume."

The concern is that, with monetary policy close to the zero lower bound, and with inadequate aggregate demand, businesses have little incentive to undertake new investment—in turn, condemning the economy to slower potential growth as well. Whether, in fact, the world economy has entered a period of secular stagnation is the subject of considerable debate. Certainly, investment rates have fallen significantly in major economies since the onset of the global financial crisis (Figure 1.20). Recent data on US growth have been more encouraging—but conversely, emerging markets, which had been the one bright spot of the world economy after the global financial crisis, have now slowed considerably, and their growth prospects seem much diminished compared with even a couple of years ago (Figure 1.21).

Currency Wars

From the perspective of the international monetary system, secular stagnation raises concerns about "currency wars." With monetary policy at or close to the zero lower bound, and with limited fiscal space, the main scope for boosting aggregate demand is through exports, via currency depreciation. If this happens, the global economy could be thrown back to the interwar world of competitive devaluations.

Empirically, various unconventional monetary policy expansions in Japan, the United States, and the euro area have indeed been associated with depreciation of the corresponding currency, and some advanced economy central banks— Switzerland and the Czech Republic—have been intervening in the foreign exchange markets on grounds that their policy rates are at the zero lower bound, but they have insufficient domestic assets to undertake quantitative easing (Figure 1.22). It is noteworthy, however, that these central banks generally do not consider that they are deliberately depreciating their exchange rates—rather, the defense is that they are seeking to fulfill their (typically, 2 percent a year) inflation targets. But with "divine coincidence," meeting the inflation target is equivalent to closing the output gap, which requires boosting aggregate demand—including by raising net exports. Meanwhile, for trading partners, it makes little difference whether the country's exchange rate depreciation (and hence trading partners' loss of competitiveness) is the result of monetary policy (quantitative easing) or exchange rate policy (foreign exchange intervention).[19] In this sense, a world of secular stagnation is also likely to be a world of currency wars.

---

[19]As in the interwar period, competitive devaluations provide some benefit to the world economy inasmuch as they allow expansionary monetary policies. Likewise, although quantitative easing might be negatively transmitted through the exchange rate, there could be a positive benefit through reflation.

Figure 1.20. Investment, Inflation, and Growth, 2005–13
(Percent)

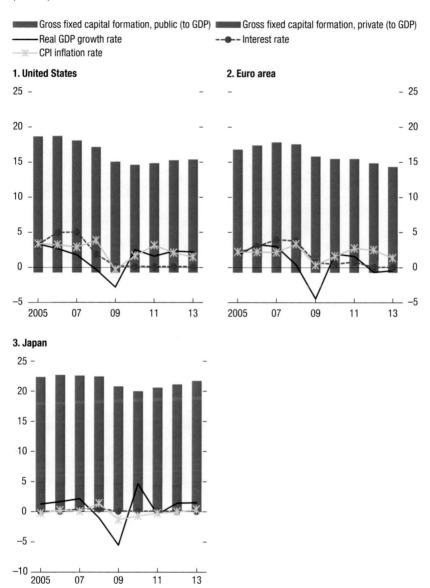

Sources: EUROSTAT; and IMF, International Financial Statistics and World Economic Outlook databases.

Figure 1.21. Projected Real GDP Growth Rates, 2008–17
(Percent)

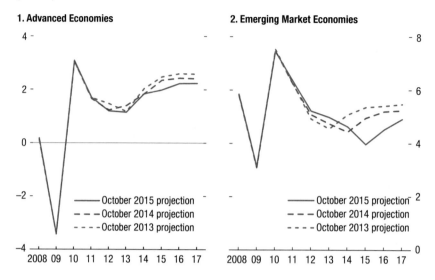

1. Advanced Economies

2. Emerging Market Economies

Source: IMF, World Economic Outlook database.

Figure 1.22. Quantitative Easing and Real Effective Exchange Rate, 2008–13

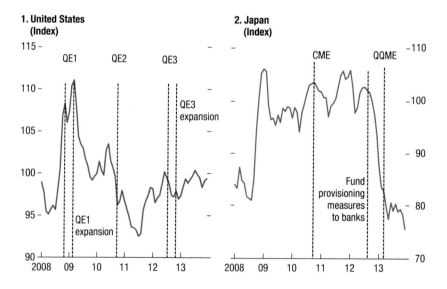

1. United States
(Index)

2. Japan
(Index)

Source: IMF, Information Notice System database.
Note: QE dates are from IMF 2013. CME = comprehensive monetary easing; QE = quantitative easing; QQME = quantitative and qualitative monetary easing program.

VOLUME OVERVIEW

With this broad narrative as a backdrop, the chapters in this book delve deeper into particular aspects of the international monetary system over the past century. The chapters are wide ranging, but they may be grouped under four broad rubrics:

Part I, "Perspectives from the Past: Imbalances and the Asymmetric Burden of Adjustment," looks at historical antecedents of today's challenges. In Chapter 2, Harold James reexamines the interwar period from the perspective of current and capital account imbalances (or, put differently, in terms of net and gross flows). In Chapter 3, Emmanuel Mourlon-Druol looks at European adjustment experiences in the 1960s and 1970s to draw lessons for today. Catherine Schenk takes a more global perspective in Chapter 4 and recounts how policy coordination failures since Bretton Woods have contributed to large and persistent imbalances; and in Chapter 5, Michael Bordo and Harold James explain the problem of adjustment in terms of four distinct policy constraints or "trilemmas" that arise from international capital mobility.

Part II, "International Monetary Negotiations and the International Monetary System," goes "behind the scenes" of how the modern international monetary system has been—and continues to be—shaped through international financial diplomacy. In Chapter 6, Eric Helleiner debunks the myth that Bretton Woods was the brainchild of Keynes and White alone; although these men were undoubtedly the main protagonists, he argues that there were substantial and important contributions from the delegates of many of the 44 nations represented at the conference, including developing countries and colonies. Benn Steil brings the same theme forward in time in Chapter 7, asking whether, or to what extent, emerging markets today are trying to craft new institutions that will result in a less G7-centric international monetary system. James Boughton reminds us in Chapter 8 of the central role the IMF has played—and continues to play—in the modern-day international monetary system.

Part III, "Currency Wars and Secular Stagnation—The New Normal?" brings the discussion to the present day. Richard Cooper proposes an indicator-based approach in Chapter 9 to discipline exchange rate policies, particularly of surplus countries that are typically not subject to market discipline. In Chapter 10, Robert McCauley looks at monetary spillovers and the possibility of national policies being at cross purposes in globally integrated bond markets where assets are close substitutes. Edwin Truman in Chapter 11 assesses the issue of global liquidity and asks whether the IMF has sufficient resources to assist countries facing balance of payments difficulties (he also proposes ways that the rest of the IMF membership could move forward on quota reform without the participation of the United States—and such thinking likely helped spur the US Congress to approve the quota increase in December 2015).

Part IV presents a brief overview of the analytics of international policy coordination by Atish Ghosh, and the proceedings of a panel discussion (moderated by Olivier Blanchard) on "Prospects for the Future: Toward a More Cooperative

System," with Maurice Obstfeld, José Antonio Ocampo, Alexander Swoboda, and Paul Volcker as panelists. The key takeaways from the discussion—summarized by Atish Ghosh and Mahvash Qureshi—wrap up this volume.

REFERENCES

Bernanke, B. 2005. "The Global Saving Glut and the US Current Account Deficit." Remarks made at the Sandridge Lecture, Virginia Association of Economists, Richmond, Virginia, March 10.

Bloomfield, A. 1968. "Patterns of Fluctuation in International Investment before 1914." Princeton Studies in International Finance No. 21. Princeton, NJ: International Finance Section, Department of Economics, Princeton University.

Bolt, J., and J. L. van Zanden. 2014. "The Maddison Project: Collaborative Research on Historical National Accounts." *The Economic History Review* 67 (3): 627–51.

Bordo, M. 1993. "The Bretton Woods International Monetary System: A Historical Overview." In *A Retrospective on the Bretton Woods System: Lessons for International Monetary Reform*, edited by M. Bordo and B. Eichengreen. Chicago: University of Chicago Press.

———. 2007. "Gold Standard." In *Concise Encyclopedia of Economics*, edited by D. Henderson. Indianapolis, IN: Liberty Fund, Inc.

Boughton, J. 2002. "Why White, Not Keynes? Inventing the Post-War International Monetary System." Working Paper 02/52, International Monetary Fund, Washington, DC.

Brown, B. 1987. *The Flight of International Capital: A Contemporary History*. London: Croom Helm.

Cassel, G. 1928. *Postwar Monetary Stabilization*. New York: Columbia University Press.

Coombs, C. 1976. *The Arena of International Finance*. New York: Wiley.

Crabbe, L. 1989. "The International Gold Standard and US Monetary Policy from World War I to the New Deal." *Federal Reserve Bulletin* 75 (6): 423–40.

Eichengreen, B. 1992. *Golden Fetters*. New York: Oxford University Press.

———. 2008. *Globalizing Capital: A History of the International Monetary System*, 2nd ed. Princeton, NJ: Princeton University Press.

Friedman, M. 1953. "The Case for Flexible Exchange Rates." In *Essays in Positive Economics*, edited by M. Friedman, 157–203. Chicago: University of Chicago Press.

Galicia-Escotto, A. 2005. "Liability Aspects of SDRs." Issues Paper (Resteg) No. 10, International Monetary Fund, Washington, DC.

Gardner, R. 1980. *Sterling-Dollar Diplomacy in Current Perspective: The Origins and the Prospects of Our International Economic Order*. New York: Columbia University Press.

Ghosh, A., and P. Masson. 1994. *Economic Cooperation in an Uncertain World*. Cambridge, MA: Blackwell.

Hansen, A. 1939. "Economic Progress and Declining Population Growth." *American Economic Review* 29 (1): 1–15.

Helleiner, E. 1994. *States and the Re-emergence of International Finance: From Bretton Woods to the 1990s*. Ithaca, NY: Cornell University Press.

International Monetary Fund (IMF). 2013. "Unconventional Monetary Policies: Recent Experience and Prospects." IMF Board Paper, International Monetary Fund, Washington, DC.

Irwin, D. 2014. "Who Anticipated the Great Depression? Gustav Cassel versus Keynes and Hayek on the Interwar Gold Standard." *Journal of Money, Credit and Banking* 46 (1): 199–227.

Kindleberger, C. 1973. *The World in Depression, 1929–1939*. Berkeley: University of California Press.

League of Nations. 1932. *World Economic Survey, 1932*. Geneva, Switzerland: League of Nations.

Mills, J. 1922. *The Genoa Conference*. London: Hutchinson & Co.

Oudiz, G., and J. Sachs. 1984. "International Policy Coordination in Dynamic Macroeconomic Models." NBER Working Paper No. 1417, National Bureau of Economic Research, Cambridge, MA.

Putnam, R., and N. Bayne. 1984. *Hanging Together: The Seven Power Summits*. London: Royal Institute of International Affairs.

Reinhart, C., and K. Rogoff. 2009. *This Time Is Different: Eight Centuries of Financial Folly*. Princeton, NJ: Princeton University Press.

Shin, H. 2012. "Global Banking Glut and Loan Risk Premium." *IMF Economic Review* 60 (2): 155–92.

Solomon, R. 1982. *The International Monetary System, 1945–1981*. New York: Harper & Row.

Steil, B. 2013. *The Battle of Bretton Woods: John Maynard Keynes, Harry Dexter White, and the Making of a New World Order*. Princeton, NJ: Princeton University Press.

Summers, L. 2013. "Have We Entered an Age of Secular Stagnation?" Remarks made at the IMF's Fourteenth Annual Research Conference in Honor of Stanley Fischer, Washington, DC, November 8.

Volcker, P., and T. Gyohten. 1992. *Changing Fortunes: The World's Money and the Threat to American Leadership*. New York: Three Rivers Press.

PART I

Perspectives from the Past: Secular Stagnation and Asymmetric Burden of Adjustment

Learning Lessons from Previous Crises: The Capital Account and the Current Account

Harold James

The phenomenon of financial globalization has become a ubiquitous way of understanding the world, but people who have used the concept as a tool of analysis have failed to understand its inherent volatility and instability. This chapter presents two sets of lessons about the difficulty of establishing international cooperation and coordination, derived from the experience of two international financial crises: the Great Depression and the Panic of 1907. In particular, this chapter suggests that the analysis of the determinants and the institutions underlying financial flows are crucial to understand the character of crises and to develop effective policy responses. The question of financial flows does not just raise issues of financial governance; it relates directly to debates about security. The vision of 1944–45 (that a global governance system needed to look at both economic and security aspects) is more relevant than ever in today's discussions about the international monetary system.

1929 AND 1931

After the global financial crisis of 2007–08, policymakers were gripped by the fear of a repetition of the Great Depression. Even before the September 2008 Lehman Brothers failure, it became standard to refer to conditions that had "not been seen since the Great Depression." Some even went further: the deputy governor of the Bank of England, for example, called the crisis the "worst financial crisis in human history." In the April 2009 *World Economic Outlook*, the IMF explicitly considered the depression analogy not only in terms of the collapse of financial confidence but also in the rapid decline of trade and industrial activity around the world (IMF 2009). Almost every contemporary use of the analogy takes the year 1929 as a reference point, but there were really two completely

---

This chapter is based on James 2009 and Borio, James, and Shin 2014.

different pathologies at work during the Great Depression, and they involve different diagnoses and different remedies.

The first and most famous pathology is the crash of the US stock market in October 1929. No country had ever had a stock market panic of that magnitude, primarily because no country had ever experienced the euphoric run-up of stock prices that had sucked large numbers of Americans from very different backgrounds into financial speculation. The second pathology was decisive in turning a bad recession into the Great Depression: a series of bank panics emanated from central Europe in the summer of 1931, spreading financial contagion to Great Britain and then to the United States and France, eventually engulfing the whole world.

The 1929 panic has dominated the literature for two rather peculiar reasons. First, no one has ever been able to give a rational explanation for the collapse of the market in October 1929, in which market participants reacted to a specific news event, as there was no obviously game-changing development in the day or days before the crash. So the crash presents an intriguing intellectual puzzle, and economists can build their reputations on trying to find innovative ways to explain it. Ben Bernanke once called the search for an explanation of the Great Depression the macroeconomic counterpart of the quest for the Holy Grail (Bernanke 1995). Some people conclude that markets are simply irrational, while others produce complicated speculations; for example, that investors might have been able to foresee the Depression or that they were pondering the likelihood of protectionist reactions in other countries to the American tariff act, which had not yet even been cast in its final form.

The second reason that 1929 has been popular with academic and political commentators is that it provides a clear motive for taking particular policy measures. Keynesians have been able to demonstrate that government fiscal demand can stabilize the expectations of the market and thus provide an overall framework for stability. Monetarists tell an alternative but parallel story of how stable monetary growth means that radical perturbations are avoided.

The 1929 crash has no obvious cause but two very plausible solutions, while the 1931 disaster is exactly the other way around: the origins are obvious but the solutions are not. The destructive character of 1931 lay in the series of contagious financial crises that rippled out from central Europe (with origins in Austria), producing a new wave of economic downturns. Without those panics, the stock market crash would have caused a severe but short recession; in other words, it would not have been the Great Depression.

The European banking crises of 1931 are easy to explain; economists will not win any academic laurels by finding innovative accounts of causation. The collapses were the result of bank weakness in countries that had been wrecked by bad policies that produced inflation, hyperinflation, and the destruction of banks' balance sheets. An intrinsic vulnerability made for a heightened exposure to political shocks, and disputes about a central European customs union and about the postwar reparations issue were enough to topple the house of cards. But finding a way out of the damage proved to be very tough. Unlike the situation in 1929, there were no obvious macroeconomic answers to financial distress.

DIFFERING FRAMEWORKS

The lack of an answer reflects the fact that analysts have generally looked in the wrong place, leading to the wrong kind of interpretation and explanation. One version of the history of the international monetary and financial system—the most popular and influential approach—focuses on current accounts. It goes back (at least) to David Hume's view of the gold specie standard (Hume 1752). It sees the economic havoc in the interwar years from the perspective of the *transfer problem* (Keynes 1929a, 1929b; Ohlin 1929a, 1929b). It identifies a systematic contractionary bias in the global economy because of an asymmetric adjustment problem: deficit countries are forced to retrench while surplus countries are under no pressure to expand (Johnson and Moggridge 1980). It traces the 1970s woes and the 1980s Latin American crisis to the recycling of oil exporters' surpluses (Lomax 1986; Congdon 1988). It argues that a saving glut, reflected in large Asian current account surpluses, was at the root of the global financial crisis that erupted in 2007 (Bernanke 2005, 2009; Krugman 2009; King 2010). This version of events is the focus of G20 discussions, which have been preoccupied with global imbalances (shorthand for current account imbalances).

There is a parallel history that focuses on capital accounts. It is less popular and as yet mostly unwritten, although Shin (2012, 2013) attempts a corrective narrative. This parallel version highlights the role of the mobility of financial capital in the gold standard (Bloomfield 1959; De Cecco 1974) and perceives the economic turmoil of the interwar years through the lens of large cross-border flows (Schuker 1988). It focuses on biases and asymmetries that arise from countries' playing the role of bankers to the world (Triffin 1960; Kindleberger 1965; Despres, Kindleberger, and Salant 1966). It argues that a financial surge unrelated to current accounts was the origin of the global financial crisis (Borio and Disyatat 2011; Shin 2012). It laments the peripheral attention that the G20 pays to financial, as opposed to current account, imbalances.

The Achilles' heel of the international monetary and financial system is not so much a contractionary bias that reflects an asymmetric current account adjustment problem (what might be termed a propensity to generate "excess saving"); rather, it is the propensity to amplify financial booms and busts—financial cycles—that generate crises (what might be termed "excess financial elasticity"; Borio and Disyatat 2011; Borio 2014). Surges and collapses in credit expansion, whether through banks (banking gluts) or securities markets, are key ingredients (Shin 2012, 2013), typically along with equivalent surges and collapses in asset prices, especially property prices (Drehmann, Borio, and Tsatsaronis 2012).

Once we focus on the system's excess financial elasticity, we have to look beyond the capital account. For one, the decision-making units, be they financial or nonfinancial, often straddle borders. The residence principle that defines the boundary for the national accounts (and hence for the balance of payments) is inadequate; we need to consider the consolidated income and balance sheet positions of the relevant players. In addition, the currencies underpinning financial and real transactions—in which goods and services are invoiced and, above all, assets are denominated—are often used outside national boundaries. Some currencies (most notably the US dollar) play a huge role in the international monetary and financial system. Finally, it is not so much the international component of the balance sheet position of a country that matters but how it fits into the overall balance sheet of the economy. Financial and macroeconomic vulnerabilities can be properly assessed only in that context.

In a world in which firms increasingly operate in multiple jurisdictions, consolidated income and balance sheet data are more informative. Decision-making units of these firms determine where to operate, what goods and services to produce at what prices, and how to manage risks. Importantly, it is these units that ultimately come under strain. It is nationality, rather than residence, that reflects the consolidated balance sheet of firms and often sets the more relevant boundary. ("Nationality" in this context generally refers to the country in which the company is headquartered. Different criteria may determine where the decision-making unit is located, but the principle of consolidation is not affected by this.) Indeed, the Bank for International Settlements (BIS) consolidated banking statistics were created in the 1970s specifically to address this issue (Borio and Toniolo 2008). In addition, international currencies are used well beyond the boundary of the currency jurisdiction (McCauley, McGuire, and Sushko 2014). The intersection between the nationality of the players and the currencies they use is what matters most to understand currency and funding exposures, vulnerabilities, and the dynamics of financial distress.

THE INTERWAR EXPERIENCE

In the interwar story, the current account imbalance gives only a partial picture. Although the German current account deficit and the US surplus attracted an enormous amount of attention at the time and since, the financial flows and round-tripping between Germany and its neutral neighbors, the Netherlands and Switzerland, were largely under the radar as regards public policy. The implications became clear only after a major financial crisis in 1931, in which foreign short-term credits in Germany were frozen. Foreign borrowing by the German private and public sectors occurred in foreign currencies, with dollar-denominated bonds and credits from the United States and sterling-denominated bonds and credits from the United Kingdom. German agents also accumulated foreign-currency-based claims in other countries, especially the small neutral neighbors; these sums were then re-lent to German corporations. In the lead-up to the financial crisis, as German capital flight accelerated, it was financed in part by drawing on credit lines from US and U.K. banks. As a result, in 1931 net gold inflows to France, Switzerland, and the Netherlands totaled $771 million, and there were gold outflows from Germany but also from the United Kingdom and the United States (Allen and Moessner 2011). Figure 2.1 is a schematic of the 1920s flows.

Figure 2.1. The Geography of Capital Flows in the Interwar Years

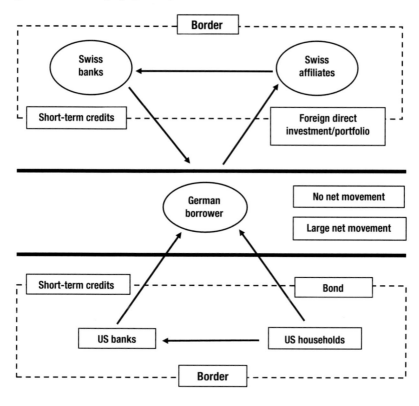

Source: Author's illustration.

It was in the 1920s that the phenomenon of excess financial elasticity appeared in its modern form. Although in the classical (pre-1914) gold standard regime, financial instability was a feature of many countries on the periphery—including the United States—the core countries of the gold standard, Great Britain, France, and also Germany, were comparatively stable and did not experience systemic crises after 1873. That relative stability was admired by the National Monetary Commission in the United States after the Panic of 1907; it was attributed to certain European institutional arrangements and put forth as a reason for instituting a European-style central bank (Mitchell 1911).

The contrast between the generally modest prewar fluctuations at the core and the postwar emergence of an outsize cycle is dramatically evident from comparative data on bank loans. Before the war, bank loans relative to GDP grew gradually in all countries (panel 1 of Figure 2.2), and even the sharp crisis of 1907 caused only a brief interruption in the trend. On the other hand, some (but not all) countries experienced very substantial bank gluts, or excess financial elasticity, in the 1920s, with a collapse during the Great Depression. There is little sign of such a glut in France or Great Britain, but the cycle is very noticeable in the Austrian, German, and US cases, as well as in the Netherlands and Switzerland. (Switzerland is not included in the Schularick and Taylor 2012 data set.) The severity of the Great Depression—measured conventionally by output, industrial production, or unemployment—was significantly greater in the countries that experienced a glut. In the view of Accominotti and Eichengreen (2013), the flows were chiefly driven by the outsized cycle in the principal exporting country, the United States.

The gluts were linked through capital flows, but they were not necessarily correlated with current account positions. The United States, with a substantial surplus, and Germany, with a substantial deficit, both saw large credit and property price booms (panel 2 of Figure 2.2). By contrast, France, with a large surplus, and Britain, with trade deficits, did not experience that phenomenon. Germany and the United States were linked by a substantial gross capital flow in the form of both bond issues and bank lending. Financial fragility played a major role in the buildup of vulnerability and then in the propagation of crisis.

The choice of currency regime alone does not explain the interwar pattern. France and Great Britain returned to the gold standard, the former at a rate conventionally thought to be undervalued and the latter at an overvalued rate as policymakers sought to restore the pre-1914 parity. Banks in both countries engaged in international lending. Some of the relatively small London merchant banks were heavily engaged in South America and central Europe and consequently faced illiquidity or even insolvency threats during the Great Depression (Accominotti 2014). But the segmentation of British banking into merchant banks and clearing banks meant that there was no general glut and no generalized banking crisis after the central European collapse in the summer of 1931. Thus, attempts to explain interwar weakness primarily in terms of the gold standard and its constraints (Temin 1989; Eichengreen 1992; Eichengreen and Temin 2010) build on the argument about asymmetric adjustment (Johnson and Moggridge 1980), but they miss a central element in the vulnerability of the international monetary and financial system in the interwar period.

A key distinction between the pre-1914 world and that of the restored gold standard or gold exchange standard in the 1920s was the centrality of bond financing before World War I, in contrast with the rise of bank credit afterwards. The most common explanation of the 1920s peculiarity lies in the preoccupation with normalization, a return to peacetime normality. With normality, there was an expectation that bond yields would fall. Consequently, short-term bank financing was regarded as an attractive way of bridging the gap before normalization and the return to lower yields, and thus to less expensive financing. In addition, the increased prominence of bank credit was driven by the financial reconstruction of European countries (especially in central Europe) following inflation and hyperinflation during and after the war. The promise of a restoration of prewar conditions provided grounds for the initial optimism ("displacement," in

Figure 2.2. Bank Loans Relative to GDP, 1896–1913

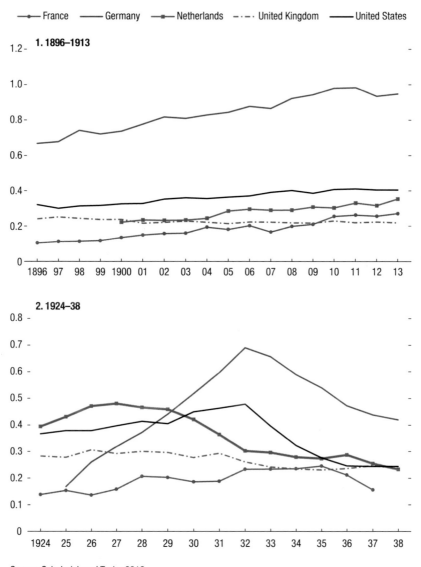

Source: Schularick and Taylor 2012.

Kindleberger's terminology) that generated cross-border capital flows, which pushed the banking glut.

The principal creditor country, the United States, experienced considerable financial innovation, with a new market for foreign bonds developing as a supplement to the old market for domestic bonds (Flandreau and others 2009). In addition, while the traditional issuing houses (notably J.P. Morgan) were very cautious about the burgeoning European market, innovative and pushy houses such as the Boston investment bank Lee, Higginson & Co. saw an opportunity to win market share.

For the debtor countries, financial innovation offered a return to a past that seemed to have been destroyed by World War I and its legacy. In the course of inflation, German bank capital had been destroyed; and in the stabilization of the mid-1920s, banks began with severely reduced levels of capital relative to their prewar positions. They found it expensive to raise new capital, and their new lending consequently occurred on a very thin capital basis. They also found it much harder than before the war to attract retail deposits; consequently, they funded lending with interbank credit from both domestic and international sources. The external source of finance drove the German expansion. It was only at the height of the credit boom that bank loans relative to GDP reached prewar levels (which were high in an international comparison). Paradoxically, this reflection that German growth simply represented a catch-up, with Germany moving back to its prewar position, offered one ground for creditors to believe that their claims might be secure (Balderston 1993).

This vulnerability was increased by the persistence of a German prewar tradition of thinking of the central bank as a lender of last resort. That perception was the fundamental flaw in the domestic policy regime. The safety net provided by the Reichsbank allowed a thinner capital basis and gave misguided confidence to both the banks and their creditors (James 1998). While the banks appeared to have no liquidity constraints, the central bank in the poststabilization world (after 1924) was constrained by the convertibility requirements of the gold standard.

The expansion of borrowing by central European banks occurred in an informational or statistical fog (BIS 1932, 1934). Although the extent of bond financing was quite well known because bond issues were managed publicly, the extent of foreign borrowing was not apparent. Bimonthly and then monthly bank balance sheets (whose publication was required by law in Germany) did not distinguish between foreign and domestic liabilities, although they did give figures for different terms or duration of borrowing. Thus the Reichsbank's assessment of the size of short-term debt in early 1931, on the eve of the crisis, was one-quarter lower than it should have been (Schuker 1988, 57). It was only after the reversal of flows and the inability to make foreign exchange payments after the summer of 1931 that the extent of commercial short-term bank indebtedness became known and statistical overviews could be prepared. The initial assessment of the extent of Germany's short-term debt was presented in August 1931 by the Wiggin-Layton Committee (Wiggin 1931), but the estimates rose over the following months (Special Advisory Committee 1931).

Thus, although the government banking and regulatory authorities knew about the phenomenon, they were ignorant of its extent. Their ignorance casts some doubt on a theory that explains the large expansion of international credit in terms of a well-defined and deliberate strategy on the part of the borrowers. It has been suggested that reparations debtors (above all, Germany) tried to build up their foreign debt liabilities in order to engineer a payments crisis in which the claims of reparations creditors and commercial and bank creditors would come into conflict. According to this logic, when the debt level approached the point of unsustainability, it would trigger a crisis in which the commercial creditors would assert the priority of their claims and press for the cancellation or radical reduction of the reparation burden (Ritschl 2002). Schuker (1988) laid out the argument this way: "Schacht [the president of the German central bank] appeared to be letting German banks run up their short-term liabilities to correspondent institutions in Britain and America so that the latter, fearing for their own liquidity, would entreat their governments to go easy in the next reparations round" (46).

This argument was certainly accepted by some of the lenders and became a way of boosting creditor confidence. A politically well-connected British banker, Reginald McKenna of the Midland Bank, observed,

> under pressure of circumstances when political and commercial forces are in the exchange market with marks to get foreign currencies [to service debt], in practice the commercial would always get priority and success and leave the political in the lurch. … Each bank will act as a clearing house of marks against sterling for its own customer. Each trade operation sets in motion its own demand and offer of one of the two currencies. There would be a private arrangement within the walls of the bank to clear these against each other before the balance of demand was released to the open exchange market. (Johnson 1978, 307–08)

The international flow of capital followed a complex web of linkages, often through decision units that straddled borders. The tangled connections of Germany, a major borrower in the 1920s, and its immediate neighbors, the Netherlands and Switzerland, provide a powerful illustration. Especially in the immediate aftermath of World War I, many German companies, including non-financial corporations as well as banks, acquired stakes in or formed close relations with banks in the Netherlands and Switzerland. There was an initial outflow of funds to build these external relationships. The Dutch and Swiss companies were then used as vehicles to borrow money that was re-lent to Germany, often to the parent company. International credit could be leveraged up in a foreign country, and the resulting capital inflow could in turn be leveraged up in the recipient country. Within Germany, a substantial discussion of the phenomenon of capital flight began even while US money was still flooding into Germany (James 1986).

The motivation for the development of the outward flow from Germany was complex. One reason may have been tax advantages from buying a foreign subsidiary and running substantial operations through it. Initially, many of the fiscal advantages were related simply to saving on stamp duty and stock exchange taxes in Germany. A second reason was that the wartime neutrality of the Netherlands and Switzerland meant that companies there had been used to camouflage German ownership during World War I. But in the 1920s, a third reason was probably the decisive one: borrowing through a non-German corporation substantially reduced the cost of credit, as carry trade developed with interest rates in

Figure 2.3. Swiss Bank Assets, 1906–38
(Millions of Swiss francs)

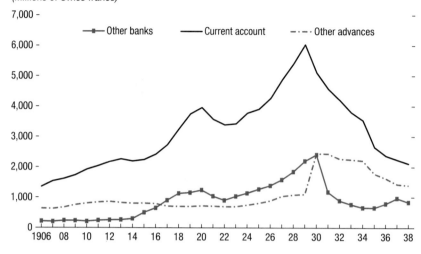

Source: Borio, James, and Shin 2014.

the United States and in the neutral countries substantially lower than rates in Germany.

Direct lending to German industrial, commercial, or agricultural businesses from Switzerland and the Netherlands amounted to no less than 45 percent and 67 percent, respectively, on July 28, 1931 (when the credits were frozen). In the United States, these direct loans represented a much smaller proportion, 28 percent. The prominence of Switzerland and the Netherlands as intermediaries is revealed by the calculation that corporations and individuals in those two countries held 32.2 percent of Germany's short-term debt and 29.2 percent of its long-term debt (Statistisches Reichsamt 1932; Schuker 1988, 117).

The rundown during the financial crisis occurred in parallel in German and Swiss banks. There was substantial capital flight as the economic situation worsened and the fragile political stability of Germany was eroded. Such operations involved repaying German loans from Swiss banks; German banks also saw their deposits fall, and they liquidated some of their foreign holdings. By the time the banking crisis hit in July 1931, the Wiggin-Layton Committee estimated that the short-term foreign assets of German banks had contracted by 40 percent. Swiss bank claims against other banks contracted by a similar amount, 52 percent, over the course of 1931 (Figure 2.3).

The movement of funds out of Germany occurred well before the major US banks started to cut credit lines; for example, it was not until June 23, 1931, that the Bankers Trust Company cut the credit line of Deutsche Bank. On July 6, only a week before the failure of a large German bank, the Guaranty Trust Company announced immediate withdrawals. These outside banks, unlike the insiders involved in the intricate Germany-Netherlands-Switzerland loop, were relatively ill-informed and probably reluctant to trigger a panic in which they were bound to lose a substantial part of their assets.

There has been a considerable controversy about the extent to which the German banking crisis was a banking crisis or a general currency and political crisis set off by the German government's desperate reparations appeal of June 6, 1931. The latter case is made by Ferguson and Temin (2003). However, a look at the positions of individual banks suggests that the withdrawals were not made equally from all German banks; those with a weak reputation suffered the most dramatic outflows (Schnabel 2004; see also James 1984). Thus the Darmstädter und Nationalbank (Danat)—the bank with the most vulnerable reputation—suffered an almost complete collapse of the bulk of its short-term deposits (between seven days and three months maturity); there was also a run, although less significant, on the more solid Deutsche Bank und Disconto Gesellschaft.

Withdrawals from banks meant that the banks demanded more discounting facilities at the central bank, but the Reichsbank refused because it was under pressure from the Bank of England and the Federal Reserve Bank of New York to restrict its credit to stem the developing run on the German currency. The central bank no longer had the currency reserves it would have needed to satisfy the demand for foreign currency that arose in the course of credit withdrawal. The Reichsbank no longer had operational freedom but was tied under the gold-exchange standard system into a network of agreements and dependent on the willingness of other central banks to engage in swaps or other forms of support.

In short, the fragility that had built up in the banking glut was a major cause of the reversal of confidence and of the major financial crisis that hit central Europe in the summer of 1931. Ostensibly, excess financial elasticity was at work.

CONTEMPORARY APPLICATIONS

We can identify similar forces behind the recent great financial crisis. As is well known, the crisis in the United States was preceded by a major financial boom. Credit and property prices surged for several years against the backdrop of strong financial innovation and an accommodative monetary policy.

In comparison with other credit booms, much of the credit expansion was financed from purely domestic sources. But the fraction of external funding as measured by balance of payment statistics was low compared to, say, the credit booms in Spain or the United Kingdom at roughly the same time.

Even so, this aggregate picture conceals the key role that foreign banks, especially European banks, and cross-border flows more generally played in this episode. Indeed, the subprime crisis illustrates well the importance of drawing the correct boundary for capital flow analysis. In particular, European global banks sustained the *shadow banking system* in the United States by drawing on dollar funding in the wholesale market to lend to US residents through the purchase of securitized claims on US borrowers (Shin 2012).

Figure 2.4 illustrates the direction of flows. It shows that European global banks intermediate US dollar funds in the United States by drawing on wholesale dollar funding (for instance, from money market funds in the United States), which is then reinvested in securities that are ultimately backed by mortgage assets in the United States. Capital first flows out of the United States and then flows back in. In this way, the cross-border flows generated by the European global banks net out and are not reflected as imbalances in the current account. In the run-up to the crisis, money market funds in the United States played the role of the base of the shadow banking system, in which wholesale funding is recycled to US borrowers via the balance sheet capacity of banks, especially European banks.

The gross capital flows into the United States in the form of lending by European banks via the shadow banking system no doubt played a pivotal role in influencing credit conditions there in the run-up to the subprime crisis. However, because the euro area had a roughly balanced current account while the United States was a deficit country, the euro area collective current account position (net capital flows) vis-à-vis the United States did not reflect the influence of European banks in setting overall credit conditions in the United States.

This episode clearly illustrates the interaction between the nationality of the banks and the foreign currency in which they operate. Policymakers were completely caught by surprise by the US dollar funding squeeze on European institutions. Why was the need for US dollars so large? The account above provides an explanation. More generally, the BIS international banking statistics reveal that combined US dollar assets of European banks reached approximately $8 trillion

Figure 2.4. European Banks in the US Shadow Banking System

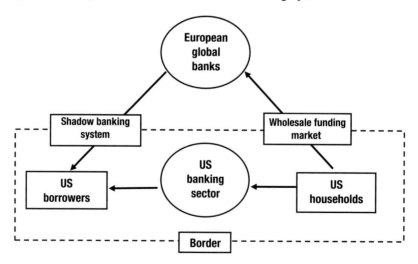

Source: Shin 2012.

in 2008, including retail and corporate lending as well as holdings of US securities: Treasury, agency, and structured products (Borio and Disyatat 2011). Of this amount, between $300 billion and $600 billion was financed through foreign exchange swaps, mostly short term, against the pound sterling, euro, and Swiss franc. Estimates indicate that the maturity mismatch ranged from $1.1 trillion to as high as $6.5 trillion (McGuire and von Peter 2009). Hence the unexpected funding squeeze that hit the US dollar positions of these banks, and the associated serious disruptions in foreign exchange swap markets—the so-called US dollar shortage (Baba and Packer 2008).

US money market funds played a key role. In particular, the Lehman Brothers failure stressed global interbank and foreign exchange markets because it led to a run on money market funds, the largest suppliers of dollar funding to non-US banks, which in turn strained the banks' funding (Baba, Packer, and Nagano 2008; Baba, McCauley, and Ramaswamy 2009). However, the role of the US dollar as the currency that underpins the global banking system is undiminished. McCauley, McGuire, and Sushko (2014) report that more than 80 percent of the dollar bank loans to borrowers resident outside the United States have been booked outside the United States.

NATIONAL POWER AND FINANCE

The discussion of the relationship between financial decision-making units and webs that span national frontiers on the one hand and nation-states as centers of political power on the other raises the issue of how the international system can be appropriately managed. Since the middle of the nineteenth century, the presence of financial centers was often discussed in terms of enhancement of national power. Walter Bagehot (1873) described the city of London in the aftermath of the Franco-Prussian war as "the greatest combination of economic power and economic delicacy that the world has ever seen." When the new German Empire, established only two years earlier, was hit by a financial crisis in 1873, the lesson was clearly drawn: Germany needed something like the Bank of England. In 1875 the Imperial Bank (Reichsbank) was created. By the beginning of the twentieth century some countries still did not have central banks. Indeed there is no inherent reason under the gold standard why a central bank would be needed.

The financial operations of the world in the early 1900s were concentrated in Britain, and specifically in the city of London. Since exporters could not have financial agents in every city that imported from them, the trading finance of the world was run through London merchant banks. If Hamburg or New York merchants wanted to buy coffee from Brazil, they would sign a commitment (a bill) to pay in three months' time on arrival in their port. The commitment might be drawn on a local bank, or it could be turned into cash by the exporter (discounted) at a London bank. A physical infrastructure—the transoceanic cable—provided the basis for the financial links. In addition, most of the world's marine insurance, even for commerce not undertaken on British ships or to British ports, was underwritten by Lloyds of London.

The vulnerability of the world was displayed very abruptly with the outbreak of a financial crisis. The panic of October 1907 showed the fast-growing industrial powers the desirability of mobilizing financial power. The crisis unambiguously originated in the United States, where it had been preceded by financial stress in late 1906 and a stock market collapse in March 1907. At first the October panic affected the new trust companies, but the New York banks were forced to restrict convertibility of deposits into currency. The demand for cash produced an interest rate surge that drew in gold imports but also pushed spikes in interest rates elsewhere, causing great bank strains in Egypt, Italy, and Sweden, but also in Germany.

Only one country seemed quite immune to the panic, even though its market was the central transmission mechanism of price information and interest rate behavior. British observers congratulated themselves on their superiority in a world that was increasingly "cosmopolitan" as a result of the "marvellous developments of traffic and telegraphy," as the *Economist* (1907) put it. "We have no reason to be ashamed. The collapse of the American system has put our supremacy into relief. ... London is sensitive but safe." The central bank in the central financial economy of the world did significantly better in fighting off the financial crisis than any other central bank anywhere else. (Does that sound familiar? The Bank of England then, the Federal Reserve now: people in other countries wanted their institutions to be more like those bulwarks.)

How would the United States and Germany respond to the unique advantages of the Bank of England? The 1907 experience convinced some American financiers that New York needed to develop its own commercial trading system that could handle bills the way the London market did (Broz 1997).

On the technical side, the central figure pushing for the development of an American acceptance market was Paul Warburg, the immigrant younger brother of the great fourth-generation Hamburg banker Max Warburg, who was the personal advisor to Kaiser Wilhelm II. Paul Warburg was a key player in the bankers' discussions on Jekyll Island in 1910 and in drawing up the institutional design of the Federal Reserve System. The Warburg banking brothers were energetically pushing on both sides of the Atlantic for German-American institutions that would offer an alternative to the British industrial and financial monopoly. They were convinced that Germany and the United States were growing stronger year by year, while British power would erode.

Paul Warburg's first contribution appeared well before the panic of October 1907 demonstrated the terrible vulnerability of New York as a financial center and was a response to the market weakness of late 1906. That initial contribution, "Defects and Needs of Our Banking System," appeared in the *New York Times Annual Financial Review* on January 6, 1907; its primary message was the need to learn from continental Europe. Warburg started by complaining, "The United States is in fact at about the same point that had been reached by Europe at the time of the Medicis, and by Asia, in all likelihood, at the time of Hammurabi. ... Our immense National resources have enabled us to live and prosper in spite of our present system, but so long as it is not reformed it will prevent us from ever becoming the financial center of the world. As it is, our wealth makes us an important but dangerous factor in the world's financial community" (Warburg 1907a). The Cassandra-like warning about the danger posed by the American financial system would make Warburg look like a true prophet in the renewed period of tension after October 1907. The panic, the need for a response—coordinated by J.P. Morgan—and the debate about whether Morgan profited unduly from his role as lender of last resort is one of the most celebrated incidents in US financial history. By 1910 Warburg had firmly established himself as the preeminent banking expert on reform of the monetary system.

In Warburg's mind, the problem with the American system was that it relied on single-signature promissory notes: when confidence evaporated in a crisis, the value of these notes became questionable and banks would refuse to deal with them. Warburg proposed emulating the trade finance mechanism of the city of London, where the merchant banks (acceptance houses) established a third signature or endorsement on the bill—a guarantee that they would stand behind the payment. The addition of this guarantee provided a basis on which a particular bank favored by a banking privilege conferred by law, the Bank of England, would rediscount the bill; that is, pay out cash (Warburg 1907b). The second element of the Warburg plan was fundamentally a state bank, an innovation that recalled the early experimentation of Alexander Hamilton but also the controversies about the charter renewals of the First and the Second Bank of the United States.

Warburg was very mindful of international politics in the response to the 1907 crisis. Great Britain was the most mature economy and the financial center of the world, but it was growing more slowly than the larger challengers: the United States and the heavily export-oriented German Empire. The language of Warburg's public appeals made analogies to armies and defense: "Under present conditions in the United States … instead of sending an army, we send each soldier to fight alone." His proposed reform would "create a new and most powerful medium of international exchange—a new defense against gold shipments" (Warburg 1907a). In the financial crises of 1893 and 1907, the United States, which depended on gold shipments from Europe, had been in a profoundly fragile position. Building up a domestic pool of credit that could be used as the basis for issuing money was a way of obviating this dependence. The reform project involved the search for a safe asset—one that was not subject to the vagaries and political interferences of the international gold market.

In the tense debates about the design of the new institution, Warburg consistently presented the issue in terms of a need to increase American security in the face of substantial vulnerability. The term chosen in the original Aldrich Plan, and the eventual name of the new central bank, suggested a clear analogy with military or naval reserves. Warburg (1916) said,

> The word "reserve" has been embodied in all these varying names, and this is significant because the adoption of the principle of co-operative reserves is the characteristic

feature of each of these plans. There are all kinds of reserves. There are military and naval reserves. We speak of reserves in dealing with water supply, with food, raw materials, rolling stock, electric power, and what not. In each case its meaning depends upon the requirements of the organization maintaining the reserve.

Many features of this early twentieth century world have been reproduced in the modern era of hyperglobalization. Like Bagehot's world, it is both highly complex and vulnerable to dislocation and interruption. The modern equivalent to the financial and insurance network that underpinned the first era of globalization is the connectivity established through electronic communications. Like the nineteenth-century trading and insurance network, it is in principle open to all on the same terms. But its complex rules are set in a limited number of jurisdictions—to some extent in Europe but mostly in the United States. The data that connect the information economy depend on complex software and interaction systems managed by large and almost exclusively American corporations such as Google, Microsoft, and Facebook, and American telecom firms such as Sprint and Verizon.

CONCLUSIONS AND OUTLOOK

In a highly globalized world, we need ways to deal with financial policy spillovers, both to other countries and to aggregate conditions. Regulatory and monetary authorities are attached to countries, but financial decision makers often are not. The management of spillovers is especially urgent, as we are in a moment of geopolitical transition that has some fascinating parallels with the world of a century ago. The most mature economy then was Great Britain, but it was growing more slowly than the larger challengers: the United States and the German Empire. Today, the United States is playing the role of Britain a century earlier, and China looks like Imperial Germany: authoritarian but with a politically modernizing society and a quickly growing economy. Today, as then, there is a widespread perception that financial power can be mobilized in security disputes. At the time of Bretton Woods, international security and economic issues were treated in tandem. The United Nations Security Council had five permanent members: China, France, the United Kingdom, the United States, and the USSR. The original Bretton Woods plan put the same five countries on the IMF Executive Board. However, the USSR never ratified Bretton Woods, and the China seat was held by the Republic of China (Taiwan Province of China). It was only in 1980 that the People's Republic came to represent China at the IMF. As a consequence of the exclusion of the Soviet Union and China from the IMF board, financial and economic discussions moved in a different direction than the security discussions at the United Nations. Since 2008—and especially since the April 2009 London G20 meeting—the need to make the IMF more reflective of the real political and economic geography of the world has become more apparent. Realizing this objective would be an appropriate response to the legacy of two major financial crises—in 1907 and 1929–31—that were both tragically soon followed by world wars.

REFERENCES

Accominotti, O. 2014. "London Merchant Banks, the Central European Panic and the Sterling Crisis of 1931." *Journal of Economic History* 72 (1): 1–43.

Accominotti, O., and B. Eichengreen. 2013. "The Mother of All Sudden Stops: Capital Flows and Reversals in Europe, 1919–1932." Working Paper 9670, Center for Economic and Policy Research, Washington, DC.

Allen, W. A., and R. Moessner. 2011. "The International Propagation of the Financial Crisis of 2008 and a Comparison with 1931." Working Paper 348, Bank for International Settlements, Basel, Switzerland.

Baba, N., R. McCauley, and S. Ramaswamy. 2009. "US Dollar Money Market Funds and Non-US Banks." *BIS Quarterly Review* (March): 65–81.

Baba, N., and F. Packer. 2008. "Interpreting Derivations from Covered Interest Parity During the Financial Market Turmoil of 2007–08." Working Paper 267, Bank for International Settlements, Basel, Switzerland.

Baba, N., F. Packer, and T. Nagano. 2008. "The Spillover of Money Market Turbulence to FX Swap and Cross-Currency Swap Markets." *BIS Quarterly Review* (March): 73–86.

Bagehot, W. 1873. *Lombard Street: A Description of the Money Market.* London: H.S. King & Co.

Balderston, T. 1993. *The Origins and Course of the German Economic Crisis: November 1923 to May 1932.* Berlin: Haude & Spener.

Bank for International Settlements (BIS). 1932. *Second Annual Report.* Basel, Switzerland.

———. 1934. *Fourth Annual Report.* Basel, Switzerland.

Bernanke, B. 1995. "The Macroeconomics of the Great Depression: A Comparative Approach." *Journal of Money, Credit, and Banking* 27 (1): 1–28.

———. 2005. "The Global Saving Glut and the U.S. Current Account Deficit." The Sandridge Lecture, Virginia Association of Economists, Richmond, Virginia, March 10.

———. 2009. "Financial Reform to Address Systemic Risk." Speech at the Council on Foreign Relations, Washington, DC, March 10.

Bloomfield, A. 1959. *Monetary Policy under the International Gold Standard, 1880–1914.* New York: Federal Reserve Bank.

Borio, C. 2014. "The Achilles' Heel of the International Monetary System: What It Is and What to Do about It." Paper prepared for a keynote lecture at the Festschrift in honor of Niels Thygesen, University of Copenhagen, December 5.

Borio, C., and P. Disyatat. 2011. "Global Imbalances and the Financial Crisis: Link or No Link?" Working Paper 346, Bank for International Settlements, Basel, Switzerland. Revised and expanded version of "Global Imbalances and the Financial Crisis: Reassessing the Role of International Finance." *Asian Economic Policy Review* 5 (2010): 198–216.

Borio, C., H. James, and H. S. Shin. 2014. "The International Monetary and Financial System: A Capital Account Historical Perspective." Working Paper 457, Bank for International Settlements, Basel, Switzerland.

Borio, C., and G. Toniolo. 2008. "One Hundred and Thirty Years of Central Bank Cooperation: A BIS Perspective." In *The Past and Future of Central Bank Cooperation,* edited by C. Borio, G. Toniolo, and P. Clement. Studies in Macroeconomic History Series. Cambridge, U.K.: Cambridge University Press.

Broz, J. L. 1997. *The International Origins of the Federal Reserve System.* Ithaca, New York: Cornell University Press.

Congdon, T. 1988. *The Debt Threat: The Dangers of High Real Interest Rates for the World Economy.* Oxford, U.K.: Basil Blackwell.

De Cecco, M. 1974. *Money and Empire: The International Gold Standard.* Oxford, U.K.: Blackwell.

Despres, E., C. Kindleberger, and W. Salant. 1966. *The Dollar and World Liquidity: A Minority View.* Washington, DC: Brookings Institution.

Drehmann, M., C. Borio, and K. Tsatsaronis. 2012. "Characterising the Financial Cycle: Don't Lose Sight of the Medium Term!" Working Paper 380, Bank for International Settlements, Basel, Switzerland.

Economist 1907. "The Money Market." Issue 3357 (December 28): 2285–86.

Eichengreen, B. 1992. *Golden Fetters: The Gold Standard and the Great Depression, 1919–39.* Oxford, U.K.: Oxford University Press.

Eichengreen, B., and P. Temin. 2010. "Fetters of Gold and Paper." *Oxford Review of Economic Policy* 26 (3): 370–84.

Ferguson, T., and P. Temin. 2003. "Made in Germany: The German Currency Crisis of 1931." *Research in Economic History* 21: 1–53.

Flandreau, M., J. H. Flores, N. Gaillard, and S. Nieto-Parra. 2009. "The End of Gatekeeping: Underwriters and the Quality of Sovereign Bond Markets, 1815–2007." NBER Working Paper 15128, National Bureau of Economic Research, Cambridge, MA.

Hume, D. 1752. *Political Discourses.* Edinburgh, Scotland: A. Kincaid and A. Donaldson.

International Monetary Fund (IMF). 2009. *World Economic Outlook.* International Monetary Fund, Washington, DC, April.

James, H. 1984. "The Causes of the German Banking Crisis of 1931." *Economic History Review* 38: 68–87.

———. 1986. *The German Slump: Politics and Economics 1924–1936.* Oxford, U.K.: Oxford University Press.

———. 1998. "Die Reichsbank 1876 bis 1945." In *Deutsche Bundesbank, Fünfzig Jahre Deutsche Mark: Notenbank und Währung in Deutschland seit 1948,* 29–89. Munich: C.H. Beck.

———. 2009. *The Creation and Destruction of Value.* Cambridge, MA: Harvard University Press.

Johnson, E., editor. 1978. *The Collected Writings of John Maynard Keynes, Volume 18. Activities 1922–1932: The End of Reparations.* Cambridge, U.K.: Royal Economic Society.

Johnson, E., and D. Moggridge, editors. 1980. *The Collected Writings of John Maynard Keynes, XXV, Activities 1940–1944 Shaping the Post-War World—The Clearing Union.* Cambridge, U.K.: Macmillan.

Keynes, J. M. 1929a. "The German Transfer Problem." *Economic Journal* 39: 1–7.

———. 1929b. "The Reparations Problem: A Discussion. II. A Rejoinder." *Economic Journal* 39: 179–82.

Kindleberger, C. 1965. "Balance-of-Payments Deficits and the International Market for Liquidity." *Princeton Essays in International Finance* 46 (May).

King, M. 2010. Speech delivered at the University of Exeter, Exeter, United Kingdom, January 19. http://www.bankofengland.co.uk/archive/Documents/historicpubs/speeches/2010/speech419.pdf.

Krugman, P. 2009. "Revenge of the Glut." *New York Times,* March 1.

Lomax, D. 1986. *The Developing Country Debt Crisis.* London: Macmillan.

McCauley, R., P. McGuire, and V. Sushko. 2014. "Global Dollar Credit: Links to US Monetary Policy and Leverage." Paper prepared for the 59th Panel Meeting of Economic Policy, Izmir, Turkey, April 25–26.

McGuire, P., and G. von Peter. 2009. "The US Dollar Shortage in Global Banking and the International Policy Response." Working Paper 291, Bank for International Settlements, Basel, Switzerland.

Mitchell, W. C. 1911. "The Publications of the National Monetary Commission." *Quarterly Journal of Economics* 25 (3): 563–93.

Ohlin, B. 1929a. "The Reparation Problem: A Discussion." *Economic Journal* 39 (June): 172–83.

———. 1929b. "Mr. Keynes' Views on the Transfer Problem. II. A Rejoinder from Professor Ohlin." *Economic Journal* 39: 400–404.

Ritschl, A. 2002. *Deutschlands Krise und Konjunktur 1924–1934: Binnenkonjunktur, Auslandsverschuldung und Reparationsproblem zwischen Dawes-Plan und Transfersperre.* Berlin: Akademie Verlag.

Schnabel, I. 2004. "The Twin German Crisis of 1931." *Journal of Economic History* 64: 822–71.

Schuker, S. 1988. "American 'Reparations' to Germans, 1919-33: Implications for the Third World Debt Crisis." *Princeton Studies in International Finance* 61 (July).

Schularick, M., and A. M. Taylor. 2012. "Credit Booms Gone Bust: Monetary Policy, Leverage Cycles, and Financial Crises, 1870-2008." *American Economic Review* 102(2): 1029–61.

Shin, H. 2012. "Global Banking Glut and Loan Risk Premium." Mundell-Fleming Lecture, *IMF Economic Review* 60 (2): 155–92.

———. 2013. "The Second Phase of Global Liquidity and Its Impact on Emerging Economies." Keynote address at the Federal Reserve Bank of San Francisco, Asia Economic Policy Conference, San Francisco, November 3–5.

Special Advisory Committee. 1931. *Report of the Special Advisory Committee.* Basel, Switzerland, December 23.

Statistisches Reichsamt. 1932. "Die Deutsche Auslansverschuldung." *Wirtschaft und Statistik* (August): 490–93.

Temin, P. 1989. *Lessons from the Great Depression.* Cambridge, MA: MIT Press.

Triffin, R. 1960. *Gold and the Dollar Crisis: The Future of Convertibility.* New Haven, Connecticut: Yale University Press.

Warburg, P. 1907a. "Defects and Needs of Our Banking System." *New York Times*, January 6.

———. 1907b. "A Plan for a Modified Central Bank." *Proceedings of the Academy of Political Science in the City of New York, No. 4, Essays on Banking Reform in the United States,* July 1914 (originally 1907).

———. 1916. "The Reserve Problem and the Future of the Federal Reserve System." Address by Hon. Paul M. Warburg before the Convention of the American Bankers Association, Kansas City, Missouri, September 29. http://fraser.stlouisfed.org/docs/historical/federal%20 reserve%20history/bog_members_statements/Warburg_19160929.pdf.

Wiggin, A. 1931. *Report of the Committee Appointed on the Recommendation of the London Conference 1931.* 59th Panel Meeting of Economic Policy, Basel, Switzerland.

CHAPTER 3

Debates about Economic Adjustment in Europe before the Euro

EMMANUEL MOURLON-DRUOL

Economic adjustment in Europe had been a source of intense debate and frustration long before the inception of the European Economic Community (EEC) in 1957.[1] The ambitious desire to create a European common market aimed at an "ever closer union" and the decision to create a single currency in 1992 have led to even more vivid debates, which have come to the fore since the beginning of the European debt crisis in 2009 (Mourlon-Druol 2014).

Design failures of the euro area are apparent—academics and some policymakers clearly identified them as early as the 1990s (Feldstein 1997; Verdun 1996). The absence of a redistributive budget at the European Union (EU) level, the lack of coordination in economic policymaking across the euro area, and the nonmutualization of sovereign debt are but a few elements that have often been cited as shortcomings in the euro area's institutional setup. The euro crisis has provided a stark reminder of these problems and has reignited the debate about necessary reforms in the single currency area. The advantages and weaknesses of current reforms are a hotly debated topic and are likely to remain so in the future (De Grauwe 2012; Vallée 2014).

As a consequence of the design failures of the euro area, there is a widespread perception that European policymakers were largely uninterested in the wider economic and financial implications of monetary integration in Europe. A conclusion of the 1975 Marjolin report on Economic and Monetary Union (EMU) remains true:

> the decision of 1969 to create an EMU in the course of the next ten years [was taken] without any precise idea of what was being undertaken. At government level, there was no analysis, even approximative, of the conditions to be fulfilled. It was

---

[1] For a sense of these debates, see, for example, Bussière, Dumoulin, and Schirmann 2006; Schirmann 2006; and Stevenson 2012. This chapter presents some preliminary ideas of my project "The Making of a Lopsided Union: Economic Integration in the European Economic Community, 1957-1992," funded by a Starting Grant of the European Research Council.

just as if the governments had undertaken the enterprise in the naïve belief that it was sufficient to decree the formation of an EMU for this to come about at the end of a few years, without great effort nor difficult and painful economic and political transformations."[2]

The Treaty on European Union (also known as the Maastricht Treaty) of 1992 focused exclusively on currency relations and thus overlooked many aspects of economic adjustment, which indicates that the euro's inception had not been thoroughly thought out. In short, the sustainability of EMU was a question left unanswered by the Maastricht Treaty (Dyson and Featherstone 1999). This confusion is reflected in the debate about optimum currency areas (OCAs), which seeks to define the economic characteristics of countries for which the use of a common currency would be optimum—that is, would not create any loss of well-being. In his seminal article, economist Robert Mundell identified several factors that defined an OCA, such as the mobility of factors of production (labor and capital) and the symmetry of external shocks (Mundell 1961). Other scholars have since added to the list: Ronald McKinnon (1963) stressed the openness of the economy; Peter Kenen (1969), the diversification of production; James Ingram (1969), the financial dimension; Gottfried Haberler (1970) and Marcus Fleming (1971), the convergence of inflation rates; and Charles Kindleberger (1986), the homogeneity of preferences within the zone. From the beginning, the euro area was not an OCA, as it did not meet several of the criteria, and too little thought had been given to how to compensate for these shortcomings, which were likely to threaten the very existence of the area.

Currency-related issues have dominated the process of European integration for the past 50 years or so of European integration. The story is well-known (James 2012). It all started with some modest proposals in the 1960s, in particular the so-called Barre memoranda, named after the European economic and financial commissioner Raymond Barre. Most famous is the 1970 Werner Plan, named after the Luxembourg finance minister, Pierre Werner, who chaired a working group on the creation of an economic and monetary union, which called for such a union in three stages. The implementation of the plan failed as early as 1974, partly owing to disagreements among the EEC members and partly as a result of the collapse of the Bretton Woods system, which created monetary turbulence in Europe. In the late 1970s, the EEC launched a new exchange rate system, the European Monetary System (EMS), which was meant to be a step toward the adoption of a single European currency. This currency was finally designed by the Delors report (which bore many similarities to the 1970 Werner report), enshrined in the 1992 Maastricht Treaty, created in 1999, and physically introduced in 2002. But although they achieved a single currency, European policymakers were careless about actual economic integration. They overlooked the other key components of what constitutes, both in theory (as shown in

---

[2]Report of the study group "Economic and Monetary Union 1980" (Brussels: European Commission, 1975).

political science, economics, and history) and in practice, a properly functioning monetary union: the fiscal, supervisory/regulatory, and political components.

This carelessness is apparent if we consider the level of high politics and grand bargains. At the key lower levels—bureaucratic, technocratic, and academic—interesting discussions took place about missing elements such as macroeconomic policy coordination, fiscal transfers, banking regulation and supervision, and the completion of the single market. This chapter outlines some of the debates in each of these areas during the formative period of the EU, then still known as the EEC. Taken together, these four areas highlight the richness of the debates about European economic integration before the creation of the euro and underline the long-standing challenges to European economic integration. The chapter concludes with some reflections on past and current efforts to enhance integration and on the overall flexibility of the European polity.

MACROECONOMIC POLICY COORDINATION

The idea that macroeconomic policy cooperation among EU member states should be improved is not a new one; it has been a constant feature of discussions since the creation of the EEC in 1957. Throughout the 1960s, the European Commission took on the issue of macroeconomic policy coordination. The two successive European commissioners for economics and finance, Robert Marjolin (1958–67) and Raymond Barre (1967–73), stressed the need to better synchronize European economic policymaking in the short, medium, and long terms. Their thinking was strongly influenced by French economic planning. The results were limited, as their efforts mostly led to the creation of various committees, including the Short Term Economic Policy Committee established in 1960 and the Budgetary Policy Committee and the Medium-Term Economic Policy Committee set up in 1964.

Macroeconomic policy coordination—or economic convergence, as it was sometimes called—remained on the agenda in the 1970s. The Werner Plan, published in 1970, emphasized the need for EEC member states' economies to converge for the monetary union to be successful. This materialized in an EEC Council decision in February 1974 on "the attainment of a high degree of convergence of the economic policies of the member states of the EEC." The Council explained, "There can be no gradual attainment of Economic and Monetary Union unless the economic policies pursued by the member states henceforth converge and unless a high degree of convergence is maintained."[3] However, the directive was not binding, and EEC member states did not put it into practice; for example, the so-called stop-and-go economic policies practiced by the French government throughout the 1970s were not coordinated with other EEC

---

[3]Council Decision of February 18, 1974, on the attainment of a high degree of convergence of the economic policies of the Member States of the European Economic Community, 74/120/EEC.

Figure 3.1. Inflation Rates in France, Germany, Italy, and the United Kingdom, 1970–90
(Percent)

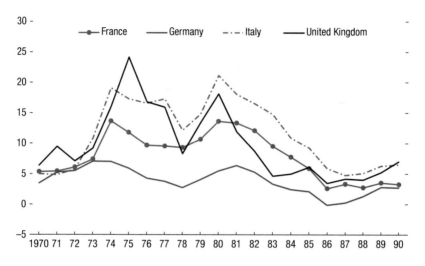

Source: Organisation for Economic Co-operation and Development statistics.
Note: Annual percentage change of consumer prices for all items.

member states. This contributed to significant differences in inflation rates (see Figure 3.1), which in turn made monetary cooperation more difficult.

In addition to the initiatives originating from the Commission, the Council, and the Werner report, some attempts at improving macroeconomic policy coordination occurred at the bilateral level, primarily the Franco-German joint effort at the end of the 1970s, in the run-up to the creation of the EMS. French President Valéry Giscard d'Estaing and German Chancellor Helmut Schmidt showed their willingness to better coordinate the French and German governments' macroeconomic policymaking by developing regular and frequent consultations, especially between their finance ministries and central banks, in the framework of the Élysée Treaty (Mourlon-Druol 2012). This effort stemmed from the stability-oriented economic policy pursued since 1976 by French Prime Minister Raymond Barre, who was much closer in his economic philosophy to German conceptions than the French government before him. However, these Franco-German economic consultations bore little fruit after Barre's premiership. In particular, economic policy measures were little coordinated from 1981 on, after François Mitterrand became president of France (Duchaussoy 2011).

The history of the Commission's efforts in the 1950s and 1960s, the 1974 Council directive, and the Franco-German attempts of the late 1970s show that the quest for greater macroeconomic policy coordination in the EU has not been just a post-euro endeavor. The Stability and Growth Pact of the late 1990s raised this endeavor to a formal, structured level (Heipertz and Verdun 2010).

But its vicissitudes ever since, and the debates over implementing the 2012 Treaty on Stability, Coordination, and Governance (TSCG or Fiscal Compact), underscore the difficulty of establishing proper macroeconomic policy coordination in the EU.

FISCAL TRANSFERS

The notion that financial transfers should occur from the richer to the less developed euro area members in order to create the conditions of a properly functioning monetary union is not new, although it was mostly implicit in the 1960s, the formative period of the EEC. The EEC developed (or attempted to develop) a number of common policies to effectively transfer money across the whole group of countries. Most famously, the common agricultural policy accounted for the largest part of the EEC budget (Knudsen 2009). Some other policies that engendered financial transfers (such as the common fishing policy and, most important, the creation of the European Regional Development Fund in 1975) and the existence of the European Investment Bank (EIB) were attempts, if modest and imperfect, to rebalance economic development among EEC member states and regions (Varsori and Mechi 2007; Bussière, Dumoulin, and Willaert 2008; Churchill and Owen 2010).

Actual discussions focusing on the role of the European budget in the functioning of a European monetary union were more vivid in the 1970s. These discussions centered on the idea that, if the Community were to move forward on the road to monetary union, such a budget would be required as a stabilization mechanism and to run countercyclical policies. Two reports tackled these issues specifically. The Marjolin report, published in 1975, painted a very bleak picture of EMU prospects: "Europe is no nearer to EMU than in 1969. In fact, if there has been any movement it has been backwards."[4] But the report also contained interesting reflections about the wider implications of the establishment of a monetary union in Europe, including comments on European fiscal transfers. The report mentioned the need for a sizable Community budget, the development of sectoral policies (for example, industrial and energy), and the possibility of introducing a Community unemployment benefit.

Two years later, in 1977, the MacDougall report looked into "the role of public finances in European integration."[5] This report suggested increasing the EEC budget from 0.7 percent of GDP to 2.0–2.5 percent: "We have considered whether the Community budget could or should be used as an instrument for helping to stabilise short-term and cyclical fluctuations in economic activity. We conclude that this would be very limited in the 'pre-federal integration' period.

---

[4]Report of the study group "Economic and Monetary Union 1980" (Brussels: European Commission, 1975).

[5]Report of the study group on the role of public finance in European integration (Brussels: European Commission, 1977).

With a budget of the order of 1–2 percent of gross product, the budget balance would have to swing by enormous percentage fractions of this budget to have a perceptible macro-economic effect on activity in the Community as a whole; and to allow this would also weaken the link in the minds of politicians between public expenditure and the need to pay for it over a period of years by taxation." Some reflections in the report strikingly echo current discussions about austerity policies: "We would, however, favour limited powers of borrowing (and repayment) to prevent the need for a Community budgetary policy that actually accentuated cyclical movement, by forcing tax increases or expenditure cuts in recession years and vice versa. We would also favour specific counter-cyclical policies."[6]

The "less prosperous" countries of the EEC made a similar point about the need for fiscal transfers during the EMS negotiations in 1978 (Mourlon-Druol 2012). Three countries—Britain, Ireland, and Italy—made it clear that they might not be able to maintain their currencies within the new Community exchange rate system, because their economies were weaker compared with those of Germany and the Netherlands. To compensate for this, Britain, Ireland, and Italy asked their European partners to explore the possibility of increasing the actual transfer of resources from richer to less developed EEC member states. This was done through the so-called concurrent studies of the EMS negotiations, that is, studies that were run in tandem with the discussions about devising the Exchange Rate Mechanism (ERM). Overall, however, the concurrent studies did not bring results. The potential creditors—chiefly Germany but also the Benelux countries and France—were not willing to contribute, so the concurrent studies ended in deadlock. But they contributed to the debate about the need to go beyond the assumption that member states that were willing to participate in a European monetary arrangement had to adapt on their own, without financial help from the EEC, if the EEC were to become a genuine economic and monetary union.

BANKING UNION

The development of European banking regulation and supervision is the third area that is thought to have been overlooked when policymakers considered European economic integration before the introduction of the euro. However, the idea that banking regulation and supervision should be developed at the EEC/EU level and in tandem with monetary integration appeared much earlier than the recent euro area crisis and the current discussions on the creation of a banking union (Mourlon-Druol 2016).

Of the four policy areas covered in this chapter, ambitions have been highest from the beginning in this one, although their concrete realization was limited until 2012 (Pisani-Ferry and others 2012; Dragomir 2010; Goodhart 2011). In

---

[6]Report of the study group on the role of public finance in European integration (Brussels: European Commission, 1977), 17–18.

the 1960s, the EEC Commission wanted to draw up a single directive that would harmonize the member states' banking legislation. The Commission of the European Communities—the executive arm of the community—wanted to create a common market in banking and aspired to remove the obstacles that prevented equal access to the markets. One of these obstacles pertained to the disparities that existed among the regulatory and supervisory frameworks of the six EEC member states. In July 1972 European Commissioner Wilhelm Haferkamp wrote a draft directive on "the coordination of legislative, regulatory and administrative dispositions concerning the access to the non-stipendiary activities of credit institutions and their exercise."[7] The Commission communicated the project to the six member states and the three applicants (Britain, Denmark, and Ireland), but the nine failed to agree on a common position. Although the Commission never suggested the creation of a single supranational supervisor, the directive did cover the issues of deposit insurance, winding-up procedures, and harmonization of banking regulations across Europe—the pillars of today's euro area banking union (Howarth and Quaglia 2013; Véron 2015).

Because of the failure of its initial strategy, the European Commission moved in the mid-1970s to a slower and more modest step-by-step approach. Christopher Tugendhat, British commissioner in charge of the negotiations, mentioned the link with monetary integration:

> There is the close relation between this field [banking harmonization] and the wider issue of the EMS. It would be easier to implement a common monetary policy if we had banking systems supervised according to equivalent common standards, and eventually of similar structures. Moreover, to the extent to which EMS gives rise to more capital liberalisation, we have to make sure to be able to monitor the actors in this forthcoming common capital market, i.e., the European credit institutions, on the basis of equivalent rules.[8]

In spite of the clear link between monetary integration and the development of banking regulation and supervision in Europe, the areas evolved at a different pace.

Another reason for the modesty of EEC developments was the question of where international banking regulation and supervision should take place. A series of banking failures in 1974 prompted the coordination of regulatory and supervisory efforts at the international, rather than European, level (Schenk 2014; Mourlon-Druol 2015). The failures of Bankhaus Herstatt and the Israeli-British Bank, as well as the Lloyds Lugano rogue trading scandal, highlighted lapses in international supervisory coordination. The Basel Committee on Banking Supervision—although established after the development of EEC committee

---

[7]Projet de directive visant la coordination des dispositions législatives, réglementaires et administratives concernant l'accès aux activités non salariées d'établissements de crédit et de leur exercice, Commission européenne, 1972.

[8]Historical Archives of the European Commission, HAEC, 223/1997 No.3, Record of the meeting of senior officials of the member states in the field of banking legislation and bank supervision held in Brussels on December 7, 1978.

structures on the same policy areas—quickly took precedence, especially in setting out the successive Basel Agreements. In that sense, the development of European banking regulation and supervision illustrates the wider challenges posed by the concurrent processes of financial globalization and regionalization (Bussière 2012).

SINGLE MARKET

A fourth stream of ideas relates to the completion of the single market in Europe. The crux of the single-market project from the 1980s onward was the removal of nontariff barriers (Egan 2001; Jabko 2006). Current actions regarding the development of transport and energy networks; citizen and business mobility; the digital economy; and social entrepreneurship, cohesion, and consumer confidence—presented under the umbrella term Single Market Act II—are meant to encourage economic growth in the EU.[9] But such efforts are not new; they began with the creation of the EEC in the late 1950s.

The development of European banking regulation and supervision mentioned in the previous section originates from the European Commission's policy ambition to improve the European common market by creating a genuine common market in banking. This effort often focused on nontariff barriers and developed as a complement to other projects for monetary integration, although it related more widely to the development of European capital markets (Maes 2007). Thus, far from being a recent preoccupation of European policymakers, the development of European capital markets was already an important topic in the 1960s. Claudio Segré, chairman of an expert group on the subject and director of studies in the Commission's Directorate-General for Economic and Financial Affairs, published a report on the topic in November 1966. The report presented a comprehensive look at the problems confronting the capital markets of the EEC, especially the issue of their underdevelopment:

> In all the Member States the financing of economic growth is coming to depend more and more on the capital market, and the establishment of wider markets and close co-ordination of economic policies would facilitate this growth by: i) Offering enterprises new and more varied opportunities of obtaining from outside sources the financial resources that can help them expand to the size needed for efficient operation in the common market; ii) Bringing more into line the conditions on which finance can be obtained in the Community, and so reducing the distortions in competition due to present differences; iii) Increasing the supply of capital as financial savings are attracted to the market by the wider range of investment outlets; iv) Intensifying financial flows and so lessening the risk of the disturbances that are characteristic of excessively narrow markets. (Segré 1966, 15)

---

[9]See the European Commission's website: http://ec.europa.eu/growth/single-market/smact/index_en.htm.

However, liberalization of capital flows faced much opposition in the EEC during the 1960s and 1970s, and the development of European capital markets was largely postponed. The influence of Bretton Woods thinking—in particular the distrust of capital flows—and different policy priorities limited progress in that policy area.

The idea of focusing on the removal of nontariff barriers did not originate in the 1980s but dates back at least to the late 1970s. In the run-up to the EMS negotiations, the European Commission was split into two camps: one, led by Commission President Roy Jenkins, prioritized monetary integration; the other, led by Vice President for Economic and Financial Affairs François-Xavier Ortoli, gave precedence to improving economic cooperation (Mourlon-Druol 2012, 134–42). As early as 1978, Ortoli advocated the elimination of the remaining obstacles to the four fundamental freedoms of the EEC (goods, capital, services, and people). His argument was that economic convergence (and thus the deepening of the common market) was a necessary precondition of the establishment of a monetary union. However, the negotiations over the creation of the ERM took center stage, and Ortoli's ideas were largely sidelined until the renewed political impetus given to the single market project in the mid-1980s.

CONCLUSIONS

Discussions about economic adjustment in Europe before the creation of the euro were often very ambitious and made a clear connection with monetary integration, although the traditional narrative inherited from the Single European Act (SEA)/Maastricht agenda (which focused on liberalization and currency union) tends to deemphasize the richness of the debates that took place in the 1950s, 1960s, and 1970s. Examining these early debates shows that many current efforts originated much earlier than is usually thought.

What can we learn from these past discussions? A strict comparison between then and now is very difficult to make. For example, calling for the creation of a single banking regulatory regime throughout the EEC, as the Commission did in the late 1960s and early 1970s, is very different from what is going on today. The context has changed enormously. The first efforts in this direction by the European Commission took place in a world with very limited capital movements, very different banking systems among the EEC member states, no single currency, and only six members in the Community. But leaving aside comparability of the past and present, a couple of important elements emerge from reviewing history: the political will and flexibility.

Political will was as central to past successes and failures as it is to today's discussions, improvements, and setbacks in the euro area. The lack of political will to back up the Commission's efforts in the 1960s and 1970s, for instance, partly explains why its proposals failed; why no redistributive mechanism accompanied the creation of the exchange rate mechanism; and why various attempts to coordinate budgetary policies across the EEC/EU (1974 directive, 1997 Stability and Growth Pact, 2012 TSCG) have been so difficult to implement. The EU's institutional setup is another dimension of European economic adjustment. The independence or supranational character of some institutions have proved to be paramount in their evolution and their role in EEC/EU integration. The European Central Bank, the European Court of Justice, and the Single Supervisory Mechanism of the euro area banking union have all asserted strong influence over the integration process, as a result of their independence and supranational dimension. The independence of these institutions continues to fuel the debate about EU legitimacy and constitutes a key dimension of EU economic policymaking (Sternberg 2013; Vauchez 2016).

The second important element that emerges from the historic overview in this chapter is that although the euro area's design failures were anticipated in the 1990s, both in the literature and by some of the architects themselves, the high degree of flexibility of the overall system has been largely underestimated. A discussion of design failures often focuses on inflexibility in the single currency area; for instance, the fact that the Maastricht Treaty prevented the European Central Bank from purchasing government bonds has often been criticized. But the bank's January 2015 decision to launch its "quantitative easing" program proved how flexible the institutional setting of the euro area can be. This raises questions about the legitimacy of the EU institutions and about the usefulness of such a program under current conditions. But in any case, it highlights the flexibility and plasticity of the overall institutional and policy framework of the euro area over the past 14 years.

REFERENCES

Bussière, Éric, ed. 2012. "Régionalisme Européen et Mondialisation." *Les Cahiers Irice* 9 (1).

Bussière, Éric, Michel Dumoulin, and Sylvain Schirmann, eds. 2006. *Europe Organisée, Europe du Libre-Échange?: Fin XIXe Siècle-Années 1960*. Brussels: Peter Lang.

Bussière, Éric, Michel Dumoulin, and Emilie Willaert. 2008. *The Bank of the European Union: The EIB 1958–2008*. Luxembourg: European Investment Bank.

Churchill, R. R., and Daniel Owen. 2010. *The EC Common Fisheries Policy*. Oxford, U.K.: Oxford University Press.

De Grauwe, Paul. 2012. "The Governance of a Fragile Eurozone." *Australian Economic Review* 45 (3): 255–68.

Dragomir, Larisa. 2010. *European Prudential Banking Regulation and Supervision: The Legal Dimension*. New York: Routledge.

Duchaussoy, Vincent. 2011. *La Banque de France et l'État: de Giscard à Mitterrand, Enjeux de Pouvoir ou Résurgence du Mur d'Argent ?1978–1984*. Paris: L'Harmattan.

Dyson, Kenneth H. F., and Kevin Featherstone. 1999. *The Road to Maastricht: Negotiating Economic and Monetary Union*. Oxford, U.K.: Oxford University Press.

Egan, Michelle P. 2001. *Constructing a European Market: Standards, Regulation and Governance*. Oxford, U.K.: Oxford University Press.

Feldstein, Martin. 1997. "The Political Economy of the European Economic and Monetary Union: Political Sources of an Economic Liability." *Journal of Economic Perspectives* 11 (4): 23–42.

Fleming, Marcus. 1971. "On Exchange Rate Unification." *Economic Journal* 81: 467–88.

Goodhart, Charles A. E. 2011. *The Basel Committee on Banking Supervision: A History of the Early Years, 1974–1997*. Cambridge, U.K.: Cambridge University Press.

Haberler, Gottfried. 1970. "The International Monetary System: Some Developments and Discussions." In *Approaches to Greater Flexibility of Exchange Rates*, edited by George N. Halm, 115–23. Princeton, NJ: Princeton University Press.

Heipertz, Martin, and Amy Verdun. 2010. *Ruling Europe: The Politics of the Stability and Growth Pact*. Cambridge, U.K., and New York: Cambridge University Press.

Howarth, David, and Lucia Quaglia. 2013. "Banking Union as Holy Grail: Rebuilding the Single Market in Financial Services, Stabilizing Europe's Banks and 'Completing' Economic and Monetary Union." *Journal of Common Market Studies* 51: 103–23.

Ingram, James. 1969. "Comment: The Optimum Currency Problem." In *Monetary Problems of the International Economy*, edited by Robert Mundell and A. Swoboda, 95–100. Chicago: Chicago University Press.

Jabko, Nicolas. 2006. *Playing the Market: A Political Strategy for Uniting Europe, 1985–2005*. Ithaca, New York: Cornell University Press.

James, Harold. 2012. *Making the European Monetary Union: The Role of the Committee of Central Bank Governors and the Origins of the European Central Bank*. Cambridge, MA: Belknap Press of Harvard University Press.

Kenen, Peter. 1969. "The Theory of Optimum Currency Areas: An Eclectic View." In *Monetary Problems of the International Economy*, edited by Robert Mundell and A. Swoboda, 41–60. Chicago: Chicago University Press.

Kindleberger, Charles. 1986. "International Public Goods without International Government." *American Economic Review* 76 (1): 1–13.

Knudsen, Ann-Christina L. 2009. *Farmers on Welfare: The Making of Europe's Common Agricultural Policy*. Ithaca, New York: Cornell University Press.

Maes, Ivo. 2007. *Half a Century of European Financial Integration: From the Rome Treaty to the 21st Century*. Brussels: Mercatorfonds.

McKinnon, Ronald. 1963. "Optimal Currency Areas." *American Economic Review* 53: 717–24.

Mourlon-Druol, Emmanuel. 2012. *A Europe Made of Money: The Emergence of the European Monetary System*. Ithaca, New York: Cornell University Press.

———. 2014. "Don't Blame the Euro: Historical Reflections on the Roots of the Eurozone Crisis." *West European Politics* 37 (6): 1282–96.

———. 2015. "'Trust Is Good, Control Is Better': The 1974 Herstatt Bank Crisis and Its Implications for International Regulatory Reform." *Business History* 57 (2): 311–34.

———. 2016. "Banking Union in Historical Perspective: The Initiative of the European Commission in the 1960s and 1970s." *JCMS: Journal of Common Market Studies* 54 (4): 913–27.

Mundell, Robert. 1961. "A Theory of Optimum Currency Areas." *The American Economic Review* 51 (4): 657–65.

Pisani-Ferry, Jean, André Sapir, Nicolas Véron, and Guntram B. Wolff. 2012. *What Kind of European Banking Union?* Bruegel Policy Contribution, Brussels.

Schenk, Catherine. 2014. "Summer in the City: Banking Scandals of 1974 and the Development of International Banking Supervision." *English Historical Review* 129 (540): 1129–56.

Schirmann, Sylvain. 2006. *Quel Ordre Européen?: De Versailles à la Chute du IIIe Reich*. Paris: Armand Colin.

Segré, Claudio. 1966. *The Development of a European Capital Market*. Brussels: Publishing Services of the European Communities.

Sternberg, Claudia Schrag. 2013. *The Struggle for EU Legitimacy: Public Contestation, 1950–2005*. Basingstoke, U.K.: Palgrave Macmillan.

Stevenson, David. 2012. "The First World War and European Integration." *International History Review* 34 (4): 841–63.

Vallée, Shahin. 2014. "From Mutual Insurance to Fiscal Federalism: Rebuilding the Economic and Monetary Union after the Demise of the Maastricht Architecture." *International Economics* 136: 49–62.

Varsori, Antonio, and Lorenzo Mechi. 2007. "At the Origins of the European Structural Policy: The Community's Social and Regional Policies from the Late 1960s to the Mid 1970s." In *Beyond the Customs Union: The European Community's Quest for Deepening, Widening and Completion, 1969-1975*, edited by Jan Van Der Harst. Brussels: Bruylant.

Vauchez, Antoine. 2016. *Democratizing Europe*. Basingstoke, U.K.: Palgrave Macmillan.

Verdun, Amy. 1996. "An 'Asymmetrical' Economic and Monetary Union in the EU: Perceptions of Monetary Authorities and Social Partners." *Journal of European Integration* 20 (1): 59–81.

Véron, Nicolas. 2015. *Europe's Radical Banking Union*. Brussels: Bruegel.

CHAPTER 4

Coordination Failures during and after Bretton Woods

Catherine R. Schenk

"If you cannot keep your mouth shut, don't come into this room."

(Jelle Zijlstra, president of Nederlandsche Bank, Notes on Meeting of G10 Governors at the Bank for International Settlements, March 7, 1977)

As witnessed in the aftermath of the global financial crisis of 2008, events that expose the interdependence of national economies tend to prompt calls for greater international macroeconomic policy coordination as a way to ensure greater systemic resilience. But examples of successful coordination are relatively scarce. In 1984 in the wake of the sovereign debt crisis, Oudiz and Sachs (1984, 2) remarked that "advocacy of international coordination has been far more plentiful than actual implementation," and 30 years later Ostry and Ghosh (2013, 1) noted that "examples of international macroeconomic policy coordination have been few." It seems that little progress has been made on coordination during the past 30 years. Moreover, when international efforts have actually resulted in attempts at economic coordination, they have shown mixed success in achieving tangible outcomes (Eichengreen 2014). Nevertheless, there have been repeated initiatives to bring governments together to address seemingly persistent failures in the international monetary system. This chapter addresses the motivations for these persistent efforts at international policy coordination in the 40 years after the seminal Bretton Woods conference in 1944. Unlike existing academic assessments of the outcomes of systems of coordination such as Bretton Woods, the Bonn Summit of 1978, and the Plaza and Louvre Accords in the 1980s (see, for example, Frankel, Goldstein, and Masson 1996; Holtham 1989; Putnam and Henning 1989; Tucker and Madura 1991; Bergsten and Green 2016), this chapter highlights failed attempts—initiatives that either were waylaid by events or never got off the ground—and cites private and confidential evidence from various archives that provide evidence of informal collaboration. This approach allows a broader assessment of the landscape of coordination, the continuity in motivation, and the impact of informal rather than rules-based models.

The elusive quest for exchange rate stability is the main focus of the coordination efforts discussed in this chapter. The chapter describes the coordination failures at Bretton Woods, which identified the three key challenges that subsequent efforts sought to address: asymmetric burden of adjustment, the role of the dollar, and the ambiguity over when adjustment was necessary. Next, the chapter provides the context of the range of alternative frameworks to address these apparent failures during the end of the Bretton Woods system. The role played by the Bank for International Settlements' (BIS's) central bank governors meetings is described, followed by a look at a prolonged initiative to devise a new rules-based system through indicators to prompt adjustment.

COORDINATION FAILURES DURING BRETTON WOODS

The great innovation of Bretton Woods was that it created an elaborate set of formal rules to which a large number of countries adhered. The ability of British and American leadership to create consensus and obtain commitment from a wide range of countries at Bretton Woods was an extraordinary success that has not been replicated; however, the system had a mixed record of achieving monetary coordination.

Because the system was based on stable exchange rates, the problem of the accumulation of imbalances was part of the framework. Thus, the IMF was a source of funds to allow members to overcome short-term imbalances without resorting to restricting their external economic relations or adjusting their exchange rates. The issue of how countries would be encouraged to adjust their domestic price levels to retain exchange rate stability in the longer term was left to the IMF Executive Board, which imposed certain conditions when a deficit country drew heavily or at longer term from the Fund. However, the effectiveness of conditionality was mixed. For example, the United Kingdom was a frequent borrower in the 1950s and 1960s, but the terms of its letters of intent were often vague and were not always enforced (Clift and Tomlinson 2012). Fundamentally, the onus of adjustment was placed squarely on deficit countries, with no formal means to encourage surplus countries to inflate or increase demand. This asymmetry suited the United States as the world's major creditor in 1946, but the inability to bring pressure to bear on the persistent surpluses of West Germany and Japan 15 years later proved to be an important driver of the abandonment of the Bretton Woods system in 1971, and became a prominent target of future attempts at coordination.

A second asymmetry in the Bretton Woods system was the role of the US dollar in the global monetary system. Although gold had its role to play in defining the nominal par values of all currencies, the dollar was operationally necessary as an intermediary, given the uneven distribution of gold reserves. Moreover, the perils of linking to a pure commodity standard seemed evident in light of the deflationary experiences of the nineteenth- and early twentieth-century gold standards. However, as early as the 1960s, Robert Triffin famously identified a fundamental flaw in the use of a national currency as the main global currency, conferring a "poisoned 'privilege'" on the dollar (Triffin 1978, 271). The role of the dollar made the system vulnerable to national economic policy of the United States. But the US economy was somewhat insulated from the international economy by the large size of its domestic market, which meant that international trade was relatively small compared to GDP. The role of the dollar is still highly contested in claims that it confers "exorbitant privilege" on the US economy by increasing the appetite for dollar-denominated debt overseas to be held in official and private sector foreign exchange reserves, although the size of this privilege has recently been challenged (McCauley 2015). It is also argued that the pricing and settlement of international trade in US dollars insulates the US economy from the vagaries of exchange rate shocks that affect other economies and can accentuate the tendency for American domestic priorities to prevail in any conflict between US and global monetary priorities.

Even in the context of a rules-based system with broad consensus, compliance was still a problem. The IMF Articles of Agreement were particularly vague on when an exchange rate change would be condoned, relying on the notion of "fundamental disequilibrium" that defied precise ex ante definition. In practice, this ambiguity meant, first, that adjustments were delayed until there was a crisis and, second, that the IMF played a marginal role in the timing and coordination of exchange rate changes. Thus, the general devaluation of European currencies in 1949 paid scant attention to the IMF (Schenk 2010). Likewise, in 1967 the substantial devaluation of sterling involved some consultation with the IMF, but the timing and size of the change were essentially decided by the British government. Identifying the need for and timing of adjustment has been the third goal of successive efforts at coordination.

US support for the system that it designed in the 1940s dwindled in the late 1960s, as West Germany and Japan accumulated substantial surpluses but resisted calls to appreciate their currencies. In the early 1970s, Richard Nixon's government took a harder line on the collective management of the dollar-based monetary system, seeking unsuccessfully to force adjustment on surplus economies. Conversely, European governments called for the correction of American deficits that threatened to spread inflation pressure. But after the unilateral US suspension of the Bretton Woods system in August 1971, the negotiation of the Smithsonian Agreement by December 1971 demonstrated the strong international commitment to this form of rules-based coordination. The ability of the US negotiators, led by Paul Volcker, to renew the system of pegged exchange rates (albeit with some greater flexibility) is testament to the continued consensus among governments that monetary coordination, operated through the constraint of agreed-upon exchange rate targets, was achievable. However, the asymmetries that had plagued the Bretton Woods era were left unresolved, and there was no constraint on the United States that could force it to adjust its domestic monetary policy. Abrupt reversals in US monetary policy in the early 1970s prompted substantial flows of international capital that destabilized European economies, ultimately bringing an end to the dollar-based exchange rate pegs by the spring of 1973.

Thus, although the three flaws in the Bretton Woods framework (asymmetric burden of adjustment, role of the dollar, and ambiguity over when adjustment is required) were clearly identified during the 1960s, they remained unresolved at the time of the system's collapse in the early 1970s. Moreover, the persistence of these challenges after the end of Bretton Woods shows that they were not restricted to the rules-based pegged exchange rate regime.

ALTERNATIVE FORUMS FOR REFORM: G10 DEPUTIES AND THE COMMITTEE OF 20

In response to the evident weaknesses in the Bretton Woods rules, in the 1960s new mechanisms to promote coordination emerged both within the IMF and beyond it. Table 4.1 shows the range of groups that addressed the perceived need for greater cooperation and reform of the international monetary system during the 1960s and 1970s. These organizations focused primarily on restoring or reforming a rules-based framework for macroeconomic coordination, which proved an elusive goal as international capital markets were liberalized and government control over markets eroded. These efforts were also plagued by a lack of consensus regarding the problem to be solved (too little international liquidity or too much?) and the proliferation of interests that made a coherent focus more difficult to achieve as problems of unequal growth and development became more prominent during the 1960s.

The locus of the IMF as the pinnacle forum for policy coordination eroded during the 1960s as the interests of rich countries in leading reform diverged from the IMF's more inclusive structures. During the 1960s the G10 deputized an army of economic and financial bureaucrats who toured the major centers to debate new rules, including the Special Drawing Right (SDR). This cadre converged in various forums, including formal meetings of deputies of the Group of Ten (G10) and Working Party 3 of the Organisation for Economic Co-operation and Development (OECD; Solomon 1982; Helleiner 1996). But despite the huge commitment in time and energy, tangible outcomes were limited by a failure to achieve consensus on either the diagnosis of the problem or its solutions, even among a group of relatively homogeneous high-income industrialized countries. The SDR proposed in 1967 was a last-ditch effort to deliver on repeated promises that reform would be forthcoming, but there was no consensus on whether the dollar should be replaced or on whether the SDR was a form of credit or a form of international money (Schenk 2010; Wilkie 2012). Most important, the US administration was not convinced that reducing the role of the dollar in the global system was desirable. In the wake of the failure to achieve wider reform that would sustain a stable exchange rate system, the European states moved more deliberately toward monetary integration on a regional basis with the Hague Summit of 1969, and their interest in global reform declined (Mourlon-Druol 2012).

Table 4.1. Overlapping Organizations Addressing International Monetary Reform

	Function	Originating Organization	Membership
G10 Deputies	Reform of international monetary system	G10 governments/ General Agreement to Borrow (IMF)	Bureaucrats from G10 industrialized countries
OECD Working Party 3	Promotion of better international payments equilibrium	OECD	Bureaucrats from member states of OECD
Committee of 20	Reform of international monetary system	IMF	Appointed by Executive Committee members of IMF (including both developing and advanced economies)
G5/G7	International cooperation	Governments of G5/G7	Finance ministers and governors of central banks
Interim Committee		IMF	Appointed by Executive Committee members of IMF (including both developing and advanced economies)
Group of 24 on International Monetary Affairs (G24)	International monetary affairs	Developing countries	Intergovernmental group

Source: Author.

Note: G5/G7 refers to the five and seven, respectively, largest economies in the global economy, comprising France, Germany, Japan, the United Kingdom, and the United States (G5), along with Canada and Italy (G7). The G10 comprises Belgium, Canada, France, Germany, Italy, Japan, the Netherlands, Sweden, the United Kingdom, and the United States. OECD = Organisation for Economic Co-operation and Development.

Concerns over the governance of the global economy after the end of Bretton Woods led the IMF to propose a more inclusive forum through the Committee of 20 (C20) nominated by the Executive Board of the IMF. This group included both developing and developed economies and was tasked in 1972 with devising plans to reform the international monetary system. This laudable goal was quickly overtaken by events as the Smithsonian Agreement crumbled and most currencies floated against the US dollar beginning in April 1973. Like the OECD and G10 deputies, the C20 became mired in detailed discussions with little prospect of achieving the consensus necessary to promote effective reform. Its deliberations were comprehensively reviewed by a junior negotiator from the IMF, John Williamson, who identified five reasons for failure (Williamson 1977). The first three are symptomatic of most efforts to deliver comprehensive international reform: the "unsettled" global economy, conflict between national interests, and lack of political will. Williamson also cited the lack of responsibility given to technical bureaucrats, which resulted in decisions deferred to busy ministers who could not grasp the technical aspects sufficiently well to find consensus. Finally, he blamed the C20's expedient decision to recommend a return to an adjustable pegged system, which reflected an innate aversion to floating or crawling pegs among many members, even though this was already an unrealistic goal by the time the committee's report was published in mid-1974.

After the indeterminate outcome from the C20, the IMF embarked on a revision of the Articles of Agreement that was completed in 1978 (James 1996). The IMF continued to be a forum for debate and exercised some influence through the system of surveillance over the exchange rate policies of members. Under the revised Articles, members were required to pursue "orderly" exchange markets and to consider the impact of exchange market intervention on other members; a strict rules-based system was not restored. But during the inflationary 1980s, the urgency of domestic economic policy objectives meant that interest rate and exchange rate volatility increased significantly. This generated spillover effects to smaller economies and renewed interest in more formal coordination mechanisms. The annual review of the IMF's surveillance procedures and the *World Economic Outlook* provided regular opportunities for debate over whether and how to constrain the spillover effects of new monetarist policies, but the fight against inflation remained paramount.[1] The minutes of IMF Executive Board meetings reveal increasing frustration with the inability of the IMF's surveillance structures to deliver greater exchange rate stability, both because national consultations were too infrequent and broad and because recommendations could not be enforced unless the country was drawing on IMF resources.[2] In January 1984, the IMF staff described surveillance as "a complex problem of analysis and persuasion and its effectiveness largely rests on the hope that competent analysis and clear identification of the problems will persuade policymakers to take more account of the effects of their decisions on the exchange rates of their partners" but concluded that "it remains the case ... that ... a national authority may deliberately choose not to take required actions or even to take perverse actions because of what it perceives to be domestic constraints."[3]

In November 1983 the question of a more thorough reform of the international monetary system returned to the G10 deputies, who reported in July 1985.[4] Lamberto Dini, the chair of the group, reported to the G10 central bank governors in May 1985 that the view of the G10 deputies was that "the present international monetary system on the whole was sound and was working reasonably well. Moreover there was no practical alternative to the present arrangements and no major reform or institutional change was warranted at this time."[5] The report recommended that "it would be helpful for major countries to engage in consultations and policy discussion in case of significant movements in real exchange rates" and called for greater surveillance by the IMF "to promote sound and

---

[1]See, for example, "Review of the Implementation of the Fund's Surveillance over Members' Exchange Rate Policies," March 11, 1981, SM/81/54. IMF Archives [hereafter IMFA].

[2]See, for example, Minutes of Executive Board Meeting, March 28, 1983, EBM/83/55. IMFA.

[3]"The Organization and Substance of IMF Surveillance," January 5, 1984, SM/84/8. IMFA.

[4]The G24 report in August 1985 was more critical of the floating exchange rate regime and called for more coordination to limit detrimental effects on developing countries.

[5]Reported to the G10 Governors Meeting at the BIS, May 13, 1985, by Lamberto Dini, Chairman of the G10 Deputies. Note on the G10 Governors Meeting, Reserve Bank of New York Archives [hereafter FRBNY] Cross Papers, Box 198389.

consistent policies through enhanced dialogue and persuasion through peer press-ing rather than through mechanical rules." Dini noted that this depended on willingness to "accept a measure of compromise between national and interna-tional objectives." The G10 central bank governors were more critical of exchange rate misalignments. When discussing the G10 deputies' report, Michel Camdessus, Governor of the Banque de France, was the strongest critic of the floating regime, but few others viewed a return to pegged rates as an option given open capital markets. Karl Otto Pöhl, governor of the Bundesbank, doubted the willingness of governments to subvert their domestic policy interests to adapt to exchange rate movements, noting that "the 1978 [Bonn] Summit effort at concerted action was a failure." In Pöhl's view, "at present neither the US, Germany or Japan were prepared to change domestic policies merely to change the exchange rate or exter-nal balances," but he concluded that "closer cooperation among central banks would help improve the functioning of the system."[6] He thus drew a stark con-trast between formal summits involving governments and the informal coopera-tion possible among central banks.

INFORMAL FORUMS FOR COORDINATION: THE BANK FOR INTERNATIONAL SETTLEMENTS

More functional and effective systems were deployed at the Bank for International Settlements in Basel (Helleiner 1996; Toniolo 2005). The ability of the G10+2 central banks to act quickly to provide substantial short-term credits to support exchange rate stability proved much more effective than the public, time-consuming, and conditional support available through the IMF (Bordo and Schenk 2017).[7] In 1960 the central banks agreed formally to support the gold value of the dollar through coordinated intervention in the London gold market. The Banque de France was the only holdout from this agreement, but it took part less formally from the sidelines. From 1963 the Bilateral Concerte created a more formal network of bilateral swaps that supported the dollar value of the lira, franc, and pound (Toniolo 2005). The central bank governors' support for sterling was particularly strong because sterling was still the main reserve currency for a large number of countries and because sterling remained an important symbolic bul-wark of the Bretton Woods system (Schenk 2010). Should sterling fail, specula-tion in an increasingly nimble international capital market would quickly turn to the US dollar, with potentially fatal implications for the Bretton Woods system as a whole. Indeed, these prophesies were borne out when the sterling devaluation in November 1967 was followed by a run on the dollar that exhausted the resolve of the Gold Pool members to defend the gold price and effectively led to the decoupling of the dollar and gold in March 1968. The collapse of this example of

---

[6]Note on the G10 Governors Meeting, FRBNY Cross Papers, Box 198389.

[7]G10+2 included the G10 countries plus Luxembourg and Switzerland (both important financial centers).

coordination in the wake of speculative pressure emphasized the importance of credibility once the private capital market swamped the resources of central banks to defend exchange rates and marked the beginning of the final stages of the Bretton Woods system.

Despite the end of the gold anchor, the G10+2 central bank governors continued their attempts at coordination to manage the transition of the Bretton Woods system. The collective Basel Agreement line of credit to the United Kingdom agreed on in September 1968 was conditional on the British government offering a dollar-value guarantee for the bulk of sterling held in the reserves of 34 countries to forestall a wholesale conversion of these reserves (and to minimize the likelihood that the credit would be drawn). While this might have marked the end of sterling's reserve role, the accumulation of substantial sterling surpluses by primary product producers, especially oil exporters in Nigeria and the Middle East, meant that the British government was soon forced actively to try to reduce the amount of sterling accumulating in the reserves of other countries. Indeed, the consensus that a volatile sterling exchange rate was still a threat to collective interests meant that the coordinated support for sterling outlasted the pegged exchange rate system itself, culminating in the January 1977 Third Group Arrangement among G10 central banks to support the pound (Schenk 2010).

After the collapse of the pegged rate system, the G10 central bank governors continued their coordinated efforts to manage the operational aspects of the system by extending their informal meetings, and the more formal swap network developed in the 1960s (Toniolo 2005). During the first decade of the floating regime, the Federal Reserve intervened regularly, selling foreign currencies to support the dollar and then repurchasing or repaying swaps when the dollar strengthened (Bordo, Humpage, and Schwartz 2015, Chapter 5). The volatility ushered in by the Organization of the Petroleum Exporting Countries (OPEC) oil crisis in October 1973 and subsequent gyrations in the US dollar exchange rate against the deutsche mark and Swiss franc also periodically drew central banks into coordinated intervention. For example, as the dollar fell in March 1974, the Federal Reserve drew on the Bundesbank swap line and, in a coordinated effort, the Bundesbank also bought US$78.4 million. At the May 1974 meeting of central bank governors at the BIS, the German, Swiss, and US officials agreed to a "concerted intervention" in the exchange markets to counter excessive speculation against the dollar. Their resolve was made public on May 14, 1974, and markets scrambled to cover short dollar positions, resulting in a 4.75 percent depreciation of the deutsche mark and Swiss franc the next day.[8] Intervention by the Federal Reserve in 1974 was partly direct in the markets ($437.7 million) and partly through prearranged swap lines ($760.7 million). By the end of the year, however, the dollar/deutsche mark exchange rate was 34.5 percent below the peak

---

[8] "Operations in Foreign Currencies during 1974," report prepared for the Federal Reserve's Federal Open Market Committee (FOMC) by FRBNY, March 1975.

levels of January and 18.65 percent below the January Swiss franc rate. These coordinated interventions were aimed at ameliorating short-term fluctuations rather than protecting permanent exchange rate levels.

The meetings of the G10+2 central bank governors at the BIS were also an important forum for sharing information that was the foundation for common understanding and goals. The meetings were private and secret, with no formal minutes, and this promoted a frank exchange of views. After views expressed around the table in March 1977 were leaked to the press, the chairman, Jelle Zijlstra of the Nederlandsche Bank, advised members, "If you cannot keep your mouth shut, don't come into this room."[9] Each meeting featured a tour de table of the governors' views on their domestic economic situations and policies. Special topics were also addressed, such as the Third Group Arrangement to support sterling in January 1977 (Schenk 2010), coordinating sanctions on Iranian banks in 1979,[10] and discussing reports from BIS standing committees, including those on banking supervision, gold and foreign exchange, and Eurocurrency markets. In addition, the governors usually discussed the state of the foreign exchange markets. Recently released archive records show that all governors were persistently averse to instability or disarray in exchange markets and tended to offer at least moral support to their colleagues who were pursuing anti-inflationary policies. They often reflected on the credibility of monetary policy and market interventions, exchanging views on market opinion in their respective jurisdictions. Through these regular meetings, the G10+2 central bank governors created an epistemic community with shared goals for inflation and a general commitment to avoid destabilizing short-term exchange rate changes. As the operational arm for coordination, this forum was important for sharing information and opinions (Bordo and Schenk 2017).

Some of the views exchanged were critical, particularly among the French, German, and US representatives. For example, in November 1978, the US government's new anti-inflationary program was warmly endorsed around the table despite doubts about its credibility. Paul Volcker, who was representing the Federal Reserve Bank of New York (FRBNY) at the meeting (his colleague Henry Wallich from the Federal Reserve Board also attended), noted that "the exchange markets have remained skeptical, especially in Europe." The Bundesbank governor Otmar Emminger challenged the Federal Reserve representatives about the likelihood that their policies would be relaxed if the US economy began to slow down. Bernard Clappier of the Banque de France "was impressed with the courageous acts by the US government, but worries that they are more to the consequences than the cause and that the US will back away quickly for fear of recession. He hopes the US will continue with determination." The open exchange of

---

[9]Notes on Meeting of Governors at the BIS, March 7, 1977, by Scott Pardee, FRBNY Cross Files, Box 107314.

[10]Notes on G10 Governors Meeting at the BIS, January 7, 1980, by Margaret L. Greene, FRBNY Cross Files, Box 107314.

views may have had an effect of creating greater coordination of national monetary policies, but it is difficult to discern direct evidence for this influence.

The spillover effects of gyrations in the dollar exchange rate were frequently discussed and prompted coordinated intervention. In January 1978, the Bundesbank-Federal Reserve swaps were extended to include the US Treasury, which the governors believed would increase the political credibility of the intervention. But Arthur Burns, then chairman of the Federal Reserve, noted that

> developments in the exchange markets have been a source of considerable anxiety—even anguish—to all of us. The United States recognizes, because of the central role of the dollar worldwide, that a declining dollar releases forces that could bring difficulties—economic stagnation if not worse—around the world. … The United States is also aware that the enormous appreciations of some currencies have hurt some export industries of these countries and may thus slow down their overall economies. However much a depreciation of the dollar may help the competitive position of US industry, the beneficial impact could be swamped by the recessionary elements it introduces abroad.[11]

The persistent inflationary environment in the United States and the weak credibility of anti-inflationary policies was finally tackled aggressively by Paul Volcker, who took the reins of the Federal Reserve in August 1979 as the second oil price shock loomed. When Volcker attended the G10 central bank governors meeting for the first time as chairman of the Federal Reserve on September 10, 1979, most governors around the table reported that they were raising interest rates.[12] Volcker noted that in the United States, "interest rates have been tightened, but it was not clear how far tightening could continue" given declining business activity. Emminger of the Bundesbank remarked on the commentary in the press and from US Congressman Henry Reuss about the prospects of an interest rate war after German interest rates were raised but argued that "increases in German interest rates had not been exaggerated but were necessary in view of the situation in Germany while the increases in interest rates in the US were justified by the US domestic situation." Volcker countered that he had "emphasized [in congressional testimony] that this was the case <u>so far</u> [underlined in original FRBNY record] and that he told Congress he would be discussing the situation with colleagues in other central banks."[13] A week later Volcker narrowly carried his proposal for a further modest increase in the federal funds rate at the Federal Open Market Committee, a decision that sparked another round of controversy over the credibility of US interest rate policy.

An important departure from coordinated monetary policy was the Volcker "shock" of October 1979 when the Federal Reserve began a fresh anti-inflation campaign, deploying unconventional policy aimed at bank reserves and leaving

---

[11]Notes on Meeting of Governors at the BIS, January 9, 1978, by Margaret L Greene, FRBNY.

[12]Notes on G10 Governors Meeting, September 10, 1979, FRBNY, Cross Papers, Box 107314.

[13]Notes on G10 Governors Meeting, September 10, 1979, FRBNY, Cross Papers, Box 107314. See also Scott E. Pardee, Notes for FOMC Meeting, September 18, 1979.

interest rates to respond. The first G10 central bank governors meeting after the October policy departure was in mid-November, when Wallich represented the Federal Reserve and explained the new reserve requirements to his G10 partners. With four weeks of experience, the markets seemed to be orderly, interest rates had increased, and "the early results of the shift of emphasis to controlling other financial aggregates were almost too good to be true," with the growth rate of money supply, bank credit, and business loans all slowing.[14] There was some controversy around the table about the new approach and whether the reserves limits could be evaded by US banks lending to American companies overseas and letting the funds flow back to the US monetary system. This point was picked up by the Federal Reserve, which subsequently sent a letter to foreign banks asking them not to undermine the marginal reserve requirements imposed on US banks by lending to US corporations. In December, Zijlstra as the chair asked what support Volcker needed from those around the table and Volcker asked each of his counterparties to "urge their banks to cooperate."[15] In general, despite concerns about the impact on their own economies in the short or medium term, Volcker's policy demarche was greeted with approval as an important contribution to the collective fight against inflation.

However, the Federal Reserve's contractionary monetary policy soon contributed to the onset of a recession in the United States. Interest rates fell sharply in the second quarter of 1980 as inflation expectations receded, and so did the growth of the monetary aggregates. These gyrations in interest rates provoked criticism at the BIS, as they had at the IMF. The FRBNY's records of the December 1980 governors meeting noted that "Zijlstra (Netherlands) … continued to scold about the volatility of US interest rates … [Cecil] de Strycker (Belgium) waded in to complain that US interest rates were simply too high. The US should pay more attention to the international effects of its policies on other countries. The swings in interest rates and the rise in rates to such extreme levels has triggered heavy volumes of short-term capital movements."[16] Gerald Bouey (Bank of Canada) "supported the effort in the US to combat inflation, but found interest rate volatility a problem." Six months later, in July 1981, the complaints continued: Pöhl of the Bundesbank remarked that "he had never complained in public but the high US rates did create a lot of problems" through higher local rates and a strong dollar.[17] Renaud de la Geniere for Banque de France "said he would be frank … interest rates were higher in France than they otherwise would be if US policy was different" and while he approved of the battle against

---

[14] Notes on G10 Central Bank Governors Meeting, November 12, 1979, by Robert Sleeper, FRBNY, Cross Files, Box 107314.

[15] Notes on G10 Governors Meeting at the BIS, December 10, 1979, by Scott E. Pardee, FRBNY Cross Files, Box 107341.

[16] Notes on G10 Governors Meeting at the BIS, December 8, 1980, by Scott E. Pardee, FRBNY Cross Files, Box 107341.

[17] Notes on G10 Governors Meeting at the BIS, July 13, 1981, by Scott E. Pardee, FRBNY Cross Files, Box 107341.

inflation, "he hoped we [the United States] would hurry. The foreign exchange consequences were serious for medium-sized countries with open economies." But Volcker held firm and warned that US interest rates were not likely to come down unless the economy began to contract; at the evening meeting over dinner Zijlstra (as chair) "concluded that no one was very enthusiastic about the high US interest rates but that perhaps the US has no other alternative at the moment."

The effects of informal efforts at coordination during this period were mixed. There were certainly opportunities through the BIS G10 central bank governors for sharing information, learning from each other, and arranging short-term coordinated interventions in the foreign exchange markets in the 1970s. However, the major monetary policy initiative, inaugurated by Volcker, was almost purely unilateral, although some advance warning was given to the Bundesbank in October 1979 (Silber 2012). The disruptive effects on other economies among the G10 led to complaints, but there was broad consensus that reducing inflation in the United States was a common good.

DEVISING NEW RULES: THE INDICATORS PROPOSALS

As the Bretton Woods system struggled through its final years, the combination of asymmetric adjustment and the inadequacy of the vague concept of "fundamental disequilibrium" to trigger adjustment prompted a lengthy period of strategic planning. With the Japanese economy in persistent surplus and a huge accumulation of US dollar reserves overseas from 1969 through 1971, the US Treasury and the Federal Reserve focused on new rules to increase pressure on surplus countries to adjust. In particular, they sought ways to monitor incipient imbalances and to trigger currency appreciation by reluctant surplus countries (still a vital policy issue in the 2000s). In 1969, a special policy group was established under the leadership of Paul Volcker, then Treasury Under-Secretary of State for International Monetary Affairs.[18] The group's proposals included an international Ministerial Adjustment Committee (analogous to the Mutual Assessment Process of the G20) that would monitor imbalances and make recommendations for adjustment policies, applying sanctions where corrective action was not forthcoming.[19] By April 1972, the proposal included provision for

> a set of presumptive criteria to guide the committee in making judgments regarding the adjustment required in the balance of payments positions of individual

---

[18]Members included Fred Bergsten, Dewey Daane, Henrik Houthakker, and Nathaniel Samuels. In 1969 R. N. Cooper also promoted the use of reserve changes as an objective indicator on a week-by-week basis linked to a "gliding" parity of greater exchange rate flexibility (T. G. Underwood, "Analysis of Proposals for Using Objective Indicators as a Guide to Exchange Rate Changes," June 27, 1972, IMFA DM/72/53).

[19]Volcker Group Paper, April 27, 1972, Foreign Relations of the United States (hereafter FRUS), 1969–76, Vol. III, Doc. 228.

members. Ideally, such criteria would also provide the basis for a scale of reference that could indicate the degree of disruptiveness of a given country's failure to adjust. One possibility would be to establish a set of bands based on reserve holdings of members.[20]

The Volcker Group's final recommendations in early June 1972 identified two objectives in forthcoming negotiations: greater exchange rate flexibility and a system of guidelines to promote prompt adjustment of imbalances.[21] This system included

> agreement on procedures and guidelines for multilateral consultations and actions designed to stimulate corrective steps by governments pursuing seriously disruptive behaviour in the international economic area; possible actions should include withholding of access to international assistance funds and placing burdens on the international transactions of the offending nations.[22]

On June 21, 1972, sterling floated free of its dollar peg, prompting the US Treasury and the Federal Reserve to reassess the future of pegged exchange rates. In July, Federal Reserve Chairman Arthur Burns tried to lure National Security Advisor Henry Kissinger (and by extension the president) into his agenda to reform the international monetary system, promising that the United States had an opportunity "to rebuild the world." Burns proposed establishing "the principle of symmetry between deficit and surplus nations. Right now, when a country has a deficit, it is an international sin. With a surplus, it is practicing an international virtue. We should do away with morality in our thinking. Apply rules that surplus countries have the obligation to reduce and eliminate surpluses and deficit countries have a similar obligation to reduce their deficits. We should establish rules to achieve this."[23] As for sanctions on surplus countries, Burns suggested radical changes to the principle of multilateral convertibility established at Bretton Woods, recommending that "in the first year, a warning. In the second year, if it continues, then withdraw convertibility. Previously convertibility has been taken for granted. It was felt there was a right to convertibility. No longer should it be an automatic right. The country would have to accumulate foreign currencies and could not necessarily convert them." The loss of sovereignty required for a rules-based scheme (for both deficit and surplus economies) would make it difficult to

---

[20]These institutional plans drew on a paper from early April 1972 by Geza Feketekuty, an early career economist with the Office of Management and Budget. He subsequently led the US team in the Tokyo Round of the General Agreement on Tariffs and Trade (GATT). FRUS, 1969–76, Vol. III. Doc. 228.

[21]"Recommended Premises and Objectives of the US in Forthcoming Reform Negotiations," June 5, 1972, FRUS, 1969–76, Vol. III, Doc. 230.

[22]"Recommended Premises and Objectives of the US in Forthcoming Reform Negotiations," June 5, 1972, FRUS, 1969–76, Vol. III, Doc. 230.

[23]Memorandum of Conversation, Washington, July 25, 1972, 4:30 p.m., Henry A. Kissinger; Arthur F. Burns, Chairman, Federal Reserve System; Robert D. Hormats, NSC Staff Member. FRUS, 1969–76, Vol. III, Doc. 236.

sell such a plan to Congress, but Kissinger promised to lend Burns his support with this agenda.[24]

Meanwhile, with the support of incoming Treasury Secretary George Shultz, by the end of July 1972 the Treasury had devised "Plan X," which aimed to mobilize the SDR as a primary reserve asset and promote a symmetrical rules-based system of adjustment (Sargent 2015).[25] Primary reserves would consist of gold, SDRs, and IMF gold tranches. Each country would have an identified level of "normal reserves" calibrated against its IMF quota. The suggested threshold for normal reserves was four times a country's IMF quota. In 1972 Japan's foreign exchange reserves, not including gold, were 13.7 times its IMF quota; Germany's, 10 times; and those of the United States, 1.8 times. The plan clearly privileged the United States with its large quota. During a predetermined "open season," countries could exchange their dollars and other foreign exchange for SDRs. Allocations of SDRs from the IMF would make up any shortfall to reach the predetermined level of normal reserves. So long as they maintained central exchange rates, countries acquiring foreign exchange could present it to the issuing country for primary reserves (gold, SDRs). The system would not encourage or discourage the holding of foreign exchange in reserves, although the United States "would negotiate limits on foreign official holdings of dollars." Countries where reserves fell below the "normal" level would be permitted or required to devalue their exchange rate by 3 percent to 4 percent a year. Revaluation by at least 3 percent a year would be required once primary reserves hit 150 percent of normal. If reserves reached 175 percent of normal, the country would lose the right to convert foreign exchange reserves. Finally, a country that maintained "primary reserves (primary plus foreign exchange) at 200 percent of normal level and maintained for period (e.g., six months) would indicate a persistent surplus country, which would be expected, e.g., to increase aid, liberalize imports and unless corrected, subject to discriminatory restrictions (e.g., surcharge)."[26] This scheme sought a new and much broader international monetary agreement encompassing trade and monetary rules, requiring a parallel restructuring of the General Agreement on Tariffs and Trade (GATT). Finally, in contrast to Williamson's critique of the C20 process, the plan sought to "politicize" the governance of the international monetary system by ensuring that IMF Executive Directors were at least at deputy minister level and by keeping the C20 in existence. Those at the table had to be able to make policy decisions rather than refer them back to governments. These ambitious plans reflected the waning enthusiasm for firmly pegged exchange rates as well as a desire to link trade and monetary issues and overcome the bias in the onus of adjustment.

---

[24]On cooperation between Burns and Kissinger over international monetary reform, see Sargent (2015, 120).

[25]Paper prepared by the Department of the Treasury, July 31, 1972, FRUS, 1969–76, Vol. III, Doc. 239.

[26]Paper prepared by the Department of the Treasury, July 31, 1972, FRUS, 1969–76, Vol. III, Doc. 239.

Beginning in the late 1960s, the reform of the international monetary system was interlinked with a wider debate about ways to broaden the governance of the global system to include developing countries as a challenge to G10 leadership (de Vries 1985). As noted earlier, at the September 1972 meeting of the IMF and the World Bank, the C20, under the chairmanship of Indonesian Finance Minister Ali Wardhana, was tasked with developing proposals to reform the international monetary system in ways that promoted development, including "international trade, the flow of capital, investment, and development assistance." US Treasury Secretary George Shultz chose this meeting to launch his rules-based system based on "indicators" that would identify the need for internal and external adjustment by persistent surplus and deficit countries (Sargent 2015). Shultz noted, "I believe disproportionate gains or losses in reserves may be the most equitable and effective single indicator we have to guide the adjustment process" (Shultz 1972).[27] He proposed that the burden of adjustment should be shared between surplus and deficit countries to introduce greater symmetry into the system, while greater flexibility in exchange rates was an additional route for adjustment. Deficit countries could be required to devalue while surplus countries could have convertibility suspended if they refused to revalue. Alternatively, a surplus country could increase aid expenditure, reduce trade barriers, and remove outward capital controls. Ultimately, that country's trading partners could impose trade surcharges to force adjustment (a threat subsequently used by President Richard Nixon in August 1973).

Under Shultz's scheme, the SDR "would increase in importance and become the formal numeraire of the system," but foreign exchange reserves "need be neither generally banned nor encouraged" because they offered monetary authorities greater flexibility in reserves management (Shultz 1972). Nevertheless, Shultz noted that "careful study should be given to proposals for exchanging part of existing reserve currency holdings into a special issue of SDR, at the option of the holder." In terms of governance, the US proposal sought to vest the monetary rules with the IMF and to harmonize IMF and GATT rules. Decisions on reform "must be carried out by representatives who clearly carry a high stature and influence in the councils of their own governments," a hint at Plan X's politicization of governance. After some undefined transitional period, Shultz claimed that "the US would be prepared to undertake an obligation to convert official foreign dollar holdings into other reserve assets as part of a satisfactory system as I have suggested—a system assuring effective and equitable operation of the adjustment process" once the United States had the capacity to do so (Shultz 1972). Sargent (2015) does not mention the link between the adjustment rules and the SDR, but it was an important part of the vision for the longer-term reform of the role of the dollar as a reserve asset and the restoration of greater US policy autonomy after the series of currency shocks exerted by financial markets from 1968 onward.

---

[27]"Needed: A New Balance in International Economic Affairs," speech by G. Shultz, at the joint IMF–World Bank meeting, September 26, 1972. The word "balance" was used eight times in the first five sentences.

In January 1973 the IMF staff prepared a paper for the deputies of the C20 that set out the technical obstacles to rules-based coordination.[28] The paper distinguished between a reserve level indicator and a "cyclically adjusted basic balance indicator," which was a flow measure deriving from the balance of payments but excluding short-term capital flows. The two were clearly closely related, as persistent deficits or surpluses in the basic balance affected the level of reserves. Moreover, reserve levels were affected by "transitory and reversible flows that should be financed rather than be taken as signifying a need for adjustment." The IMF staff put greater credence on monitoring the basic balance as an indicator of "fundamental disequilibrium," but the technical difficulties of measuring the cyclically adjusted basic balance meant that it would be difficult to operate. It was important that any indicator was "unambiguous," which argued in favor of a straightforward reserves measure. A simulation of a reserves indicator based on IMF quotas for the 1960s showed that Austria, Germany, and Portugal had twice the required amount of reserves every year. However, if the base was set in relation to the levels of reserves in the period 1956–60, France, Israel, and Spain would meet an outer limit of twice the base level in all 10 years.[29] Clearly the initial calibration of the indicator was an important issue. In a broader test of a range of "objective indicators," John Williamson showed that reserve levels and basic balances were successful in signaling the need for exchange rate adjustment in only about half of the cases where such adjustment was judged by other criteria to have been necessary.[30] While these indicators might form part of surveillance, "neither provides by itself an automatic answer to the question [of] whether adjustment action would be required; nor could any mechanical combination of the two indicators perform that function." Instead, they should be used "as triggers of a full assessment of a country's position and prospects, in addition to such regular appraisal of balance of payments situations and prospects as may be provided for."[31] This did not take the process much beyond the existing annual IMF Article IV consultations. Having been challenged by the IMF staff, Shultz's plan also did not find favor among other G10 leaders.

French Finance Minister Giscard d'Estaing expressed his misgivings to Paul Volcker at the Reykjavik summit in May/June 1973. The French priority remained a return to pegged exchange rates; if countries accepted some ineffective form of indicators, they would then have the freedom to change parities but without any rules preventing competitive devaluation and other unwarranted changes in exchange rates. Beyond this ideological disagreement over exchange

[28]"Reserves and Basic Balances as Possible Indicators of the Need for Payments Adjustment," January 11, 1973, IMFA, SM/73/7.

[29]"Reserves and Basic Balances as Possible Indicators of the Need for Payments Adjustment," January 11, 1973, IMFA, SM/73/7.

[30]"The Historical Performance of Possible 'Objective Indicators' of the Need for Par Value Changes," IMFA, DM/73/2.

[31]"Reserves and Basic Balances as Possible Indicators of the Need for Payments Adjustment," January 11, 1973, IMFA, SM/73/7.

rate flexibility, neither Giscard d'Estaing nor his advisor Claude Pierre-Brossolette believed that the proposal could realistically be implemented, partly because "there was always room for discussion as to whether a country should act when the indicators so suggested. Also, the indicators did not work the same for a large country and for a small country—they allowed greater freedom for the large country."[32] Volcker defended the scheme as a negotiating platform or "skeleton" that required flesh to be attached through international negotiation. No progress was likely without a firm "backbone" proposal to discuss, and he tried to convince Giscard d'Estaing that "if the French would agree, we could get the rest of the world to agree. Some of the LDC's [lesser developed countries] had begun to see some of the advantages of the US system to them, in that it did not leave them at the mercy of IMF control."[33] The French were key to an effective compromise, but they rejected the American scheme in the context of their distrust of flexible exchange rate regimes in general. Both sides agreed that no new system would be introduced before the Nairobi C20 meeting in September and that public expectations should be dampened by announcing that there would be no communiqué from that meeting.

At the Nairobi meeting of the C20 deputies, the reserve indicator remained on the agenda and was assigned to one of four technical groups.[34] Shultz remained hopeful, advising President Nixon,

> In recent weeks, I have made considerable efforts to discuss monetary reform with our Monetary Advisory Committee, various other groups of bankers and businessmen, and with the academic community. There is almost universal support among these groups for the US substantive proposals and for our negotiating approach—in particular, our desire for some flexibility in exchange rates; our emphasis on a reserve indicator system which will keep countries like Germany and Japan from continuing to pile up huge surpluses; and avoiding a premature move to dollar convertibility.[35]

Despite this optimism, the US attempt to develop a new rules-based system of coordination failed to achieve consensus. The uneven distribution of benefit and cost meant larger economies would have greater room for maneuver, and there were serious technical and practical challenges to designing transparent rules to trigger enforcement. The plan was also weakened by the lack of consensus on the diagnosis of the problem: European states were pursuing exchange rate stability

---

[32]Memorandum of Conversation, Reykjavik, May 31, 1973. Participants included Minister Giscard d'Estaing, Mr. Claude Pierre-Brossolette, Mr. Jean-Pierre Brunet, US Secretary George P. Shultz, and Under Secretary Paul A. Volcker. FRUS, 1969–76, Vol. XXXI.

[33]Memorandum of Conversation, Reykjavik, May 31, 1973. Participants included Minister Giscard d'Estaing, Mr. Claude Pierre-Brossolette, Mr. Jean-Pierre Brunet, US Secretary George P. Shultz, and Under Secretary Paul A. Volcker. FRUS, 1969–76, Vol. XXXI.

[34]Press Statement by C. J. Morse, Chairman of the Deputies of the Committee of Twenty, September 27, 1973, IMFA, PR/73/994.

[35]Memorandum from US Secretary George P. Shultz to President Richard Nixon, Nairobi (undated; Septtember 1973), FRUS, 1973–1976, Vol. XXXI, Foreign Economic Policy, Doc. 53.

while the United States embraced floating exchange rates. The indicator proposals survived into the C20's report in mid-June 1974, but the Substitution Account gained more traction and was pursued through the IMF Executive Board (McCauley and Schenk 2015). Thus, over the next eight years, the United States was invited to adhere to the SDR substitution element of its proposed indicators plan without the benefit of the rules to ensure symmetry of adjustment.

The persistent problem of how to press surplus countries to adjust meant that US officials returned repeatedly to indicator proposals as a way to promote international macroeconomic coordination. In May 1986 US Treasury Secretary James Baker again promoted an indicator system at the Tokyo G5 summit (Sterling-Folker 2002, 166–69). Sterling-Folker asserts that central bank governors were opposed because "the use of national indicators as a surveillance device would mean greater ministerial interference into central bank independence" and would force them to share private data too widely (2002, 168). This system is similar to the proposal attributed to US Treasury Secretary Tim Geithner in 2010, although rather than focusing on reserves, Geithner suggested quantitative indicators for current account balances that would require adjustment.[36] In the end, the 2010 G20 meeting in Seoul landed on a compromise that tasked finance ministers to develop "indicative guidelines composed of a range of indicators [that] would serve as a mechanism to facilitate timely identification of large imbalances that require preventive and corrective actions to be taken."[37] The outcome of this discussion in February 2011 was the Mutual Assessment Process, which included domestic indicators such as public debt and fiscal deficits, private savings rates, and private debt. The external indicators were more controversial, facing considerable opposition from surplus countries such as China. Rather than the entire current account balance, the trade balance and net investment income flows would be assessed, "taking due consideration of exchange rate, fiscal, monetary and other policies."[38] The G20 central bankers and finance ministers meeting in Washington in 2011 set out guidelines for these indicators, benchmarking each country's historical performance over the period 1990–2004, with some sensitivity to the stage of development and size of each country.[39] By November 2011 seven countries among the G20 had been identified as having significant imbalances, and the IMF prepared sustainability reports to identify the causes and recommend policy actions for the Cannes G20 Heads of State Summit.[40] The

---

[36]Tim Geithner letter, extracted in *Financial Times,* October 22, 2010, http://www.ft.com /cms/s/0/651377aa-ddc4-11df-8354-00144feabdc0.html#axzz1DfLI6xwl.

[37]Text of G20 Communiqué, Seoul, November 11, 2010.

[38]Communiqué, Meeting of Finance Ministers and Central Bank Governors, Paris, February 18–19, 2011, https://g20.org/wp-content/uploads/2014/12/Communique_of_Finance_Ministers _and_Central_Bank_Governors_Paris_February_18_19_2011.pdf.

[39]Communiqué, Meeting of Finance Ministers and Central Bank Governors, Washington, DC, April 14–15, 2011, https://g20.org/wp-content/uploads/2014/12/Communique_of_Finance _Ministers_and_Central_Bank_Governors_Washington_DC_14-15_April_20112.pdf.

[40]China, France, Germany, India, Japan, the United Kingdom, and the United States.

persistence of slow growth and the prolonged euro area sovereign debt crisis made growth, fiscal consolidation, and employment creation more immediate goals, while global imbalances were increasingly seen as an effect rather than a cause of international fragility. The inability until 2016 to conclude the ratification of quota reforms agreed in 2010 exposed the limits of collaborative commitment to the global leadership of the IMF.

CONCLUSIONS

Several conclusions can be drawn from this survey of attempts at coordination. First, the problems of adjustment and asymmetries identified during the Bretton Woods era have persisted in the rhetoric of international monetary reform despite the dramatic transformation of the global system since the 1950s, suggesting that they are not tied to a particular historical circumstance or exchange rate regime. Two issues in particular continue to be a strong focus of G20 deliberations: (1) how to encourage adjustment by surplus countries, and (2) the role of the dollar in the global monetary system. The Bretton Woods system established the IMF as the platform for coordination, but as the pegged exchange rate system crumbled, efforts to develop and encourage policy coordination became dispersed, resulting in several overlapping initiatives that varied in their representation, geographical coverage, breadth of goals, and level of technical resources. This complicated landscape did not enhance the ability to achieve consensus on either the problems to be resolved or the possible solutions.

Second, the enthusiasm for rules-based systems was not exhausted at the end of the Bretton Woods system. Indeed, the US Treasury led a sustained campaign to introduce a set of objective triggers for adjustment that straddled the end of the pegged exchange rate system and the advent of the floating era. In adapted form, these efforts finally came to fruition in the wake of the 2008 global financial crisis. The prospects for the Mutual Assessment Process will depend on the consistency with which the indicative guidelines are deployed and the strength of the enforcement mechanism. The historical record suggests that rules-based systems are difficult to devise because they require consensus on both the problems to be addressed and the means of solution, and this consensus has so far proved elusive. Looking across the transition from the rules-based pegged exchange rate to the flexible era of the 1970s, there is a clear continuity in the vexing problem of ensuring that surplus and deficit countries work together to resolve imbalances.

A third observation is that the most enduring form of monetary coordination has been the less visible collaboration among central bankers at the BIS. This is perhaps not surprising in the wake of the increased independence of central banks, their operational expertise (even if they did not determine exchange rate policy), and their close relationship with foreign exchange markets. Moreover, the records of the G10 governors meetings in Basel show evidence of the development of an epistemic community among central bankers. Although there was frequent disagreement on points of detail and mixed views on the benefits of floating exchange rates, this forum provided central bank governors an opportunity to share frank views in private and demonstrate their commitment to orderly foreign exchange markets and their support for anti-inflationary policies, despite mixed evidence that their interventions were effective. An important issue for these central bankers was the credibility of both their foreign exchange market intervention and their fight against inflation. Both required political as well as operational commitment, and there are frequent references to the governors' frustration with their respective governments. Conversely, the G10 deputies and the C20 (representing ministers of finance and the Executive Board members of the IMF, respectively) were less successful at agreeing on proposals for international monetary reform, both because of a lack of consensus on the problems to be resolved (for example, too much liquidity or too little, whether the dollar needed to be replaced) and because of the political traction needed to achieve substantive institutional reform.

REFERENCES

Bergsten, C. F., and R. A. Green. 2016. *International Monetary Cooperation: Lessons from the Plaza Accord after Thirty Years*. Washington, DC: Peterson Institute for International Economics.

Bordo, M., O. F. Humpage, and A. J. Schwartz. 2015. *Strained Relations: US Foreign Exchange Operations and Monetary Policy in the Twentieth Century*. Chicago: University of Chicago Press.

Bordo, M., and C. R. Schenk. 2017. "Monetary Policy Cooperation and Coordination: An Historical Perspective on the Importance of Rules." In *Rules for International Monetary Stability: Past, Present and Future*, edited by M. Bordo and J. B. Taylor. Stanford, CA: Hoover Press.

Clift, B., and J. Tomlinson. 2012. "When Rules Started to Rule: The IMF, Neo-Liberal Economic Ideas and Economic Policy Change in Britain." *Review of International Political Economy* 19 (3): 477–500.

de Vries, M. 1985. *The International Monetary Fund, 1972–1978: Cooperation on Trial*, Vol. 2. Washington, DC: International Monetary Fund.

Eichengreen, B. 2014. "International Policy Coordination: The Long View." In *Globalization in an Age of Crisis: Multilateral Economic Cooperation in the Twenty-First Century*, edited by R. C. Feenstra and A. M. Taylor, 43–90. Chicago: Chicago University Press.

Frankel, J., M. Goldstein, and P. Masson. 1996. "International Coordination of Economic Policies." In *Functioning of the International Monetary System*, Vol. 1, edited by J. A. Frankel and P. Masson, 17–60. Washington, DC: International Monetary Fund.

Helleiner, E. 1996. *States and the Reemergence of Global Finance: From Bretton Woods to the 1990s*. Ithaca, NY: Cornell University Press.

Holtham, G. 1989. "German Macroeconomic Policy and the 1978 Bonn Economic Summit." In *Can Nations Agree?: Issues in International Economic Cooperation*, edited by R. N. Cooper, 141–77. Washington, DC: Brookings Institution.

James, H. 1996. *International Monetary Cooperation since Bretton Woods*. Oxford, U.K.: Oxford University Press.

McCauley, R. N. 2015. "Does the US Dollar Confer an Exorbitant Privilege?" *Journal of International Money and Finance* 57: 1–14.

McCauley, R. N., and C. R. Schenk. 2015. "Reforming the International Monetary System in the 1970s and 2000s: Would an SDR Substitution Account Have Worked?" *International Finance* 18 (2): 187–206.

Mourlon-Druol, E. 2012. *A Europe Made of Money: The Emergence of the European Monetary System*. Ithaca, NY: Cornell University Press.

Ostry, J., and Ghosh, A. 2013. "Obstacles to International Policy Coordination, and How to Overcome Them." IMF Staff Discussion Note, December SDN/13/11.

Oudiz, G., and J. Sachs. 1984. "Macroeconomic Policy Coordination among the Industrial Countries." *Brookings Papers on Economic Activity* I: 1–75.

Putnam, R. D., and C. R. Henning, 1989. "The Bonn Summit of 1978: A Case Study in Coordination." In *Can Nations Agree?: Issues in International Economic Cooperation*, edited by R. N. Cooper, 12–140. Washington, DC: Brookings Institution.

Sargent, D. J. 2015. *A Superpower Transformed: The Remaking of American Foreign Relations in the 1970s*. Oxford, U.K.: Oxford University Press.

Schenk, C. R. 2010. *The Decline of Sterling: Managing the Retreat of an International Currency*. Cambridge, U.K.: Cambridge University Press.

Shultz, G. 1972. "Needed: A New Balance in International Economic Affairs." Speech at the joint IMF–World Bank meeting, Washington, DC, September 26.

Silber, W. L. 2012. *Volcker: The Triumph of Persistence*. London: Bloomsbury.

Solomon, R. 1982. *The International Monetary System, 1945–81*. New York: Harper and Row.

Sterling-Folker, J. 2002. *Theories of International Cooperation and the Primacy of Anarchy: Explaining US International Monetary Policy-Making after Bretton Woods*. Albany, NY: SUNY Press.

Toniolo, G. 2005. *Central Bank Cooperation at the Bank for International Settlements, 1930–1973*. Cambridge, U.K.: Cambridge University Press.

Triffin, R. 1978. "The International Role and Fate of the Dollar." *Foreign Affairs* 57 (2): 269–86.

Tucker, A. L., and J. Madura. 1991. "Impact of the Louvre Accord on Actual and Anticipated Exchange Rate Volatilities." *Journal of International Financial Markets, Institutions and Money* 1 (2): 43–59.

Wilkie, C. 2012. *Special Drawing Rights (SDRs): The First International Money*. Oxford, U.K.: Oxford University Press.

Williamson, J. 1977. *The Failure of World Monetary Reform 1971–1974*. New York: Nelson.

CHAPTER 5

Capital Flows and International Order

Trilemmas and Trade-Offs from Macroeconomics to Political Economy and International Relations

MICHAEL BORDO AND HAROLD JAMES

Globalization—the establishment of cross-national linkages—is rarely a simple, unidirectional process. It creates major strains as different economic, social, and political systems adapt to each other's influences. This chapter describes the challenges of globalization in terms of the logic underpinning four distinct policy constraints or "trilemmas" and their interrelationship, in particular, the disturbances that arise from capital flows. The analysis of a policy trilemma was first developed as a diagnosis of exchange rate problems (the incompatibility of free capital flows with monetary policy autonomy and a fixed exchange rate regime), but the approach can be usefully extended. The second trilemma we describe is the incompatibility between financial stability, capital mobility, and fixed exchange rates. The third extends the analysis to politics and looks at the strains inherent in reconciling democratic politics with monetary autonomy and capital movements. Finally, we examine the security aspect and look at the interaction of democracy with capital flows and international order. These four trilemmas show how domestic monetary, financial, economic, and political systems are connected within the international system. They can be described as the impossible policy choices at the heart of globalization. Frequently, the trilemmas conjure up countervailing antiglobalization tendencies and trends, as we describe in this chapter.

In practice, as scholars investigating the exchange rate trilemma have demonstrated, it is empirically hard to determine a pure policy stance: there are varying degrees of commitment to a fixed exchange rate regime, varying degrees of openness to international capital, and varying extents of monetary autonomy (Obstfeld, Shambaugh, and Taylor 2005). Thus, in practice, policy is hardly ever positioned at the corners of the trilemma, and actual policy stances fall somewhat in between the corner positions—where the corners simply represent the boundaries of the possible. The discussion of the exchange rate trilemma thus serves as a Weberian ideal type, rather than an exposition of the real world. The same reservation applies to the other trilemmas that we identify: there is obviously neither pure financial stability nor pure instability, no absolute democracy, and no completely binding treaty organization or international system. There are always trade-offs. But identifying the choices as borders can help us define problems and sources of tension and establish potentially effective remedies. Finally, we address forms of cooperation—with regard to financial stability and the building of agreements across borders—that can take the sharp edges off the trilemmas and reduce the likelihood of sudden and traumatic reversals and shocks.

THE MACROECONOMIC TRILEMMA

The first trilemma is undoubtedly the most familiar of the four sets of issues examined here. Mundell (1963) formalized the point that free capital movements and a fixed exchange rate rule out the possibility of conducting independent monetary policy. Padoa-Schioppa (1994) reformulated this proposition as the "inconsistent quartet" of policy objectives by bringing in commercial policy, another central part of the globalization package: free trade, capital mobility, fixed or managed exchange rates, and monetary policy independence. In both the Mundell and Padoa-Schioppa formulations, the impossible choice provided a rationalization for building a more secure institutional framework to secure cross-border integration, especially to deal with the problem of small or relatively small European countries. Both were major architects of the process of European monetary union. They justified this step of further integration on the grounds that the exchange rate was a useless instrument—the monetary equivalent of a human appendix or tonsils—that could be usefully and painlessly abolished. However, some countries continued to regard the exchange rate as a useful tool for obtaining trade advantages.

The policy constraint following from free capital movements has recently been posed in a more severe form by Rey (2013), who shows that in a globalized world of free capital movements, monetary policy is limited even with flexible or floating exchange rates. A choice to have a floating exchange rate thus does not give a free pass to monetary policy. Rey identifies "an 'irreconcilable duo': independent monetary policies are possible if and only if the capital account is managed, directly or indirectly, via macroprudential policies" (287). This argument does not necessarily lend itself to the demonstration of the necessity of monetary union: If the aim is to preserve national policy autonomy, a better choice is to control capital movements, as was envisaged in the 1944 Bretton Woods Conference and provided for in the Articles of Agreement of the International Monetary Fund. Capital movement across borders—through both inflow surges and the consequences of reversals—may fundamentally limit the scope of national monetary policy. Since the 2008 global financial crisis, the articulation and elaboration of macroprudential policies has become a way of trying in practice to limit or manage the extent to which capital may be mobile; consequently, the discussion of the monetary policy trilemma leads in a straightforward way to the discussion of financial policy issues.

Figure 5.1. The Macroeconomic Trilemma

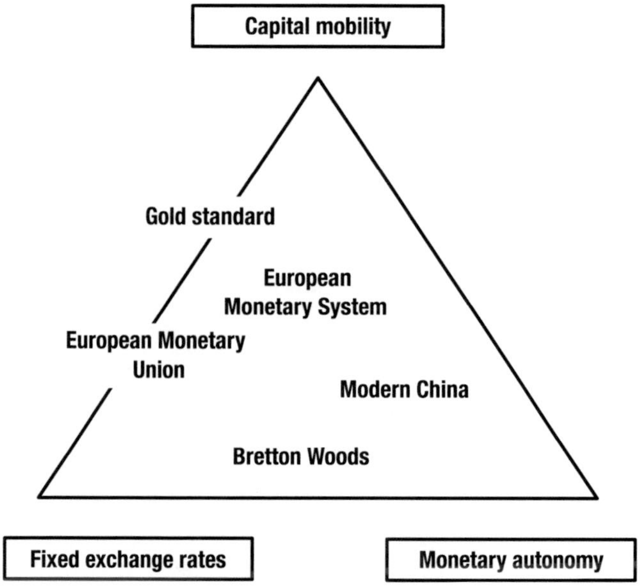

Source: Authors' illustration.

Capital mobility, however, continues to be attractive. Financially constrained borrowers—corporations as well as governments—see capital inflows as a way of obtaining access to financial resources. In addition, the inflows may be linked to institutional innovation and governance reform. After waves of overborrowing, the costs may be clearer: capital flows, in the nice analogy of Stiglitz (1998), generate such large waves as to upset the delicate rowing boats of small countries afloat on the sea of globalization. But many participants in the process quickly forget the possibility of the large waves and tides.

The logic of the original Mundell trilemma (Figure 5.1) thus points either in the direction of closer cooperation (including perhaps political arrangements that constrain domestic choices) or toward capital controls as a way of rescuing national policy autonomy. In light of the gains that may be lost as a result of capital controls (and of an awareness of the necessarily incomplete character of capital controls that makes them prone to evasion), the process of globalization requires cooperation and coordination.

THE FINANCIAL STABILITY TRILEMMA

The new formulation of the constraints on monetary policy follows from evidence of the enhanced volatility induced by the financial sector, and the proclivity of the world to lurch into credit cycles of large amplitude. Financial (particularly banking) stability is incompatible with capital flows, when exchange rates are fixed and create misleading incentives for capital to move.

To understand the character of the constraint, we must reflect on the origins of the new sources of financial instability. The formulation of the classical macroeconomic trilemma says little about the sequencing of policy measures. The original Mundell formulation implies that policy formulation began in an idealized nineteenth-century world, in which capital mobility and a fixed metallic exchange rate were assumed and central banks mechanically responded to gold inflows or outflows by loosening or tightening monetary policy. The third element—a flexible monetary policy—is necessarily ruled out if the rules of the game are followed. Indeed, almost no nineteenth-century analyst depicted monetary policy as a discretionary instrument. But this approach does not describe nineteenth-century reality. Most countries, in fact, engaged in considerable experimentation with the monetary standard (Bloomfield 1959); it was only in the last decades of the century that the gold standard became a nearly universal norm.

Why did the gold standard appear attractive? Countries adopted it (as they would later engage in fixed exchange rate arrangements) mostly in the hope that it would enhance their credibility, provide a "good housekeeping seal of approval" (Bordo and Rockoff 1996), and attract substantial capital inflows (Obstfeld and Taylor 2004). A stable exchange rate could be used to compensate for inadequate availability of domestic capital. The beneficial effect of an inflow of foreign capital would be realized only if the domestic financial system started to intermediate the new flows; thus, domestic financial expansion or the beginning of an expansive financial cycle was a consequence of regime choices.

Such domestic financial expansion often (but not always) occurred on an inadequate institutional basis; indeed, financial underdevelopment and inexperience were often the very flaws the policy choice was intended to correct. But underdeveloped financial systems had little experience in managing credit allocation or running banks. Countries wanted to adopt the gold standard in the nineteenth century (or open their capital accounts in the late twentieth century) to develop their financial institutions, but the resulting financial inflows often increased the vulnerability of fragile domestic institutions. However, as long as the inflows persisted, they sustained a false confidence that additional capital was indeed producing more stable and mature financial systems.

Eventually a learning process about finance set in. It took time for countries to adapt their institutions to the capital inflows and the risks of crises. In many cases, countries failed to adapt efficiently and capital flows simply reinforced existing rent-seeking and corrupt institutions (Haber and Calomiris 2014). In these cases, capital inflows increased rather than decreased vulnerability.

The interplay of international capital movements and a weak banking system in emerging markets has been a constant source of major international financial crises. Well-known examples include the United States in the 1830s, Argentina in the late nineteenth century, central Europe in the 1920s, some emerging Asian countries in the 1990s, and southern Europe in the 2000s. In many cases, the surge of capital also produced fiscal crises in the aftermath of excessive public debt issuance, driven by bailouts of insolvent banks or by explicit or implicit guarantees. Some countries attempted to compensate for financial instability by providing government guarantees that, in the end, involved promises that could not be fulfilled and only enhanced financial instability.

In the late 1830s, US states went on a borrowing spree. At the same time, President Andrew Jackson launched a Bank War, in the course of which he vetoed the rechartering of the Second Bank of the United States (a powerful institution that controversially combined central banking with commercial banking functions) and encouraged other banks to seek charters. Jackson achieved his immediate objective of decentralizing credit. But then the new banks (the "pet banks" as they were disparagingly called) immediately expanded lending, primarily to the states and the political elites that had facilitated their establishment. The upshot was an orgy of bank credit to individual states, often structured in a complex way so that debt securities could be repackaged and sold on foreign markets. Beginning in 1841 the borrowing states started to default, and the banks themselves were brought down by bank runs.

At the end of the nineteenth century, the 1890 bankruptcy of Argentina triggered a rethinking of how capital flows were handled. At the time Argentina was the world's largest borrower in terms of share of GDP, with "some of the most spectacular capital inflows of the history of the world economy" (Taylor 2003, 178). A modern calculation suggests that Argentina imported capital amounting to 18.7 percent of its GDP between 1870 and 1889 (Flandreau and Zumer 2004); by the 1880s Argentina accounted for almost half of British foreign lending (Ford 1962; Mitchener and Weidenmier 2008). The availability of foreign money prompted a fiscal expansion and general economic overheating. In parallel, the 1887 Law of National Guaranteed Banks is a fine example of a law that appears to constrain banking activity and thus guarantee stability, but in practice it led to a bank glut. Under the law, banks were required to buy National Gold Bonds issued by the Treasury as a requirement for note issue. The banks raced to borrow as much as they could on foreign markets, mostly in London, and deposited the gold with the Treasury. They could then use the banknotes as a basis for domestic credit expansion. After 1887 money creation surged (Cortes Conde 1989; della Paolera and Taylor 2007). Price increases made Argentina uncompetitive, tax revenue fell off, and a debt crisis erupted in 1890.

Banks in central Europe had their capital largely wiped out by hyperinflation in the aftermath of World War I. Stabilization involved returning to the gold standard with the expectation that this would make financially and fiscally stricken countries the recipients of capital inflows. In the course of postwar inflation and hyperinflation, central European bank capital had been destroyed; in the stabilization of the mid-1920s, banks began with severely reduced levels of capital relative to their prewar position. It was expensive to raise new capital, and new lending occurred on a very thin capital basis. Banks also found it much harder than before the war to attract retail deposits, so they funded lending with interbank credit—both from domestic sources and from international borrowing, largely from the United States (Kindleberger 1973; Eichengreen 1992). The external source of finance drove banking expansion in Germany and elsewhere. It was only at the height of the credit boom that bank loans relative to GDP reached prewar levels (which were high in an international comparison). Paradoxically, this reflection on catch-up offered one ground for creditors to believe that their claims might be secure (Balderston 1993). The vulnerability was increased by the persistence of a German prewar tradition of considering the central bank as a lender of last resort and a belief that the government would ultimately step in to guarantee debt. That represented the most fundamental flaw in the domestic policy regime. The safety net provided by the Reichsbank allowed a thinner capital basis and gave both the banks and their creditors misguided confidence (Schuker 1988; James 1999). The expansion of borrowing by central European banks occurred in an informational or statistical fog (BIS 1932, 1934). The vulnerability of the banks—in a banking crisis that accompanied a currency crisis—was a major cause of the financial collapse in 1931 and the reversal of capital flows (James 1986; Schnabel 2004).

The 1997 East Asian financial crisis had its origins in financial liberalization, when in 1993 the Thai government established the Bangkok International Banking Facility, allowing a substantial number of domestic and foreign banks to operate an international banking business. These banks engaged in heavy foreign exchange borrowing, which they then used to expand credit domestically. Again there were implicit guarantees of the foreign currency exposure of the banks, as it was (correctly) believed by the foreign creditors that the borrowing banks were too important to fail (Dooley 2000).

The introduction of the euro in 1999 prompted a surge of capital into southern Europe, as well as Ireland. As in Asia in the 1990s, there were large current account deficits and, as in east Asia, there were in some cases imbalances that were limited to the private sector, with the public sector fiscal position appearing strong in countries, and with a borrowing surge (notably, Ireland and Spain). There was also great confidence that the inflows were modernizing and building more resilient financial and indeed political systems. Investors also assumed some sort of implicit guarantee. As a prominent Greek politician, Yiannos Papantoniou, explained in 2005, "Greece completed a cycle of substantial modernization over the previous decade. Overcoming the economic instability and stagnation of the previous era, it managed to consolidate its finances, reduce inflation, accelerate growth and promote structural changes conducive to a friendlier environment for enterprise and investment" (Lynn 2011, 54). Political scientists spoke of the Europeanization and modernization that allowed Greece to morph into a "first-rate liberal democracy with a good economy" (Kalaitzidis 2009, 1).

The general lessons from these historical episodes is that liberalized financial systems weaken financing constraints, thereby providing more room for the buildup of financial imbalances (Borio, James, and Shin 2014). Not every surge of foreign lending had the same effect: Canada was able to digest capital inflows, and sustain a long current account deficit in the nineteenth century, without incurring financial fragility.

The most extreme cases of the damaging effects of capital inflows occur in fixed exchange rate regimes (the nineteenth-century gold standard, Europe in the 1920s, the Asian boom of the 1990s) or in a monetary union (Europe in the 2000s). Thus it is sometimes argued that a flexible exchange rate curbs the excesses, as capital inflows bring an exchange rate appreciation that lowers trade competitiveness and reduces the attractiveness for new inflows. But this approach blocks off many of the potential beneficial effects that borrowers expect to obtain from the inflow of capital.

After a series of financial crises around the world, the problem has been discussed as an issue of appropriate sequencing: that is, the wisdom of building stronger domestic institutions before seeking mechanisms to encourage capital inflows. A country should not open a capital account until it has deepened its domestic financial system; otherwise, the inflow of money might create financial imbalances. But this argument misses the fundamental point that the domestic system may never develop adequately on its own; it needs external resources. In a sense, then, financial instability is inherent to the development process. Opening the capital account in a fixed exchange rate regime is hard to reconcile with financial stability. This logic leads us to the second trilemma (Figure 5.2).

THE POLITICAL ECONOMY TRILEMMA

After a period of financial opening, the consequent development of financial imbalances may strain the political system. States (whether they are autocracies or democracies) initially like the benefits of open capital markets. Democracies, in which governments are responsive to the short-term demands of voters, are also likely to want to set monetary policy independently. They need to work out a trade-off between present monetary autonomy and the ability to attract inflows. In addition, both policies have time consistency problems of a different character. First, the monetary stimulus will bring immediate benefits only if it is unanticipated; if there is an expectation that the behavior will be repeated, agents will build the future into their responses to the stimulus. The stimulus relies on the noncontinuation of the policy. Second, by contrast, capital inflows may also bring short-term effects, but if there is a sudden stop, investment projects will remain unfinished and repayment will be problematic. The benefits rely on the expectation that the flows will continue. But states, especially democratic states, find it hard to commit to policies that will lock in the institutional basis on which long-term inflows can occur; there is instead an incentive to derive simply short-term advantages (such as those following from monetary stimulus) and leave the longer-term problems to successor governments.

The economic and financial problems that arise when capital inflows end or reverse can be severe. The collapse of unstable financial structures has immediate and severe economic effects that may include most or all of the following features: bank collapses, withdrawal of bank credits, rise in bankruptcies, collapse of prices, and rise in unemployment. In a celebrated article by Irving Fisher (1933), these effects were referred to as "debt-deflation." In Fisher's presentation there was no

Figure 5.2. The Financial Stability Trilemma

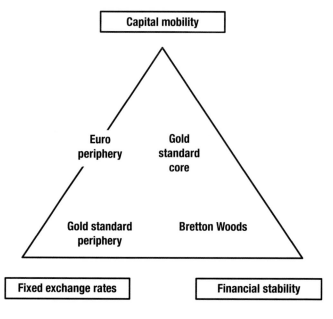

Source: Authors' illustration.

lender of last resort, but even with a lender of last resort and deposit insurance, guarantees and rescues can lead to fiscal crises.

While capital inflows continue and the financial imbalances build up, the system looks as if it is politically attractive and stable. Indeed, political parties often make compromises to support governments that can promise the institutional reforms needed to allow the inflow of capital to continue. Because inflows are generally the result of external financial conditions, they should not be interpreted as a response to particularly suitable or well-designed economic policies; but that is how they are commonly interpreted by voters, who view economic success as a key determinant in their choice (Kayser 2009). In practice, large inflows may weaken effective economic policymaking, because they relax the constraints under which governments operate and because the generally rising tide means that signals are suppressed that might indicate problematic features of the economy (Fernández-Villaverde, Garicano, and Santos 2013). Capital flows thus may suppress basic signals about government effectiveness that are essential to the functioning of democracy, because voters are not correctly informed about the level of competence of their governments. Warning against the potentially deleterious effects is a business that is unattractive, and left to outsiders, who make Cassandra-like prophecies. The insiders who benefit from inflows can in aggregate behave to ridicule the Cassandras.

However, when financial strains appear as a result of capital account openness, political parties no longer wish to be associated with the consequences. Voters blame the parties that have been associated with power for their past mistakes and flock to parties that define themselves as being against the system. In modern parlance, these parties are often described as "populist." The populist parties may be on the left or on the right; in fact, most antisystem parties combine elements of a left-wing and a right-wing critique of the system they are trying to overthrow. The left-wing critique is that the burden of crisis adjustment of incomes and wealth falls unequally and unfairly on the poor. The right-wing critique emphasizes that the adjustment works to the benefit of foreign creditors and represents a derogation of national sovereignty. These opposing arguments are not really contradictory; they can be (and are) easily combined. In these circumstances, the democratic principle is simply recast as a defense of national sovereignty.

Examples of the disintegration of traditional party systems in the aftermath of severe financial turbulence can be found in twentieth-century history and in the contemporary euro crisis. The Great Depression produced disintegration of democratic systems in central and eastern Europe and Latin America. The iconic case of democratic failure is that of Weimar Germany, which had a constitution and political system that had been carefully designed by distinguished political theorists (notably Max Weber and Hugo Preuss) to be as perfect a reflection as possible of popular voting preferences: the system featured both a direct election of the president and proportional representation designed so that there would be no "lost" votes. However, the parties committed to democracy progressively lost voting shares, and the parties associated with government lost especially badly. By the time of the Great Depression, both the center-left (the Social Democratic Party) and the center-right (the Democratic Party and the German People's Party) had lost significantly and were no longer capable of commanding a parliamentary majority. In terms of policy, the governments could do little, and their policy options were profoundly limited (Borchardt 1991).

The disintegration of system parties in the face of economic constraints is also a key element in the modern financial and political crisis in Europe. In Greece, the center-right New Democracy was defeated in elections in October 2009 and succeeded by the center-left Pasok (with 43.9 percent of the vote). Pasok was then discredited by its negotiations with creditors and by the wavering of Prime Minister George Papandreou on whether to hold a referendum on the terms of the plebiscite. After new elections in May 2012 (which were inconclusive) and June 2012, New Democracy returned to head a coalition government. The center-right party had only 29.7 percent of the vote, and it depended on Pasok, which had collapsed to 12.3 percent and had been squeezed into third place by the radical left, populist Syriza party. In January 2015, votes for New Democracy had shrunk to 27.8 percent and Pasok to 4.7 percent; Syriza, with 36.3 percent, could form a government with a populist right-wing party (Independent Greeks, 4.8 percent of the votes).

Likewise, in Spain, in the November 2011 elections, the socialists who had been in government in the first part of the financial crisis were punished with a fall in the vote from 43.9 percent to 28.8 percent, and power changed to the center-right Popular Party. But by 2015 the latter was threatened by a populist left party, Podemos, which used Syriza as a model. In Italy's 2013 elections, the party of Silvio Berlusconi, which had formed the government in the first phase of the crisis, won 29.1 percent of the vote and narrowly lost to the center left (29.5 percent). By 2014 in European Parliament elections, Berlusconi's movement was in third place with only 16.8 percent of the vote, and a populist leftist movement headed by comedian and political activist Beppe Grillo had 21.2 percent of the vote (it had done even better in the 2013 elections to the Italian parliament). The technocratic prime minister, Mario Monti, who had stepped in when Berlusconi's government collapsed under international pressure, founded a new political party (Civic Choice) but got only 8.3 percent of the vote in 2013—a showing similar to that of the liberal parties in the late years of Weimar Germany.

Even if the antisystem parties do not succeed in gaining majorities, their enhanced electoral support and the ensuing political pressure push the old or traditional parties to take a less accommodating and more radical stance.

In hard times—when politicians demand sacrifices from their voters—they often explain their position by saying that their hands are tied. While that may be a plausible argument in very small countries, the larger the country, the less compatible this stance is with the idea of national sovereignty. Consequently, the demand for an enhanced national sovereignty appears as a frequent response to setbacks, and even small countries may rebel. As Greece's flamboyantly radical finance minister Yanis Varoufakis put it in 2015, "The notion that previous Greek governments signed on the dotted line on programmes that haven't worked, and that we should be obliged to just follow that line unswervingly, is a challenge to democracy."[1]

The demand for national policy autonomy affects the policy equilibrium that arises out of the first trilemma. But when monetary independence could lead to the possibility of short-term stimulus at the cost of longer-term credibility, such autonomy would be undesirable. Monetary independence would lead to political pushes to manipulate monetary policy for short-term advantages without providing any long-term gains. The Mundell trilemma in these circumstances points in the direction of constraining national monetary autonomy. If the outcome of a likelihood of turning to a more national monetary policy is known in advance, it will influence investors' calculations. They will see commitment to a gold standard or fixed exchange rate regime as ultimately lacking credibility.

The possibility of such a reversal seemed less likely in the nineteenth century, at the time of the classic gold standard. In fact, investors often made the argument that the extension of constitutional rights was more rather than less likely to

---

[1] *Financial Times*, February 2, 2015, "Greece Finance Minister Reveals Plan to End Debt Stand-off."

protect their rights. The phenomenally successful banking house of Rothschild consistently pressed for political reforms, imposing a sort of political conditionality (Ferguson 1999). The people who were represented in parliaments were on the whole creditors; making policy dependent on their assent meant ruling out the possibility of an expropriation of creditors. However, as the franchise was extended, parliaments no longer reflected a preponderance of creditors; they came more and more to represent groups that benefited from state transfer payments. Such payments stood as alternative claims on the public purse to the requirement to service debt. The experience of the first major cycle of the political process in which democracy turned against creditors led Polanyi (1944) to make the famous argument that the gold standard (and, by implication, analogous regimes) was impossible in a democratic age.

The memory of the politics of turning against creditors during the Great Depression faded as the credit supercycle emerged in the second half of the twentieth century, when the argument began to resurface about the compatibility of globalization with democracy in emerging markets (Eichengreen 1996). Rodrik (2000, 2007) formulated the point in this way as a general argument about the incompatibility of hyperglobalization, democracy, and national self-determination: "democracy, national sovereignty and global economic integration are mutually incompatible." He presented the European Union as the best template of a new form of global governance with supranational rulemaking (Rodrik 2011). After the global financial crisis, the same problems and policy dilemmas appeared in rich industrial countries, and globalization appeared vulnerable again.

Democratic politics can be thought of as evolving two sorts of operations: the formulation of laws based on general principles of conduct, and redistribution of resources. The capacity to redistribute is limited if there is a large cross-border mobility of factors of production: capital is most obviously mobile, and it escapes if rates of capital taxation are too high; but the same process may also hold true in the case of taxation of high incomes, and income earners will try to operate in a different national and tax setting. Even the capacity to formulate general laws may be limited, in that incompatible principles in different countries may produce anomalies or loopholes and possibilities for forum-shopping.

Politicians are often painfully aware of the restraints. Jean-Claude Juncker, the veteran prime minister of Luxembourg and current president of the European Commission, formulated the constraint in the following way: "Politicians are vote maximisers ... for the politician, the Euro can render vote-maximising more difficult, as a smooth and frictionless participation in the monetary union sometimes entails that difficult decisions have to be undertaken or that unpopular reforms have to be initiated" (Marsh 2011, 269). The third trilemma (Figure 5.3) can thus be formulated as the incompatibility of capital flows, independent monetary policy, and democracy. This incompatibility poses a severe problem for people who believe that a major area of policy in a modern state should be capable of being decided by a democratic process.

Figure 5.3. The Political Economy Trilemma

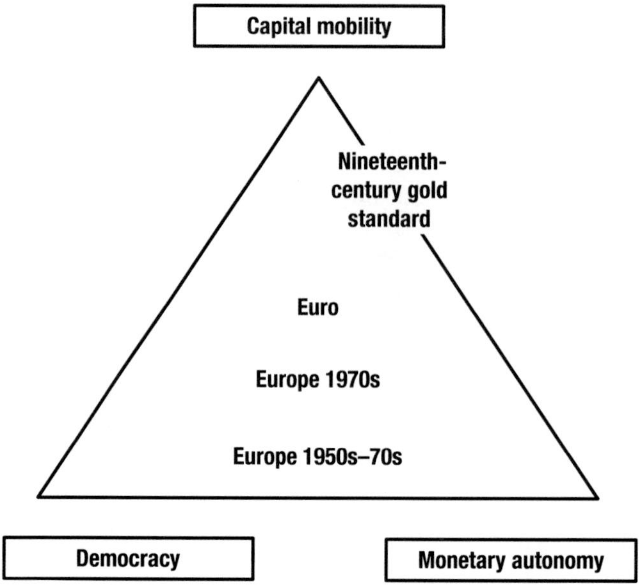

```
                    ┌─────────────────────────┐
                    │     Capital mobility     │
                    └─────────────────────────┘
                              /\
                             /  \
                            /    \
                           / Nineteenth-
                          /  century gold
                         /    standard
                        /
                       /      Euro
                      /
                     /     Europe 1970s
                    /
                   /    Europe 1950s–70s
                  /
     ┌────────────────────┐        ┌──────────────────────┐
     │     Democracy      │        │   Monetary autonomy  │
     └────────────────────┘        └──────────────────────┘
```

Source: Authors' illustration.

THE INTERNATIONAL RELATIONS TRILEMMA

Democracies like international order when it helps them attract beneficial capital inflows. But both capital mobility (as we have seen) and the limits imposed by international order narrow the scope for democratic politics.

The "tied hands" argument with regard to ensuring that democratic decisions were compatible with a longer-term framework of stability was frequently presented in the form of treaties or security arrangements. Often the reassurance creditors needed to convince them to lend was political rather than simply a monetary commitment mechanism (such as participation in the gold standard, an exchange rate mechanism, or the monetary union). Alliances offered investors the security that creditor governments would put pressure on banks to continue lending, and hence reduced the likelihood of sudden stops. The search for credibility might lead to a security commitment, in which countries would seek ties with powerful creditor countries because of the financial benefits. This kind of argument about the security bulwark that locks in capital movements applies to both democratic and nondemocratic regimes.

In addition, in democratic societies the redistributory impulse generated by the political process may—especially when the limits of domestic redistribution become apparent—translate into a wish to redistribute the resources of *other* countries. The burden of an unpleasant adjustment could conceivably be shifted onto other people who are outside the national boundary and thus outside the political process. It is this impulse ("Let the others pay!") that is restrained by treaties and security commitments. An alliance system or closer political union (as in modern Europe) helps restrain destabilizing democratic impulses, in which one country's democratic choices conflict with the voting preferences of other democracies.

Like all the other mechanisms involved in the various trilemmas, the security relationship too thus may reverse. If the security regime were severely challenged, the gain in credibility would no longer look attractive. And if capital flows reversed or financial fragility appeared, there would be fewer gains from participating in the international order. Potential borrowers that had locked themselves into security or other cooperative arrangements would then be tempted to defect.

The story of how diplomatic commitments enhance credibility is especially evident in the well-known example of Russia: a nondemocracy or autocracy locking into international security commitments. The beginning of the diplomatic rapprochement between Russia and France in 1891 was accompanied by a French bond issue, which the supporters of the new diplomacy celebrated as a "financial plebiscite" on the Franco-Russian alliance. Russia survived a sharp contraction in 1900–01 as well as a political crisis, with war and revolution in 1905, with no default. It raised new money immediately after the revolution of 1905. By 1914 almost half of the Russian government's 1,733 million ruble debt was held abroad, with 80 percent in French hands and the United Kingdom holding 14 percent. The diplomatic, military, and financial calculations were intricately entwined, and were skillfully used by Russia as a way of locking in the creditors politically and economically (Siegel 2014).

In imperial systems (which again are nondemocratic), the imperial security umbrella, coupled with the extension of legal principles from the metropol, functioned in a similar way and reassured investors that the country was capable of sustaining greater debt levels. The effect has been attributed to imperial order, but it is hard to determine whether it is due more to the effects of good policy, imposed as a result of reform-minded administrators, or to the power of the empire to compel repayment (Ferguson and Schularick 2006). In the aftermath of some crises, the imperial system simply expanded to swallow up bankrupt debtor entities; well-known examples are Egypt in 1875 and Newfoundland in 1933. But even very large and powerful political units have sought financial shelter by embracing financially stronger powers. In an extreme example, in early 1915 the Russian government suggested a fiscal and political union with France and the United Kingdom to allow it continued access to credit markets (Siegel 2014).

When capital dries up, incentives to make international commitments also disappear. Interwar Italy is a good case of the consequences of the logic of the reversal—when the international system no longer promises large financial gains. When the capital market was open in the 1920s, the fascist dictatorship of Benito Mussolini stabilized its currency and entered a fixed exchange rate regime (the *quota novanta*). Mussolini also moderated his foreign policy and suppressed any proclivity for political adventurism. When the international financial system broke down in the banking crisis of 1931, foreign policy restraint no longer offered any financial benefits, so Mussolini reoriented his policy toward imperial expansion. Adolf Hitler proposed a similar response to the Great Depression: Germany should break with international constraints and enrich itself at the expense of neighboring countries. Thus, a reversal of the gains that follow from security commitments is likely to be associated with a backlash against democratic politics.

There are more modern variants of the same process. After private capital flows in Europe from north to south halted in 2008, many southern Europeans lost their enthusiasm for European integration and turned against both the euro and the European Union.

The case of modern Russia is even more striking. Initially Russian President Vladimir Putin seemed to be a rather pro-Western, modernizing leader who sought engagement with the world economy, which included access to capital markets that would allow Russia to develop. Before 2008 Russia acquiesced to the logic of global capitalism; it needed to cooperate with global multinational companies to build an economy based on raw material and energy production, as well as technologies to process the raw materials.

But in 2007–08, Russia's strategy changed. On the eve of the global financial crisis, Putin spoke to the annual Munich Security Conference about the new power potential of the BRICs (Brazil, Russia, India, and China) as an alternative to what he dismissed as an arbitrary "unipolarity." His audience was shocked, and many saw the speech as evidence of insecurity or irrationality. However, as the financial crisis spiraled out of control, Putin reached the conclusion that he had been prophetic. After the crisis (if one follows power logic instead of the logic of economic growth) there was no longer so much to be gained from global markets. Instead, the best game in town was to cooperate with other countries with more state-centered capitalism, notably China.

In a world in which capital links do not bring mutual gains, democratic politics in each country can look as though it is targeted against other countries. Varoufakis offers a striking instance of this analysis when he refers to lessons from ancient Greece and its warring states: "Sometimes the larger, powerful democracies undermined themselves by crushing the smaller ones."[2] The fourth trilemma (Figure 5.4) can thus be formulated: that capital flows, democracy, and a stable international political order cannot be reconciled with each other.

IMPLICATIONS

The multiple trilemmas may not be the apparently impossible policy strait-jackets they seem to represent. In practice, there are always intermediary solutions; in the original macroeconomic version, there is never pure capital mobility or pure monetary policy autonomy. Some restrictions on capital mobility—even

---

[2] *Financial Times*, February 7, 2015, "An Athenian Boxer Fights the Good Fight."

Figure 5.4. International Relations Trilemma

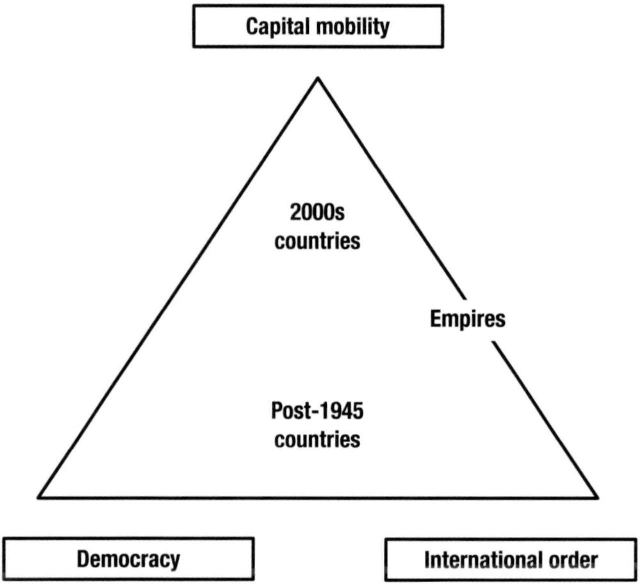

Source: Authors' illustration.

the home preference of investors or increased macroprudential controls on banking—provide room for policy maneuver. Policymakers are always making practical trade-offs.

Such an approach also indicates how practical responses to the other three trilemmas are likely to evolve. Capital mobility is central to all the trilemmas, so it might be tempting to recast the story in terms of the conclusion that capital mobility is simply not worth it (Stiglitz 1998; Bhagwati 2004). In practice, the historical experience shows that turning away from capital mobility is not that easy, and it carries an economic and political cost. Capital mobility is part of modern globalization. It is the apple in the Garden of Eden: irresistibly attractive but the cause of problems and misery. Once tasted, it is hard to spit the apple out again.

If financial stability is to be compatible with increased capital mobility, there must be more policy coordination on financial stability issues. Since 2008, such coordination has been a priority in international discussions of the Financial Stability Board (established in 2009 as a successor to the Financial Stability Forum in the wake of the Asian financial crisis). But the task of coordination is always challenged by national regulatory solutions that respond to particular local circumstances.

Absolutely irreversible fixed exchange rates—for instance, in a monetary union—require a high degree of political coordination, if not necessarily a political union. In the nineteenth century and until 1914 the gold standard economic world coexisted with political stability underpinned by an increasingly precarious international alliance system. The failure of the alliance system to contain conflict in 1914 ended the economic calculations of gold standard participants, and currency convertibility was suspended in almost every state. In the 1920s an attempt was made to restore the gold standard and to build order through the League of Nations. After 1945, in the Bretton Woods order, democracies were less constrained, as there were effective limits on capital movements. The opening of capital markets required a greater realism on the part of participants in a democratic process.

Democratic politics will not work when too many promises are made. Realistic democracy involves a commitment to longer-term sustainability. Sustainability is always threatened by rapid changes of policy or by policy inconsistency. Some commentators identify a fundamental "economic policy problem." Democratic societies find credible commitment to a long-term policy almost impossible, even with a broad consensus that such a long-term orientation would be desirable. Political scientists point out that no adequate mechanisms exist to reward current majorities for future economic performance: that is, policies that entail a current cost with payoffs that do not occur until several electoral terms in the future. Some suggest that one of the reasons fiscal reform and consolidation may work better in the United Kingdom than in the United States is that a five-year electoral cycle gives a longer horizon than a four-year cycle punctuated by midterm elections. The difficulties lie in part in the fact that present pain and future gain have often been misused as political slogans, and there is therefore a great deal of public cynicism about them. In addition, the relationship between present policy and future economic outcomes is not well understood, which leads to arguments about notions of a "free lunch" in the case of monetary policy where low interest rates are supposed to deliver greater growth, employment, and prosperity levels or in fiscal discussions that suggest that more spending and larger deficits can shift an economy from a bad to a good equilibrium.

Multilateral institutions can be thought of as commitment mechanisms that improve the quality of democracy by limiting the power of special interest organizations and by protecting individual rights (Keohane, Macedo, and Moravcsik 2009). The international relations trilemma is thus potentially solvable in the same way: through the evolution of a longer-term framework of stability. International commitments—the foundation of a stable international order—can lock in particular domestic settlements and ensure a longer-term framework of stability. The Bretton Woods international regime is often rightly regarded as a mechanism by which the United States internationalized the New Deal settlement (Ikenberry 2001).

Considering a broader concept of democracy in an international setting reduces the political logic of a zero-sum game mentality in which one country's gains can be achieved only through losses imposed on others. A larger security umbrella can therefore provide a framework for a system of rules about capital movement and a framework for stability that would limit or circumscribe the destructive capacity of capital-inflow-fueled credit booms.

But such grand compacts (of which the best historical example is the 1944–45 settlement that included Bretton Woods) are hard to achieve without a substantial amount of fear and uncertainty. The equivalent today of the time pressure that existed at the end of World War II is an urgent but also uncontrollable global crisis. The sad lesson of Bretton Woods is that things need to be extremely dangerous before a political dynamic of reform develops. It may be that today's world, for all its anxieties, is simply not obviously dangerous enough and that policymakers are too secure about the permanence of the globalization phenomenon.

REFERENCES

Balderston, Theo. 1993. *The Origins and Course of the German Economic Crisis, November 1923 to May 1932*. Berlin: Haude & Spener.

Bank for International Settlements (BIS). 1932. *Annual Report 1932*. Basel, Switzerland.

———. 1934. *Annual Report 1934*. Basel, Switzerland.

Bhagwati, Jagdhish. 2004. *In Defense of Globalization*. New York: Oxford University Press.

Bloomfield, Arthur. 1959. *Monetary Policy under the International Gold Standard, 1880–1914*. New York: Federal Reserve Bank.

Borchardt, Knut. 1991. *Perspectives on Modern German Economic History and Policy*. Cambridge, U.K.: Cambridge University Press.

Bordo, Michael D., and Hugh Rockoff. 1996. "The Gold Standard as a 'Good Housekeeping Seal of Approval.'" *Journal of Economic History* 56 (2): 389–428.

Borio, Claudio, Harold James, and Hyun Song Shin. 2014. "The International Monetary and Financial System: A Capital Account Historical Perspective." Working Paper 457, Bank for International Settlements, Basel, Switzerland.

Cortes Conde, Roberto. 1989. *Dinero, Deuda y Crisis: Evolucion Fiscal y Monetaria En La Argentina, 1862–1890*. Buenos Aires: Editorial Sudamericana Instituto Torcuato Di.

della Paolera, Gerardo, and Alan M. Taylor. 2007. *Straining at the Anchor: The Argentine Currency Board and the Search for Macroeconomic Stability, 1880–1935*. Chicago: University of Chicago Press.

Dooley, Michael. 2000. "A Model of Crises in Emerging Markets." *Economic Journal* 110 (460): 256–72.

Eichengreen, Barry. 1992. *Golden Fetters: The Gold Standard and the Great Depression, 1919–1939*. New York: Oxford University Press.

———. 1996. *Globalizing Capital: A History of the International Monetary System*. Princeton, New Jersey: Princeton University Press.

Ferguson, Niall. 1999. *The House of Rothschild, Volume 1: Money's Prophets: 1798–1848*. New York: Penguin.

Ferguson, Niall, and Moritz Schularick. 2006. "The Empire Effect: The Determinants of Country Risk in the First Age of Globalization, 1880–1913." *Journal of Economic History* 66 (2): 283–312.

Fernández-Villaverde, Jesús, Luis Garicano, and Nano Santos. 2013. "Political Credit Cycles: The Case of the Eurozone." *Journal of Economic Perspectives* 27 (3): 145–66.

Fisher, Irving. 1933. "The Debt-Deflation Theory of Great Depressions." *Econometrica* 1 (4): 337–57.

Flandreau, Marc, and Frédéric Zumer. 2004. *The Making of Global Capital 1880–1913*. Paris: OECD Development Centre Studies.

Ford, A. G. 1962. *The Gold Standard 1880–1914: Britain and Argentina*. Oxford, U.K.: Oxford University Press.

Haber, Stephen H., and Charles W. Calomiris. 2014. *Fragile by Design: The Political Origins of Banking Crises and Scarce Credit*. Princeton, NJ: Princeton University Press.

Ikenberry, G. John. 2001. *After Victory: Institutions, Strategic Restraint, and the Rebuilding of Order after Major Wars.* Princeton, NJ: Princeton University Press.

James, Harold. 1986. *The German Slump: Politics and Economics 1924–1936.* Oxford, U.K.: Oxford University Press.

————. 1999. "The Reichsbank, 1876–1945." In *Fifty Years of the Deutsche Mark: Central Bank and the Currency in Germany since 1948,* edited by Deutsche Bundesbank, 3–53. Oxford, U.K.: Oxford University Press.

Kalaitzidis, Akis. 2009. *Europe's Greece: A Giant in the Making.* New York: Palgrave-Macmillan.

Kayser, Mark Andreas. 2009. "Partisan Waves: International Business Cycles and Electoral Choice." *American Journal of Political Science* 53 (4): 950–70.

Keohane, Robert O., Stephen Macedo, and Andrew Moravcsik. 2009. "Democracy-Enhancing Multilateralism." *International Organization* 63: 1–31.

Kindleberger, Charles P. 1973. *The World in Depression 1929–1939.* London: Allen Lane.

Krugman, Paul. 1999. "Balance Sheets, the Transfer Problem and Financial Crises." Unpublished, Princeton University, Princeton, NJ.

Lynn, Matthew. 2011. *Bust: Greece, the Euro, and the Sovereign Debt Crisis.* Hoboken, NJ: Bloomberg Press.

Marsh, David. 2011. *The Euro: The Battle for the New Global Currency.* New Haven, CT: Yale University Press.

Mitchener, Kris James, and Marc Weidenmier. 2008. "Trade and Empire." *Economic Journal* 118: 1805–34.

Mundell, Robert A. 1963. "Capital Mobility and Stabilization Policy under Fixed and Flexible Exchange Rates." *Canadian Journal of Economic and Political Science* 29 (4): 475–85.

Obstfeld, Maurice, Jay C. Shambaugh, and Alan M. Taylor. 2005. "The Trilemma in History: Tradeoffs Among Exchange Rates, Monetary Policies, and Capital Mobility." *Review of Economics and Statistics* 87 (3): 423–38.

Obstfeld, Maurice, and Alan M. Taylor. 2004. *Global Capital Markets: Integration, Crisis, and Growth.* Cambridge, U.K.: Cambridge University Press.

Padoa-Schioppa, Tommaso. 1994. "Capital Mobility: Why Is the Treaty Not Implemented?" In *The Road to Monetary Union in Europe,* edited by Tommaso Padoa-Schioppa, 26–43. Oxford, U.K.: Clarendon Press.

Polanyi, Karl. 1944. *The Great Transformation.* New York: Farrar and Rinehart.

Rey, Helene. 2013. "Dilemma Not Trilemma: The Global Financial Cycle and Monetary Policy Independence." Federal Reserve Bank of Kansas City Economic Policy Symposium Proceedings.

Rodrik, Dani. 2000. "How Far Will International Economic Integration Go?" *Journal of Economic Perspectives* 14 (1): 177–86.

————. 2007. "The Inescapable Trilemma of the World Economy." http://rodrik.typepad.com /dani_rodriks_weblog/2007/06/the-inescapable.html.

————. 2011. *The Globalization Paradox: Democracy and the Future of the World Economy.* New York: Norton.

Schnabel, Isabel. 2004. "The Twin German Crisis of 1931." *Journal of Economic History* 64: 822–71.

Schuker, Stephen. 1988. "American 'Reparations' to Germans, 1919–33: Implications for the Third World Debt Crisis." *Princeton Studies in International Finance* 61 (July).

Schularick, Moritz, and Alan M. Taylor. 2012. "Credit Booms Gone Bust: Monetary Policy, Leverage Cycles, and Financial Crises, 1870–2008." *American Economic Review* 102 (2): 1029–61.

Siegel, Jennifer. 2014. *For Peace and Money: French and British Finance in the Service of Tsars and Commissars.* New York: Oxford University Press.

Stiglitz, Joseph. 1998. "Boats, Planes and Capital Flows." *Financial Times,* March 25.

Taylor, Alan M. 2003. "Capital Accumulation." In *A New Economic History of Argentina,* edited by Gerardo della Paolera and Alan M. Taylor, 170–96. Cambridge, U.K.: Cambridge University Press.

PART II

International Monetary Negotiations and the International Monetary System

CHAPTER 6

Forgotten Foundations of Bretton Woods

Eric Helleiner

It has become commonplace to hear predictions that the rising influence of countries such as Brazil, China, and India will undermine the post–World War II international financial system centered around the Bretton Woods institutions. Policymakers in these emerging powers are said to be frustrated by a number of aspects of the Bretton Woods system, including the fact that it was designed by Anglo-American officials without their input and without regard to the kinds of development issues that concern them.

The frustrations are certainly very real, but that historical narrative about the origins of Bretton Woods needs to be corrected. Far from ignoring international development issues, the Bretton Woods architects in fact pioneered the incorporation of development issues into the international financial architecture in some innovative ways. Moreover, those architects included representatives not just from the Anglo-American powers but also from many developing countries, including Brazil, China, and India. These are the forgotten foundations of Bretton Woods, discussed here, which may serve as an inspiration for those seeking to reform the international financial system in the context of new political realities.

EMERGING POWERS AT BRETTON WOODS

Conventional histories of the origins of the Bretton Woods system focus primarily on the role of Anglo-American negotiations during the early 1940s, led by Harry Dexter White representing the United States and John Maynard Keynes from Great Britain. But the Bretton Woods negotiations also involved 42 other governments, many of which contributed actively to the discussions. Among the latter were today's emerging powers Brazil, China, and India.

China had a prominent role in postwar international monetary planning because US President Franklin Roosevelt considered it to be one of the four great powers that would govern the postwar world (alongside Great Britain, the United States, and the USSR). When US officials chose an inner circle of countries to consult on White's initial plans for the international monetary system in 1942, China was included (the others were Australia, Brazil, Canada, Great Britain,

Mexico, and the USSR—Helleiner 2014, 157). White and other US officials consulted actively with Chinese officials during the long negotiations that led to the July 1944 conference in Bretton Woods, New Hampshire. At the conference itself, US officials also made sure that China received the fourth largest quota and voting share in the Bretton Woods institutions (after the United States, Great Britain, and the USSR), thereby guaranteeing it a seat on the executive boards of these bodies (Helleiner 2014, 186–200).

Chinese officials used the opportunities they were given to contribute to the design of the Bretton Woods system. The US archives contain records of various episodes in which Chinese policymakers lobbied for specific issues during the preconference negotiations. After the publication of the initial White and Keynes plans in the spring of 1943, the Chinese government prepared a detailed, full-fledged alternative plan that was sent to the other great powers in the fall of 1943. Chinese officials also took the Bretton Woods Conference itself very seriously, contributing actively to the debates and bringing a delegation that was more than twice as large (33 members) as the British delegation (15) and second in size only to that of the host country (45; Helleiner 2014).

Indians were also deeply engaged in the debates about Bretton Woods. India was a British colony at the time and was represented at the Bretton Woods Conference by the British-run government of India. Because of the fragile nature of their rule over the subcontinent, British officials recognized the political need to involve Indians in the negotiations. In advance of the conference, the government of India solicited and received detailed comments on the White and Keynes plans from Indian experts as well as officials working for the Reserve Bank of India (RBI), including its Indian governor, Chintaman Deshmukh. After the publication of the Anglo-American Joint Statement in April 1944 (which outlined areas of common agreement), the government of India sent the document for comment to all provincial governments and chambers of commerce in India. Few other governments involved in the Bretton Woods negotiations engaged in this kind of extensive consultation of public opinion in advance of the July conference (Helleiner 2014, 245–56; Helleiner 2015).

When choosing the government of India's representation at the Bretton Woods Conference, British officials decided to include four Indians among the eight-member delegation. These included not just Deshmukh and the RBI's director of research, B. K. Madan, but also two "nonofficial delegates": economist R. K. Shanmukhan Chetty and nationalist businessman Ardeshir Darabshaw Shroff. The British head of the delegation went out of his way at the conference to make sure that these Indians played a major role in representing the views of the delegation. The delegates took on the role with great energy and made a very good impression on other delegations; for example, Brazil's finance minister told a Brazilian audience after the conference that India had "brilliant representation" at the meeting (quoted in Helleiner 2014, 250).

The Brazilian government was also actively involved in the negotiations. As noted earlier, the United States considered it to be one of an inner circle of countries to be initially consulted on White's plans. In fact, Brazil—along with other

Latin American countries—was told about White's initial plans at an inter-American meeting in January 1942, even before the British were informed (Helleiner 2014, 107). Some of the core features of the plans were already quite familiar to Latin American officials, who had worked with White and other US officials since the late 1930s, pioneering inter-American financial initiatives that foreshadowed a number of the features of White's initial plans. One of the most important initiatives had been negotiations in 1939–40 on the establishment of an Inter-American Bank, an institution that was never created because of US congressional opposition but which served as a template for White's Bretton Woods plans (Helleiner 2014, Chapters 1–2).

Like their Chinese and Indian counterparts, Brazilian officials were keenly interested in commenting on the White and Keynes plans after the latter were published in spring 1943. They offered detailed suggestions in meetings with US officials and in written analyses in advance of the Bretton Woods Conference. The Brazilian government sent a 13-member delegation to the July 1944 meeting (which was the fifth largest delegation, along with that of Canada, after those of the four great powers), and its members made many contributions to the discussions. Brazilian officials worked particularly closely with delegates from other Latin American countries to coordinate positions. Because 19 of the 44 delegations came from Latin America and the conference operated on a one-country-one-vote decision-making rule, the region had considerable influence when it voted as a bloc. The US and British officials were very aware of the need to cultivate the support of Latin America, especially of regional leaders such as Brazil and Mexico. It was no coincidence that US officials gave Brazil a formal speaking role in both the opening and closing sessions of the conference, and that the Mexican finance minister was made chair of one of the three commissions around which the conference was organized (White and Keynes chaired the other two) (Helleiner 2014, 157–72). Latin America was also guaranteed two of the 12 seats on the IMF's executive board, a form of guaranteed representation offered to no other region.

The active involvement of Brazil, China, and India (as well as other countries) shows that the Bretton Woods negotiations were much more than simply a bilateral Anglo-American affair. US policymakers were in fact deeply committed to an inclusive "procedural multilateralism" that gave a formal voice in the negotiations to all the United Nations, as well as to what were called the Associated Nations, which were neutral in the war but had broken diplomatic relations with the Axis powers.[1] This US commitment was associated partly with American efforts to strengthen the anti-Axis wartime alliance and build the foundations for the postwar United Nations system. Also significant was the preference of some New Dealers for a more "democratic procedure" in global financial negotiations than had existed in the past.[2] In addition, White made the case forcefully in his first

---

[1]The phrase "procedural multilateralism" is from Toye and Toye (2004, 18).

[2]Quote from Adolfe Berle's comments in 1943, in Helleiner (2014, 131).

drafts in early 1942 that rich and powerful countries that ignored the interests of poorer or weaker countries would "only imperil the future and reduce the potential of their own level of prosperity" (Helleiner 2014, 103). Privately, White also told a Canadian colleague that he favored wide consultation because "all the brains were not concentrated in two great powers and that many of the smaller countries might have an important contribution to a discussion of the type."[3]

Finally, US support for inclusive multilateralism also had an important strategic goal: it helped dilute the British influence. Not surprisingly, Keynes and other British officials resisted the US approach for this same reason. In his first plans, Keynes had proposed that other countries would join postwar international financial institutions only after Great Britain and the United States had designed them. As he put it, "This approach has the great advantage that the United States and the United Kingdom (the latter in consultation with the other members of the British Commonwealth) could settle the charter and the main details of the new body without being subjected to the delays and confused counsels of an international conference. . . . I conceive of the management and the effective voting power as being permanently Anglo-American" (Johnson and Moggridge 1980, 54–55). During the lead-up to the Bretton Woods meeting, Keynes continued to complain about the number of countries involved, arguing that many of them "have nothing to contribute and will merely encumber the ground" (quoted in Helleiner 2014, 223). But White and other US officials insisted on a more inclusive multilateral negotiations process that gave voice to many other countries.

WHAT DID THE EMERGING POWERS WANT?

What kind of international financial order did the Brazilians, Chinese, and Indians want to see established after the war? At the top of their agenda was the goal of creating an order that was supportive of their national economic development objectives. Before Bretton Woods, this kind of international development focus had never been part of the mandate of an international institution. Representatives from Brazil, China, and India (and from other countries, as noted later) now pushed for this innovation in world politics during the Bretton Woods negotiations.

The Chinese authorities made this preference clear very early in the negotiations. China's ruling party, the Kuomintang (KMT), was committed to launching an ambitious program of state-led industrialization and modernization after the war. In commenting on the first public White plan for a Stabilization Fund and the Keynes plan for an International Clearing Union, the Chinese Ministry of Finance noted, "neither plan gives sufficient consideration to the development of industrially weak nations." In fact, one of the motivations for the Chinese government to develop its own plan at this time was to encourage a greater focus on development issues and the concerns of poorer countries. As one official said in

---

[3]W. C. Clark summarizing White's comments, in Wardhaugh (2010, 242).

mid-1943, "it may be necessary for China, as one of the four great powers, to be the leader of the undeveloped countries."[4]

The Chinese government was particularly keen to see a new kind of international financial institution that would support development lending to poorer countries. For this reason, it strongly backed the creation of the International Bank for Reconstruction and Development (IBRD). Indeed, China saw the IBRD's establishment as bringing to fruition a highly innovative proposal that had been put forward in 1918 by the KMT's founder, Sun Yat-sen, for the creation of an "International Development Organization" with this mandate. Although Sun's proposal was ignored by the Paris Peace Conference of 1919, the head Chinese delegate at Bretton Woods, H. H. Kung (who was also Sun's brother-in-law), invoked it as a source of inspiration in his speech at the start of the 1944 conference:

> China is looking forward to a period of great economic development and expansion after the war. This includes a large-scale program of industrialization, besides the development and modernization of agriculture. It is my firm conviction that an economically strong China is an indispensable condition to the maintenance of peace and the improvement of well-being of the world. . . . After the first World War, Dr. Sun Yat-sen proposed a plan for what he termed "the international development of China." He emphasized the principle of cooperation with friendly nations and utilization of foreign capital for the development of China's resources. Dr. Sun's teaching constituted the basis of China's national policy. America and others of the United Nations, I hope, will take an active part in aiding the post-war development of China. (US State Department 1948, 1156)[5]

It is interesting to note that the views of KMT officials on this issue were not all that different from those of the leaders of the Chinese Communist Party at the time. When US officials talked with Mao Tse-tung in August 1944, they reported that he was very supportive of postwar economic cooperation with the United States aimed at promoting Chinese economic development. He reportedly told them, "China *must* industrialize. This can be done—in China—only by free enterprise and with the aid of foreign capital. Chinese and American interests are correlated and similar. . . . We and must work together." Three months later, Mao's colleague Zhou En-lai reportedly told another US official that China's "greatest economic need would be for foreign capital. . . . China had to participate in international financial organizations if she was to overcome her present backward state."[6]

Indian delegates at the Bretton Woods Conference also stressed the importance of international development goals. Like many other Indian nationalists at the time, they were committed to the goal of raising Indian standards of living through state-led industrialization. (Gandhi, who was skeptical of industrialism

---

[4]Quotes from Helleiner 2014, 192.

[5]For Sun's ideas, see Helleiner 2014, 187–90.

[6]Quotes from US officials summarizing their views in Helleiner 2014, 200.

and who favored a more decentralized, village-centered economy, was an important exception.) The businessman Shroff had in fact been one of the authors of the highly publicized 1944 Bombay Plan, which outlined an ambitious approach of this kind. In consultations in India before the Bretton Woods Conference, Shroff had argued forcefully that any international monetary plan should be judged according to "whether it would be possible for India to raise the standard of living of her people within the next 10 to 15 years to something like double the existing standard." Chetty, the other "nonofficial" Indian delegate to Bretton Woods, had expressed similar views before the conference: "in evaluating these schemes, the main consideration to be kept in mind was how far they would enable us to raise the standard of life of our own people in India by increasing employment and by increasing the national wealth of the country" (quoted in Helleiner 2014, 250–51).

On the official side, Deshmukh was also strongly supportive of state-led industrialization strategies for India, and he evaluated the Bretton Woods plans in this light. As he said a few months before the July 1944 conference, "no international economic cooperation worth the name will succeed and lay the foundations for enduring international peace and prosperity unless the retarded development of important units like India and China receive special recognition and treatment" (quoted in Helleiner 2014, 251). Not surprisingly, he and other Indian delegates strongly supported the IBRD's development lending role at the conference. They even tried to add explicit development goals to the IMF's formal purposes, an initiative that resulted in wording (much less strong than India wanted) that referred to the IMF's role of contributing "to the development of the productive resources of all members" (Article 1(ii)). This initiative also had the effect of encouraging delegates to strengthen the IBRD's development mandate to make explicit reference to "the encouragement of the development of productive facilities and resources in less developed countries" (Article 1(i)) (Helleiner 2015).

Brazilian officials also prioritized international development goals at Bretton Woods. Brazil's president, Getúlio Vargas, had committed to increasingly ambitious state-led industrialization and development goals for his country after the late 1930s. As part of his plans, Vargas had accepted US financial and technical assistance, including a high-profile US offer in 1940 to help build a massive steel mill at Volta Redonda, the first in Latin America. In 1939–40, the Brazilian government had also supported the negotiations to create an Inter-American Bank, whose mandate included long-term public development lending. After the US Congress failed to support the bank, officials from Brazil and other Latin American countries looked to the Bretton Woods negotiations as a second opportunity to create this kind of an international development lending organization. Like China and India, they were very supportive of the IBRD's creation, and they pushed successfully at the conference to strengthen its development mandate (Helleiner 2014, 38, 162–65).

Brazilian officials were also very supportive of the IMF's lending role, which they saw as useful in offsetting the kinds of seasonal and cyclical balance of payments problems experienced by commodity-exporting countries. They applauded the fact that, with the IMF in place, Brazil would no longer need to maintain large gold reserves; as one official put it in August 1943, "the conservation of such reserves has been onerous, since it may be likened to an insurance maintained exclusively by the insured" (quoted in Helleiner 2014, 166). The Brazilian delegation took a lead role at the conference in successfully pressing for a waiver clause that allowed the IMF to overrule its regular lending limits in cases that could include commodity-exporting countries. In addition, Brazil lobbied the other Bretton Woods delegates to pass a resolution endorsing a future conference to create an international organization dedicated to commodity price stabilization. Although the Brazilian officials failed to get support for that specific idea, their initiative helped generate the passage of a resolution at the conference that called on governments to seek agreement on ways and means to "bring about the orderly marketing of staple commodities at prices fair to the producer and consumer alike" (Helleiner 2014, 166, 170).

Although not all the proposals of Brazil, China, and India were endorsed, the Bretton Woods Conference did pioneer the incorporation of international development goals into global financial governance. It did so in innovative ways, not least of which involved the creation of a new kind of intergovernmental international financial institution—the IBRD—with an explicit mandate to encourage development lending. This outcome had been sought by delegates not just from these three countries but also from other less industrialized regions, such as eastern Europe (for example, Poland and Czechoslovakia) and Africa (for example, Ethiopia and Egypt—Helleiner 2014, 227, 235–45).

US PRIORITIES DURING AND AFTER THE BRETTON WOODS NEGOTIATIONS

It was particularly important that the United States, as the dominant power at the conference, backed the prioritization of international development goals during the negotiations. This aspect of US postwar planning has often been neglected by historians, perhaps because it was downplayed by US policymakers themselves after the war. But it is important to recognize the depth of the commitment of many leading US policymakers at the time to the goal of raising living standards in poorer regions of the world.

This commitment began at the top, as President Franklin Roosevelt had declared his goal of securing "freedom from want ... everywhere in the world" in his famous "Four Freedoms" speech of January 1941 (Helleiner 2014, 120). With this commitment, Roosevelt sought to internationalize the New Deal and its goal of providing greater economic security for individuals (Borgwardt 2005). As part of his Good Neighbor policy, he had already backed US initiatives in the late 1930s to support Latin American economic development; these initiatives represented the first US aid program. Roosevelt saw the promotion of higher living standards worldwide as a key foundation for global political stability (Helleiner 2014, Chapter 1, 119–23; Borgwardt 2005).

Many of the US officials working on the plans for Bretton Woods had been deeply involved in the US initiatives to support Latin American economic development during the late 1930s and early 1940s. They brought this experience, and a commitment to international development, with them to the Bretton Woods negotiations. This was particularly true of White, who had played the central role in designing both the Inter-American Bank and new kinds of short-term balance of payments financial assistance to Latin American governments. White's early drafts of the Bretton Woods institutions drew directly on those initiatives and demonstrated the depth of his commitment to international development (Helleiner 2014, Chapters 1–4).

White incorporated international development goals into his initial Bretton Woods plans in a number of ways; in fact, he referred to his plans as proposals for a "New Deal in international economics" (quoted in Helleiner 2014, 121):[7]

- Building on the Inter-American Bank model, White's proposed IBRD had a mandate from the beginning to support long-term development lending to poorer countries.

- The IMF's short-term lending role built directly on the loans to Latin America for balance of payments purposes that he had pioneered in the late 1930s.

- The IMF's rules allowing capital controls and adjustable exchange rate pegs were designed to provide policy space for poorer countries to pursue state-led development strategies. This link was made clear in foreign advising activities of White and other US officials in the early to mid-1940s to countries as diverse as Cuba, Ethiopia, Guatemala, Paraguay, and the Philippines. In his initial plans, White also made explicit reference to the role that capital controls could play in curtailing capital flight from poorer countries.

- White empowered both the IMF and the IBRD to facilitate international debt restructuring, an issue that had plagued Latin American countries throughout the 1930s.

- In his initial plans, White discussed two trade issues of interest to poorer countries. First, he defended the use of infant-industry tariffs, arguing that assumptions underlying free trade theory were "not valid" and "unsound." (quoted in Helleiner 2014, 113). Second, White's IBRD was to organize and finance the creation of an international body to stabilize international commodity prices.

- As discussed already, White was strongly committed to inclusive multilateralism that gave voice to poorer and weaker states, both in the Bretton Woods negotiations and in the membership of his proposed bank and fund.

Between White's initial plans and the Bretton Woods Conference, some of these provisions disappeared, notably those relating to debt restructuring and the

---

[7]For the following provisions, see Helleiner, Chapter 4; for details of US foreign advising in support of policy space, see Helleiner 2014, Chapter 3, 172–82, 200–06, 227–33.

two trade issues, primarily because of domestic opposition (Helleiner 2014, 115–16). But the other provisions remained, and some—such as the IBRD's development mandate, the IMF's "waiver" clause, and rules allowing capital controls and adjustable pegs as a means to protect national policy space—were even strengthened during the negotiations with the support of poorer countries. At the Bretton Woods Conference itself, US Treasury Secretary Henry Morgenthau used his opening speech to emphasize the international development content of Bretton Woods: "Prosperity, like peace, is indivisible. We cannot afford to have it scattered here and there among the fortunate or to enjoy it at the expense of others. Poverty, wherever it exists, is menacing to us all and undermines the well-being of each of us" (quoted in Helleiner 2014, 122). In an article defending the Bretton Woods agreements in early 1945, Morgenthau (1945, 188) reiterated the message: "The Bretton Woods approach is based on the realization that it is to the economic and political advantage of countries such as India and China, and also of countries such as England and the United States, that the industrialization and betterment of living conditions in the former be achieved with the aid and encouragement of the latter."

Given this history, it is interesting that so many scholars have downplayed the international development content of Bretton Woods. The neglect is more understandable, however, when we recognize how this content was dramatically watered down after the war in the context of changing US priorities.[8] In the wake of Roosevelt's death in April 1945, many of the US architects of the development provisions of Bretton Woods lost influence in the new Truman administration, including both Morgenthau (who resigned in July 1945) and White (who left government service in March 1947). Those who assumed more prominent positions in US foreign economic policymaking were figures close to the New York financial community who were more skeptical of the international development goals and of the Bretton Woods plans in general. Under their influence, the Bretton Woods institutions embraced more conservative policies, and the US government scaled back its bilateral public development lending program to Latin America and urged free trade and the acceptance of private foreign investment in the region.

The onset of the Cold War in the late 1940s renewed US interest in international development somewhat, as evidenced by President Harry Truman's well-publicized commitment in January 1949 to combat "underdevelopment" as part of the struggle against communism. But his Point Four program was very limited in scale, focusing primarily on the provision of technical advice in contrast to the broader vision of the Bretton Woods architects. Bilateral US financial assistance came to focus primarily on countries on the front line of the Cold War, and US policymakers were less supportive of state-led development strategies in Latin America and elsewhere during this period than they had been during the

---

[8]For further details (and references) on the history in the following five paragraphs, see Helleiner 2014, Conclusion.

Bretton Woods negotiations. In a political context in which economic policy debates were increasingly cast as a struggle between capitalism and communism, prominent advocates of import-substitution industrialization—such as Raúl Prebisch, who had worked closely with US officials at the time of Bretton Woods and earned their respect—were now suspect (Dosman 2008).

THE PUSH FOR REFORM: CHALLENGING BRETTON WOODS OR REVIVING THE ORIGINAL VISION?

In this context, many policymakers from Latin America and India expressed strong frustration with the lack of international development content in the existing Bretton Woods system (mainland Chinese officials ceased to participate in the system after the 1949 revolution). They soon gained new allies from African and Asian countries that became independent during the 1950s and 1960s. By the early 1970s, a broad-based coalition of developing countries was demanding a full-fledged New International Economic Order (NIEO) that would better support their development goals.

The NIEO proposal was often portrayed by both its supporters and opponents as a challenge to an Anglo-American-dominated Bretton Woods system. But many of its provisions simply resurrected priorities outlined by the Bretton Woods architects, many of whom had been representatives of developing countries. These priorities included greater long-term international development finance, more generous short-term lending for balance of payments support, strengthened policy space to pursue national development strategies, and inclusive multilateral governance practices. Some of the demands of developing countries in the 1970s even revived, unknowingly, neglected features of White's initial plans, such as proposals for an international debt restructuring mechanism, commodity price stabilization, and backing for infant-industry trade protection.

When the push for an NIEO collapsed in the context of the debt crises of the early 1980s, the original international development content of Bretton Woods unraveled further: developing countries lost policy space, state-led development policies were dismantled, money flowed from South to North, and multilateral financial governance became more narrowly centered around the G7 countries (Canada, France, Germany, Japan, Italy, the United States, and the United Kingdom). In more recent years, however, support for many of the issues promoted at Bretton Woods has begun to rebuild with the rising economic power of countries such as Brazil, China, and India. Their governments have been pushing for reforms to global financial governance that will give their countries more voice and better reflect their development priorities.

Once again, these calls for reform are frequently portrayed as challenges to the Bretton Woods system, but they are more accurately viewed as criticisms of the Bretton Woods system as it actually existed than of the original vision of the Bretton Woods architects themselves. With many of their proposals, Brazilian, Chinese, and Indian policymakers today are often simply reviving international development priorities that were shared by the Bretton Woods architects, some of whom were from the same countries.

If the Bretton Woods system is to survive and flourish in the context of contemporary power shifts in the world economy, reforms that rejuvenate the international development content of the vision of its founders may be more important than ever. The costs of not supporting this vision were well expressed by US Treasury Secretary Henry Morgenthau in a *Foreign Affairs* article he published in early 1945, during the US debates about ratifying Bretton Woods. Discussing the future of the relationship between rich and poor countries, Morgenthau (1945, 190) warned,

> Unless some framework which will make the desires of both sets of countries mutually compatible is established, economic and monetary conflicts between the less and more developed countries will almost certainly ensue. Nothing would be more menacing to have than to have the less developed countries, comprising more than half the population of the world, ranged in economic battle against the less populous but industrially more advanced nations of the west.

REFERENCES

Borgwardt, Elizabeth. 2005. *A New Deal for the World: America's Vision for Human Rights.* Cambridge, MA: Belknap Press for Harvard University Press.

Dosman, Edgar. 2008. *The Life and Times of Raúl Prebisch, 1901–1986.* Montreal, Quebec, Canada: McGill-Queen's University Press.

Helleiner, Eric. 2014. *Forgotten Foundations of Bretton Woods.* Ithaca, NY: Cornell University Press.

———. 2015. "India and the Neglected Development Dimensions of Bretton Woods." *Economic and Political Weekly* 50 (29): 31–39.

Johnson, E., and D. Moggridge, editors. 1980. *The Collected Writings of John Maynard Keynes, XXV, Activities 1940–1944 Shaping the Post-War World—The Clearing Union.* Cambridge, U.K.: Macmillan.

Morgenthau, Henry. 1945. "Bretton Woods and International Cooperation." *Foreign Affairs* 23 (1): 182–94.

Toye, John, and Richard Toye. 2004. *The UN and Global Political Economy.* Bloomington: Indiana University Press.

US State Department. 1948. *Proceedings and Documents of the United Nations Monetary and Financial Conference, Bretton Woods, New Hampshire, July 1–22, 1944.* Washington, DC: US Government Printing Office.

Wardhaugh, Robert. 2010. *Behind the Scenes: The Life and Work of William Clifford Clark.* Toronto, Ontario, Canada: University of Toronto Press.

CHAPTER 7

Hurling BRICS at the International Monetary System

BENN STEIL

In April 2013 Ukraine was facing a massive current account deficit of 8 percent and was badly in need of dollars to pay for vital imports. Yet on April 10 President Viktor Yanukovych's government rejected terms set by the International Monetary Fund for a $15 billion financial assistance package, choosing instead to continue financing the gap between Ukraine's domestic production and its much higher consumption by borrowing dollars privately from abroad. On April 12 Kiev issued a 10-year, $1.25 billion Eurobond that cash-flush foreign investors gobbled up at a 7.5 percent yield.

Everything seemed to be going swimmingly until, on May 22, the Federal Reserve's chairman Ben Bernanke suggested that the Federal Reserve might, if the economy continued improving, begin to pare back or "taper" its monthly purchases of US Treasury and mortgage-backed securities. This would mean more attractive returns on longer-maturity US bonds, making financial assets of developing markets decidedly less attractive. Investors in Ukrainian bonds reacted savagely, dumping them and thus raising their yield to about 11 percent—where it stayed for most of the remainder of the year (Figure 7.1).

Ukraine's financial problems had been growing over many years, but it was the prospect of the Federal Reserve pumping fewer new dollars into the market each month that pushed the cost of rolling over its debt beyond Kiev's capacity to pay. Ultimately, in December, President Yanukovych turned for help to Moscow, which demanded that he abandon an association and trade agreement with the European Union in return. Ukrainians took to the streets ... and the rest is history.

The Federal Reserve did not actually begin its taper until January 2014, and it is sobering to contemplate that this history might have been much different—President Yanukovych might have remained in power—had Ben Bernanke's taper talk come a few months later than it did. Such is the global power of the Federal Reserve.

Ukraine was only one of many developing nations that suffered massive sell-offs in their bond and currency markets following the taper talk. The selling was not indiscriminate, however. The countries hit hardest—Brazil, India, Indonesia,

Figure 7.1. Ukraine: Seven-Year Government Bond Yield
(Percent)

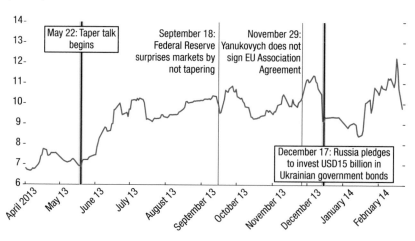

Source: Bloomberg L.P.

South Africa, and Turkey—had all been running large current account deficits, which had to be financed with imported capital. Their markets recovered modestly following the Federal Reserve's unexpected decision in September to delay the taper, but swooned again in December when the Federal Reserve announced that it would move forward with its plans. Figure 7.2 shows that there has generally been little improvement in these countries' current account balances since 2013, suggesting that they are vulnerable in the future to a "rate ruckus"—a bond sell-off triggered by an unexpectedly aggressive Federal Reserve rate increase.

As their markets tanked, many leaders of the worst-hit countries criticized Washington for its selfishness and tunnel vision. "International monetary cooperation has broken down," said Reserve Bank of India Governor Raghuram Rajan angrily, following another sell-off in his country's currency and bond markets in January 2014. The Federal Reserve and others in the rich world, he said, can't just "wash their hands off and say, we'll do what we need and you do the adjustment."[1]

To understand what Rajan had expected from the Federal Reserve and why he was so angry, the recently released transcripts of the October 2008 Federal Open Market Committee meeting are illuminating. The transcripts show that members were acutely aware of the global nature of the growing crisis; however, they were not focused on stopping its spread through emerging markets generally but on limiting blowback into the United States. Members agreed that swap lines with

---

[1]*Financial Times*, January 30, 2014, "Emerging Markets in Retreat: India's Raghuram Rajan Hits Out at Unco-ordinated Global Policy" (https://www.ft.com/content/cc1d1716-89ac-11e3 -abc4-00144feab7de).

emerging market central banks (to lend them dollars against their own currency as collateral) should be temporary and limited to large countries that were important to the US financial system: Brazil, Korea, Mexico, and Singapore, all of which could potentially spread their problems directly into American markets. For example, former Federal Reserve Governor Donald Kohn expressed concern about the potential for large-scale foreign selling of Fannie Mae and Freddie Mac mortgage-backed securities "feed[ing] back on our mortgage markets" and pushing up borrowing rates. Certain countries might go down that route, he argued, if they lacked less disruptive means of accessing dollars, like Federal Reserve swap lines. And "it would not be in our interest" for them to do so, Kohn observed.

The Federal Reserve privately rebuffed swap line requests from Chile, the Dominican Republic, Indonesia, and Peru. And two years later, when the US economy had become much less vulnerable to foreign financial instability, the Federal Reserve allowed its swap lines with Brazil, Korea, Mexico, and Singapore to expire. Two years after that, in 2012, the Federal Reserve denied a swap line request from India, which explains Rajan's anger. Yet it is unrealistic to expect the Federal Reserve to act differently, however desirable that might have been for other countries. The Federal Reserve's primary objectives—ensuring domestic price stability and maximum employment—are set by law, and it is not authorized to subordinate them to foreign concerns.

But can't developing countries take actions on their own to protect themselves, without cooperation from the United States? Indeed they can. The IMF (2013) concluded that countries whose economies have been more resilient in the face of unconventional US monetary policy since 2010 have three important characteristics: low foreign ownership of domestic assets, a trade surplus, and large foreign exchange reserves. These findings have clear policy implications: in good times, emerging markets should keep their imports and currency down, and exports and dollar reserves up.

Unfortunately, many members of the US Congress see such policies as unfair currency manipulation, harming US exporters. To prevent foreign governments from taking such steps, some influential economists such as Fred Bergsten, supported by major US corporations, have called on the White House to insert provisions against currency manipulation into future trade agreements. Others, such as economists Jared Bernstein and Dean Baker (2012), have gone so far as to call on Washington to impose taxes on foreign holdings of US Treasuries and slap tariffs on imports from alleged manipulators.[2]

These suggestions are misguided; they would only raise global trade tensions and political conflict. But the very fact that prominent commentators are calling for such actions illustrates how the functioning—or malfunctioning—of the global financial and monetary system can encourage a spiral of damaging policy actions.

Given the trajectory of US policy, the turmoil in emerging market currency and bond markets over recent years should spur more effective collective action

---

[2] *The New York Times*, November 6, 2012. "Taking Aim at the Wrong Deficit."

Figure 7.2. Emerging Market Bond Yields and Current Account Balances, 2013

1. Emerging Market Bond Yield Rises during Taper Tantrum
(Percent of GDP)

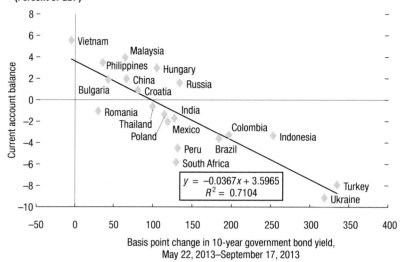

$$y = -0.0367x + 3.5965$$
$$R^2 = 0.7104$$

Basis point change in 10-year government bond yield,
May 22, 2013–September 17, 2013

2. Current Account Balances, 2013 versus 2015
(Percent of GDP)

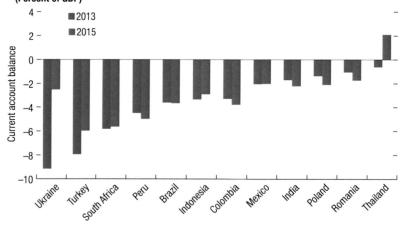

Source: Author's estimates based on Bloomberg L.P. and IMF staff.
Note: Ukraine data are for the seven-year government bond, and Brazil's September 17, 2013, data reflect the nine-year government bond yield (panel 1).

to defend the global financial system against future Federal Reserve–induced whiplash. Most emerging market countries lack the resources to protect themselves individually, but they could build sufficient currency reserves if they acted in concert. In Asia, for example, the Chiang Mai Initiative Multilateralization of 2010 allows the 13 nations involved to tap their $240 billion of combined reserves in the event of a balance of payments crisis.

Unfortunately, however, there is much less here than meets the eye. The Chiang Mai countries have not actually pooled the funds they have pledged, and members can access significant funds only if they are under an IMF program and subject to stigmatized IMF surveillance and conditionality. In reality, governments in the region are hesitant to extend credit to each other during a crisis, which is the only time it is actually needed. Chiang Mai has yet to commit a penny to mutual assistance and appears unlikely to do so in the future.

In 2014, the BRICS countries (Brazil, Russia, India, China, and South Africa) established a Contingent Reserve Arrangement (CRA) that could play a similar role. Russian President Vladimir Putin said that the CRA "creates the foundation for an effective protection of our economies from a crisis in financial markets." But does it? Is it a potential substitute for the IMF?

Clearly not, as illustrated in Figure 7.3. Under the CRA, Brazil and Russia could borrow a maximum of about $5.4 billion without being on an IMF program. To put this in perspective, the IMF approved lending to Russia of about $38 billion in the 1990s. In 2002 alone, it approved a 15-month standby credit arrangement for Brazil of about $30 billion. Net private financial flows to emerging markets today are roughly 10 times what they were in 2002, meaning that the size of the loans necessary to address balance of payments financing problems would be even larger now. The BRICS countries know this, which is why individually they hold reserves well over 50 times what they could borrow under the CRA. In fact, tapping the CRA would make a crisis more rather than less likely, as it would signal to the markets that a crisis—which the CRA is institutionally incapable of combating—is in the offing.

Of the BRICS bank initiative, President Putin said, "the international monetary system . . . depends a lot on the US dollar, or, to be precise, on the monetary and financial policy of the US authorities: the BRICS countries want to change this." But it is notable that the entire paid-in capital stock of the BRICS bank is in US dollars, whereas only 10 percent of the World Bank's paid-in capital was contributed in US dollars. So, far from making the world less dollar-dependent, the BRICS bank has actually created a significant new source of demand for dollar-denominated financial assets.

The clear limitations of the Chiang Mai, CRA, and BRICS bank initiatives suggest that it is as easy to bemoan a lack of US financial leadership as it is difficult to find a substitute for it, even when the resources required to do so are readily available. Self-help in the form of large dollar reserves with backup support from the IMF will therefore continue to be essential for developing nations as they try to cope with the vicissitudes of the dollar-dominated global monetary and financial architecture.

Figure 7.3. BRICS: IMF Disbursement and CRA Borrowing

1. IMF Disbursements to BRICS Countries (USD Billions)

2. BRICS CRA Borrowing Limit without IMF Program

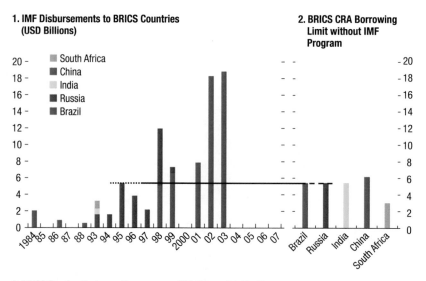

3. BRICS Foreign Exchange Reserves vs. CRA Borrowing Limits (USD Billions)

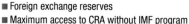
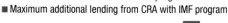
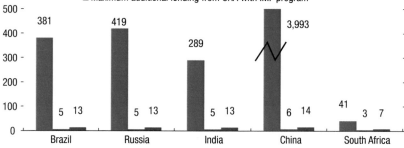

Sources: Banco Central do Brasil; Central Bank of Russia; Reserve Bank of India; People's Bank of China; South African Reserve Bank; and IMF staff.

Note: BRICS = Brazil, Russia, India, China, and South Africa; CRA = Contingent Reserve Arrangement.

REFERENCE

International Monetary Fund (IMF). 2013. "Global Impact and Challenges of Unconventional Monetary Policies." Policy Paper, International Monetary Fund, Washington, DC, October 7. https://www.imf.org/external/np/pp/eng/2013/090313.pdf.

CHAPTER 8

The IMF Is—or Was?—the Keystone of the International Financial System

JAMES M. BOUGHTON

It has become fashionable, and it is useful, to think of the international financial system as a form of architecture. That analogy can take many specific forms, but one helpful comparison is with the Gothic cathedrals of Europe, which stand among the greatest architectural triumphs in world history. The cathedrals, constructed without such modern contrivances as reinforced concrete, have stood for centuries and still evoke awe. A key element of every cathedral is the ogive arch, which is little more than a set of stones, piled in a curve and held firmly in place by a keystone at the apex of the arch. Remove the keystone, and the whole structure collapses.

The Gothic archway can serve as a metaphor for the international financial system as it has evolved since it was designed at Bretton Woods, New Hampshire, in 1944. It has many components, including private financial markets, national monetary authorities, regional institutions, multilateral development banks, and—at the apex—the International Monetary Fund. This chapter argues that, without this keystone, the system would collapse.

The IMF was in fact designed to be the keystone of the system, by a group of delegates who had known little but financial and economic chaos throughout their working lives. The entire era since the outbreak of the Great War in 1914 had been marked by autarky, mercantilist pressures, and the absence of any financial order. The Great Depression was followed by World War II. Multiple efforts to restore order had failed. Private sector financial flows were virtually nonexistent and had been quite limited for many years; enough so that everyone involved agreed that the system should be designed around stabilizing official flows, with private flows limited to those directly related to trade.

The key to stabilizing official financial flows was to create an institution—the IMF—as a forum in which representatives of trading countries could discuss how to promote trade by reestablishing currency convertibility and gradually eliminating restrictions on trade-related currency exchange. But the founders recognized that a forum would not be enough. Trade imbalances would arise and would have to be settled by official capital flows. Relying on bilateral flows (as in the classical gold standard era as well as the disorderly interwar period) would be inefficient.

The solution was to create a formal multilateral process. The founders imagined that most countries would swing between credit and debit status and would resort to drawing on IMF funding when they were temporarily in debt to other members. The United States, which completely dominated world output and finance at the time, would be exceptional as a permanent and primary creditor of the system.

The world of Bretton Woods no longer exists. We have witnessed seven decades of global economic growth, led by spectacular growth in international trade. The stock of private sector cross-border financial assets has grown to the point that it is orders of magnitude larger than official holdings. As a result, today finance drives trade, not the other way around. When countries get into trouble financing their balance of international payments, the IMF is likely to be only one of many creditors.

Today's international financial system is chaotic, but it is a totally different kind of chaos from that of the interwar period. It is chaos born of success, not failure. A point that is often missed in discussions of postwar financial history is that the Bretton Woods system collapsed in the early 1970s not because it failed but because it succeeded beyond the wildest dreams of the delegates who put it together in 1944. Instead of just stabilizing output and trade at a reasonably high level, as envisaged at Bretton Woods, the system enabled world trade to grow by nearly 9 percent a year, which in turn triggered world output growth of more than 5 percent a year. Moreover, growth was more widely shared than ever before. By the time the system ended in 1973, the number of IMF creditors had grown from one (the United States) to 17 countries on four continents. Currently that number is approaching 50.

By 1973, US economic and financial hegemony was a thing of the past, not fundamentally because of any faltering in the United States but because of the diversity of economic success around the globe. The world was no longer (if it ever had been) a common currency area, and a system based solely on the US dollar and on exchange rates pegged to the dollar was no longer viable. From an Amerocentric perspective, that might have looked like a failure, but from a global perspective it was clearly a success.

As the global need shifted toward a more flexible system, the IMF responded in three ways. First, it created the Special Drawing Right (SDR) as a supplement to dollars in foreign exchange reserves. Second, it eliminated the monetary role of gold in international finance. Third, it eliminated the system of par values for exchange rates and adopted the principle that each country could select whatever exchange rate regime it wanted (except for pegging to gold), subject to IMF oversight of restrictive policies and of the consistency of macroeconomic policies with the exchange rate regime.

Those responses were necessary and helpful, but they were not sufficient to stabilize the system, much less to sustain the growth performance of the Bretton Woods era. The devastatingly awful fact about the past four decades of international finance is that, despite moving from a rigid and narrowly constructed system to one that is far more open and dynamic, we have experienced both less stability and less growth. The frequency, severity, and geographic range of financial crises have been greater than in the Bretton Woods era, culminating in the global financial crisis that began in 2008. Meanwhile, economic growth on average since 1972 has fallen from more than 5 percent a year to around 3 percent.

WHAT HAS GONE WRONG, AND HOW CAN WE FIX IT?

Part of the problem is that economic policies have been poorly formulated and implemented. By the end of the 1970s, confidence had eroded in the ability of governments or central banks to stabilize national economies through countercyclical policy. As a result, macroeconomic policies gradually began to focus less on maintaining high employment and economic growth and more on narrower financial goals, such as fiscal deficit reduction and monetary restraint. The postwar Keynesian consensus that governments had a primary responsibility for employment and growth was lost. Perversely, the world economy ended up with neither good growth nor financial stability (price stability, yes, but accompanied by waves of financial crises). The reason for this outcome is simple and clear: high employment and sustainable economic growth are necessary conditions for financial stability. Putting the real economy on autopilot increases financial volatility.

Along with the loss of effective fiscal policy, the shift to flexible exchange rates has failed to deliver the mean-reverting tendency toward financial equilibrium that Milton Friedman and others envisioned during the Bretton Woods era. Financial globalization since the 1970s has meant that the capital account, not the trade account, has been the principal determinant of exchange rates. With the tail wagging the dog, unmanaged rates have failed to deliver equilibrium, and managing the rate to offset the financial effects has proved to be an unrealistic goal. Better regulation and oversight of international financial flows might have alleviated the problem, but for a quarter century policy toward financial regulation was moving in the other direction.

These policy mistakes and weaknesses are solvable problems, and some progress has been made since the onset of the global financial crisis. But in addition to better policies, we need to strengthen the institutional system of the global economy if we expect to restore the performance of what DeLong (2015) has called the "glorious years" of the Bretton Woods era.

The IMF was designed to be the keystone of the international financial system, and thus the first requirement for a well-functioning system is an effective IMF. As the global economy became more complex and more chaotic after 1973, the adaptation of the institution became increasingly difficult. Surveillance over a multiplicity of exchange regimes, lending to low-income countries and those making a transition toward market economics, managing the response to international financial crises, and trying to encourage or even force countries to implement extensive structural reforms—these were all new and, in combination, nearly impossible challenges. By the 1990s, the IMF was in an existential crisis from which it has been trying to extricate itself since the millennium.

Again, some progress has been made. The IMF's internal reforms have been impressive, including the adaptation of lending facilities, a greatly increased attention to staff diversity, and newly designed financial support for debt reduction and disaster relief. In 2002 the IMF adopted new conditionality guidelines with the aim of focusing and streamlining reform programs and helping to put country authorities in better control of their own reforms. In 2007 the IMF adopted new surveillance guidelines designed to give clearer signals about whether exchange rate policies were appropriate. In 2011 the IMF embedded its surveillance decision into a more holistic and multilateral approach.

Despite these changes, the IMF's ability to rise to its many challenges and its credibility as the keystone of the system remain hampered by the failure of the international community to align the institution more fully with the realities of the twenty-first century. As set out in more detail in two recent papers (Boughton 2014, 2015), three reforms would take the system a long way in the right direction.

First, modernize the governance of the IMF so that the institution can look forward and overcome the inertia that has tethered it to a postwar world dominated by Europe and the United States. The essential initial step was taken recently when the US Congress finally ratified the reform package approved by the IMF Board of Governors in 2010. That package makes permanent a modest increase in IMF resources, shifts representation and voting power slightly toward the rapidly growing emerging markets, and enables a single seat for the euro area. With that in place, attention should turn now toward more fundamental reforms—including an end to the European-US duopoly on institutional leadership—so that the IMF might no longer keep lagging behind a continually changing world.

Second, build on the revival of the SDR that began with the allocation of SDRs in 2009 (the first increase in the stock of this important reserve asset since 1981) and is continuing with the addition of the Chinese renminbi to the SDR currency basket in 2016. A strengthened SDR helps solidify the role of the IMF and is being accomplished in ways that recognize the increasing role of emerging markets. More important, it helps overcome the badly skewed supply of international reserves, which imposes heavy costs on many countries with nonreserve currencies. Large regular allocations would be the central element in this process. Creation of a substitution account in the SDR Department would be another important step, enabling countries to swap some of their US dollar reserves for a more stable currency basket. Sooner or later, central banks will seek to reduce the share of US dollars in their official reserve portfolios. A substitution account would help ensure that this was done in an orderly and predictable way, and that it would not add to market volatility.

Third, establish a more rational balance between the IMF and other international institutions, particularly the Group of Twenty (G20), specialized institutions such as the World Trade Organization (WTO) and the Financial Stability

Board (FSB), and regional agencies. As Malcolm Knight observed in a 2014 paper on financial regulation, "no institution, including the IMF, has a specific mandate to oversee the international financial system *as a whole*" (9; emphasis in the original). The silo structure that is inherent in the postwar architecture prevents effective systemic oversight and control.

Because the G20 (which became the dominant outside group on financial policy in 1999 and the prevailing summit grouping in 2008) controls more than three-quarters of the voting power in the IMF, the latter is no longer the locus of decision making on how the international financial system should function. Power and influence have shifted from the universal, treaty-based, permanent agency to a narrower, exclusive, and transient club. The G20 controls at least 80 percent of world output and trade, but it does not represent the interests of small or poor countries. Those interests, which are systemically important in the aggregate, have become marginalized. How to solve this problem is not yet clear, but the challenge must be addressed.

The proliferation of regional financial agencies such as the Chiang Mai Initiative, the BRICS (Brazil, Russia, India, China, and South Africa) Contingent Reserve Arrangement, and the Asian Infrastructure Investment Bank reflects in part a widespread dissatisfaction with the preeminent role of the IMF and the World Bank. Properly channeled, however, those agencies can serve to supplement and appropriately redirect the resources and expertise of the Bretton Woods institutions. The governance reforms sketched earlier would help promote a cooperative evolution of these relationships.

The proposed reforms are all modest, and none is radical. They do not add up to a wholesale revision of the international architecture, as has been dreamed of in calls for a "Bretton Woods II." They are, however, all feasible with political will and a commitment to act. If a Grand Bargain is never going to materialize, as seems likely, these modest steps could at least restore the IMF to its position at the apex of the archway, where its founders intended it should be.

REFERENCES

Boughton, James M. 2014. "Stabilizing International Finance: Can the System Be Saved?" CIGI Essays on International Finance 2 (June), Centre for International Governance Innovation, Waterloo, Ontario, Canada. https://www.cigionline.org/publications/cigi-essays-international -finance-volume-2-international-finance-can-system-be-saved.

———. 2015. "The IMF as Just One Creditor: Who's in Charge When a Country Can't Pay?" CIGI Paper 66 (April), Centre for International Governance Innovation, Waterloo, Ontario, Canada. https://www.cigionline.org/publications/imf-just-one-creditor-whos-charge-when -country-cant-pay.

DeLong, J. Bradford. 2015. "An Even More Dismal Science." Project Syndicate (April 30). http://www.project-syndicate.org/commentary/economy-debate-post-world-war-ii-by-j --bradford-delong-2015-04.

Knight, Malcolm D. 2014. "Reforming the Global Architecture of Financial Regulation: The G20, the IMF and the FSB." CIGI Paper 42 (September), Centre for International Governance Innovation, Waterloo, Ontario, Canada. https://www.cigionline.org/publications/reforming -global-architecture-of-financial-regulation-g20-imf-and-fsb-0.

PART III

Currency Wars and Secular Stagnation— The New Normal?

CHAPTER 9

Reform of the International Monetary System: A Modest Proposal

RICHARD N. COOPER

In recent years there have been many criticisms, explicit and implied, of the international monetary system. At the 2010 World Economic Forum in Davos, President Nicolas Sarkozy of France called for a new Bretton Woods Conference, overlooking the fact that the real Bretton Woods Conference of 1944 required two years of preparation. In my judgment, the international monetary system performed rather well after the global financial crisis of 2008, although of course it did not prevent the crisis. Nonetheless, the crisis provides an opportunity to review the international monetary system, which—like all institutions—should be subject to close reevaluation every decade or two.

Those with some experience in policymaking know that it is difficult to fight something with nothing when circumstances lead to many calls for action. With that in mind, I made a proposal for improving the international monetary system in the context of the Group of Twenty (G20) meeting chaired by President Sarkozy in 2011, before which he announced that improving the international monetary system was high on his agenda. My proposal fell like a stone. I like to think that was for reasons other than its merits, since the G20 got distracted by the euro crisis and other urgent matters.

My proposal was radical but not revolutionary: radical in that it would involve significant change in the way we manage international monetary issues; not revolutionary in that it builds on the existing institutional structure, and in that sense is evolutionary. The proposal works toward several objectives: (1) to give the Special Drawing Rights (SDRs) more, and national currencies less, prominence in the future provision of international liquidity; (2) to generate needed international liquidity without cost at the global level, through the issuance of new SDRs; (3) to introduce greater symmetry in adjustment between surplus and deficit countries; and (4) to shift emphasis in concern about global imbalances from current account imbalances, which received much attention at the G20 meeting in Seoul in 2010, to official settlement imbalances. The first three of these objectives have been under discussion in one form or another for many decades; the fourth received considerable attention in the early 1970s, the last time reform of the international monetary system was seriously on the official agenda.

The proposal is appended to this brief introduction, and the rationale and operational details can be found there. An early version was submitted to the deputies of the G20 in 2011 and was subsequently published in *Central Banking* (May 2011). In brief, it suggests that each member country should propose a target for its international reserves 5 or 10 years hence. These proposed targets would be subject to international discussion and review, and countries with exceptionally high or low targets would have to defend their proposals. After revisions, the IMF would commit to create the global total in SDRs during the target period. Allocation of SDRs would continue to be based on IMF quotas or some revised basis, not linked to the national targets. Countries with targets above their SDR allocations could "earn" the difference by running a surplus in their international payments, current account plus net capital flows. Countries with targets below their allocations would be expected to run down their reserves through deficits in international payments. Because international payments are influenced by many factors—some of which are not under the influence of individual countries—certain latitude would be allowed (for example, by averaging over several years and engaging in discussions with the IMF). But, subject to these allowances, each country would be expected to meet its target, and those that failed to do so would be subject to adjustment pressure. This approach works today for countries in deficit that undertake IMF programs. The new element would be to hold countries in surplus accountable as well—these countries would also have to adopt adjustment programs under IMF surveillance. If they failed to comply, the ultimate sanction would be permissible: coordinated trade restrictions against the offending country's exports, introduced under the balance of payments provisions of the World Trade Organization.

I am not wildly enthusiastic about my proposal, although I believe it would represent a significant improvement over current arrangements. It was the best I could think of in response to numerous complaints about the international monetary system. I put it forward as a challenge to others: if you do not like existing arrangements or my proposal for improving them, make a better proposal. If we cannot find a superior formulation for the international monetary system, even as a basis for serious discussion, the existing arrangements must be optimal (which does not mean perfect). Grumbling about something is not a serious approach to policy. We should stop mere grumbling. Fat chance!

THE PROPOSAL

Reform of the international monetary system is back on the official agenda for the first time since 1974. A start was made at the Seoul summit in November 2010, when the G20 leaders requested the IMF to identify "indicative guidelines" for large imbalances in payments.

These discussions are taking place against a background perception that imperfections in the international monetary system played a critical role in precipitating the financial crisis of 2007–09. I am not aware of a definitive statement on the alleged link, but Governor Mervyn King of the Bank of England said in 2009 that global imbalances were the main cause of the financial crisis and suggested that the world economy would remain vulnerable until they are corrected.[1] He did not define "global imbalances," but in common usage the term refers to current account imbalances (goods, services, and investment income) in international payments. My view is that imbalances were implicated in the crisis, as savings were transferred from countries such as China, Germany, Japan, and oil-exporting countries (and from smaller countries such as the Netherlands, Singapore, Sweden, and Switzerland) to countries with investment booms such as Australia, Spain, the United Kingdom, and, above all, the United States (not to mention Greece and Ireland). These transfers helped keep world long-term interest rates relatively low. But they were hardly the main cause of the crisis, which was to be found in system failure in major financial markets, especially those of the United Kingdom and the United States. Many parties, each pursuing its own narrow interests, were involved in this failure: commercial and investment banks, rating agencies, accounting firms, and excessively tolerant financial regulators. The legal advisors of all of them have undeservingly escaped censure. No one was watching the financial system as a whole.

In accepted parlance, the international monetary system is a narrower concept than the world economy or even than the financial components of the world economy. It designates the rules, conventions, and practices governing the official monetary authorities of the world, along with the relevant institutions, such as the Bank for International Settlements and the IMF.

The international monetary system (or regime, as I prefer to call it, since in some respects it is not very systematic) has actually worked during the past few years; not, of course, in preventing the crisis but in preventing it from producing an even greater economic recession than we actually experienced. The European Central Bank and the Federal Reserve acted promptly to provide liquidity in euros and dollars, respectively. When, following the failure of Lehman Brothers in the fall of 2008, demand for US dollars rose sharply outside the United States, the Federal Reserve opened swap lines with several other central banks. These swap lines exceeded $700 billion, of which $554 billion was drawn by the end of 2008. The IMF eased its lending criteria and increased its lending commitments by SDR 73 billion (over $100 billion) during late 2008 and 2009, and created a new Flexible Credit Line. The World Bank—not strictly a monetary institution but one of the two Bretton Woods institutions—pledged to double its annual rate of lending and in fact increased its lending from $25 billion in its fiscal year 2008 to $47 billion in 2009, and further to $59 billion in 2010. The first G20 summit

---

[1] Speech given by Mervyn King, Governor of the Bank of England, to the CBI Dinner, Nottingham, at the East Midlands Conference Centre, January 20, 2009 (http://www.bankofengland.co.uk /archive/Documents/historicpubs/speeches/2009/speech372.pdf).

in November 2008 called for fiscal stimulus actions by participating governments and pledged to resist protectionist actions. On the whole, both goals were achieved. The G20 agreed in spring 2009 that a new issue of SDRs should be made, the first since 1979. That was duly accomplished by August 2009, in the amount of about $250 billion. Foreign exchange markets continued to function smoothly, unlike interbank lending and commercial paper markets. True, exchange rates did not remain stable. In particular, the US dollar appreciated sharply in the fall of 2008, despite the vast injection of Federal Reserve credit through many channels, some unorthodox. Total Federal Reserve credit increased from $0.9 trillion in July 2008 to $2.3 trillion by the end of 2008. But overall, exchange rate movements cushioned the decline in aggregate demand in the countries worst hit by the recession. The evolution of events could have been much worse than it turned out to be.

This relatively good performance of the international monetary regime does not mean we should not examine its performance critically and determine whether it can be materially improved before the next crisis. As noted, the last comprehensive official examination was 40 years ago (see Solomon 1982 and Williamson 1977 for good discussions of this examination). All important arrangements should be reexamined critically every decade or two, if only to remind each new generation of participants, official and private, why the arrangements are as they are.

International monetary regimes have typically been analyzed in terms of three characteristics: adjustment, liquidity, and credibility. The first characteristic concerns how countries adjust to imbalances of international payments. The second concerns how the regime provides international means of payment and, when appropriate, how such liquidity grows over time. The third characteristic concerns whether the first two are durable over time so that the relevant public has confidence in the regime. For instance, the Bretton Woods regime, formally adopted by many countries in the mid-1940s, lacked a clear mechanism for providing additional liquidity in a growing world economy beyond acquisitions of monetary gold from new production. The world economy in the 1950s and 1960s grew much more rapidly than had been expected in the mid-1940s (haunted perhaps by a fear of secular stagnation based on the Great Depression of the 1930s). In the event, the additional international liquidity was provided partly by sales of gold from the (inordinately high) US gold reserves and even more by the acquisition of US Treasury bills by many central banks. Professor Robert Triffin of Yale University pointed out the dilemma in this arrangement: if the additional dollar holdings were restricted, world growth would be restrained; but if they continued to increase, the gold convertibility of the dollar (for monetary authorities only) would become increasingly questionable as the ratio of US dollar liabilities increased relative to US monetary gold stocks (Triffin 1960).

The Triffin dilemma, as it came to be known, was resolved through the IMF's decision to create SDRs ("paper gold," as financial journalists appropriately dubbed them) and to allocate them to member states. The decision for the first allocation of SDRs was made in 1969 and executed in 1970–72. But it was too little, too late. With its low interest rates, dollars flowed abundantly out of the United States in the recession of 1970–71, and President Richard Nixon closed the gold window in August 1971. This resolved the Triffin dilemma definitively but left the world, in effect, on a dollar standard. One country after another did not want to accept the implications for domestic monetary policy and allowed currencies to float against the dollar, violating the Bretton Woods rule calling for fixed (but, if necessary, adjustable) exchange rates, which had been realigned by international agreement in the Smithsonian Agreement in December 1971. The fixed exchange rate rule was subsequently dropped.

Under the Bretton Woods system, the adjustment problem was to be dealt with through appropriate management of aggregate demand and through adjustments in exchange rates in the presence of "fundamental disequilibrium." In principle, adjustment was to be symmetric, applying to countries in surplus as well as those in deficit. But this feature never worked very well. Countries in significant surplus had posed problems of adjustment since the inauguration of the Bretton Woods system. The problem focused on the United States in the 1950s, on Germany and the Netherlands in the 1960s, on the Organization of the Petroleum Exporting Countries (OPEC) members during the late 1970s and early 1980s, on Japan in the 1980s, and on China for the 2000s. Compliance in principle was to be brought about through the "scarce currency" clause of the original IMF Articles of Agreement, whereby countries could, if necessary, discriminate against a country in surplus that did not adjust its policies to limit the surplus (including, if necessary, through the exchange rate policy). But the scarce currency clause operated only if the country's currency became scarce within the IMF, and it was never invoked.

What is the applicability of the three criteria today? What might we mean, in a world of many allowed exchange rate arrangements, by "adjustment"? The concept is clear enough for countries that run current account deficits in their international payments that they are unable to finance on an ongoing or sustainable basis. They need to change their policies to reduce their trade deficit or to attract additional net inflows of capital. But what about the others? Concern has been expressed about current account imbalances—surpluses as well as deficits. At the Seoul summit in 2010, it was proposed that current imbalances, surpluses as well as deficits, should be held below 4 percent of GDP, at least by the systemically important countries represented at the summit. This proposal did not find favor, which spared the summiteers from addressing whether it should also apply to the many countries in excess of that limit that were not represented at the summit and from having to explain why they should or should not be covered.

Surely such a rule cannot be right in general. In a world with a globalized capital market or one that is in an advanced stage of globalization, an important benefit of international engagement is intertemporal trade—borrowing or lending in some periods and repaying or liquidating investments later. Periods of net borrowing or lending can go on for a long time. Canada, for instance, ran current account deficits for most of its first 100 years (the exceptions being during the two world wars), as foreign capital flowed into a country well endowed with resources and with sound institutions. Should this have been denied? Singapore, a small country with a high saving rate, sensibly invests a substantial amount of its saving abroad, thus running a persistent current account surplus. Profound demographic trends in the world suggest that rapidly aging societies such as Germany and Japan should be net savers while the bulk of their population is still employed; that is, these countries should build up their claims on the rest of the world, to be drawn down after large portions of their populations reach retirement age. The potential retirees highly value the preservation of principal, so they do not want to invest in countries where their investments are at risk, either through economic failure or through political action against foreign investors, as has occurred in several developing countries. Again, their surpluses may endure for many years, although eventually they will turn into deficits, first through a decline in the trade balance, as is already occurring in Japan, and then by a decline in earnings on foreign investments as they are slowly liquidated. Oil-exporting countries are selling a depletable resource into world markets. They too might sensibly run current account surpluses for years as they, in effect, diversify their portfolios by converting oil in the ground into international investments, the proceeds from which will provide income to future generations as the oil is depleted.

The arithmetic of trade balances requires that if some countries run persistent surpluses, other countries must run persistent deficits. Apart from measurement errors, the global sum of current account balances must be zero. This self-evident point is routinely ignored in much public discussion of the need for corrective action in particular countries or groups of countries.

The most obvious measure of a country's balance of payments is movement in its official foreign exchange reserves, which it acquires through intervention, directly or indirectly, in the foreign exchange market. But in a growing world economy, demand for official reserves can be expected to rise. By how much? There is no widely accepted formula linking the growth in reserves to imports or indeed to any other measure of international transactions, although early work (e.g., Olivera 1971) suggested that desired reserves (in a world with low capital mobility) might be related to the square root of imports—growing with imports but more slowly. With high capital mobility, desired reserves could grow less rapidly if capital flows were reliably related to actions (for example, interest rates) by the country concerned or much more rapidly if capital movements were volatile and not easily predicted.

To focus minds on concrete action, here's a proposal: let each country set a target level for its foreign exchange reserves five years hence. Then subject these proposed national targets to international discussion and review. Each country would be expected to defend its proposed target before its peers, especially if the target was unusually high or low. Adjustments would be made to the targets as a result of these discussions, and SDRs would be created over the coming five years to match the total of the adjusted targets. In this fashion, supply of reserves, without resort to national currencies, would be matched to the desired demand for reserves.

Current account targets, in principle, could also be set through a process of international discussion and negotiation, as proposed by Williamson and Mahar

(1998) and Williamson (2004). But they must sum to zero for the world as a whole, and the chances of reaching such an agreement on a consistent set of targets is negligible. (An effort to assign current account targets to the Organisation for Economic Co-operation and Development countries after the first major oil price increase in 1974 predictably failed, although the discussion usefully sensitized the participating governments to their interdependence in the presence of unavoidably large OPEC surpluses.) By contrast, reserve targets would enjoy an extra degree of freedom, whereby total supply could be matched to total expressed demand.

SDRs would not be allocated to countries on the basis of their targets; only the totals would match. Currently SDRs are allocated to countries on the basis of their quotas at the IMF. (All countries except for Cuba, the Democratic People's Republic of Korea, and some microstates are members of the IMF; Taiwan Province of China and Hong Kong Special Administrative Region are also excluded.) Countries with targets greater than their allocations would earn the difference by running current account surpluses or by increasing their liabilities to foreigners. Countries with allocations greater than their targets would invest abroad (net) or run current account deficits. For example, if a country targeted a level of reserves five years hence that was double its allocation of SDRs during that period, it would be expected and allowed to earn the additional reserves by running a current account surplus or by receiving net inward investment, or some combination of the two. Meanwhile, some other countries would have reserve targets less than their cumulative SDR allocations during the same period.

SDRs as constituted today can be held only by national monetary authorities and a few international financial institutions. They are meant to satisfy a demand for official reserves. They are issued by and their use is facilitated by the IMF. Although wider private use might be contemplated eventually, currencies such as the dollar, the euro, and maybe someday the Chinese renminbi would be used in the interim for private international transactions, and would be bought and sold in foreign exchange markets. Thus, they would coexist with SDRs and indeed would continue to be the media of private transactions. But the allocation of SDRs would be tailored to satisfy incremental demand for official international reserves, so the demand for currencies for these purposes would no longer exist, although of course there would be a large outstanding legacy of holdings of such currencies.

Reserves rise and fall for many reasons. A country that suddenly found itself with an improvement in its terms of trade (such as a large change in oil prices for oil exporters) or a large unexpected inflow of capital would experience a rise in reserves if it did not want its exchange rate to appreciate fully. This would not be prohibited. That is one reason for focusing on the medium term. But if the price rise persisted for several years or the capital inflows continued, the country would be expected to adjust to them by raising imports or stimulating capital outflows, or both. It would not be allowed to build reserves indefinitely beyond its targets. That is what balance of payments adjustment is all about.

A special problem could arise with economies that practice freely floating exchange rates, such as currently the euro area, the United Kingdom, and the

United States—three large markets with large IMF quotas. One might suppose that these regions would declare reserve targets involving no growth or only minimal growth to allow for unusual contingencies. In this case, their SDR allocations would be substantially above their targets. They could decline to receive their allocations; donate them to a worthy cause, such as the World Bank; or agree to sell them to any eligible country in exchange for presentations of their own currency (that is, euros, pounds, or dollars). The third option would require IMF certification that the transaction complied with the purposes of the arrangement. The proceeds could then be used to pay down their public debt (enlarged virtually everywhere by the financial/economic crisis of 2008–09).

The euro area poses a special problem, insofar as only states can be members of the IMF, yet its foreign exchange interventions would be carried out by the European Central Bank on behalf of its 19 members. The reserve target for the euro area should be a collective one, but arrangements for the use of the SDRs allocated to member states could be left to those states, provided they were consistent with the purposes of the scheme.

Rules or guidelines work only if all parties adhere to them. What methods of discipline could be used to ensure compliance over time? It is understood that reserves might be used from time to time to help smooth out shocks and take pressure off exchange rates; indeed, that is the purpose of them. "Compliance" must therefore be interpreted in a medium-term framework, say five years. Ideally, the process of multilateral surveillance in the IMF and mutual assessment by the G20 would induce compliance. However, if such pressures were not sufficient, subsequent allocations of SDRs could be denied to any offending country. Or the long-dormant Article XV of the General Agreement on Tariffs and Trade, carried into the World Trade Organization (WTO), which links trade policies to balance of payments considerations, could be activated. Violation of the adjustment to reserve targets could lead the IMF to request the WTO to activate Article XV against an offending country, which would permit importing countries to apply restrictions on products from that country higher than those levied on goods from other countries.

Some might worry that allocation of SDRs on a scale sufficient to satisfy the stated demand for reserves would be inflationary. But, by construction, the increase in SDRs would reside in reserves of the member countries, willingly held by them. Such an allocation would permit some countries that maintain exchange rates designed to ensure current account surpluses to invest their national savings at home rather than put them into foreign exchange reserves. This would permit higher domestic demand in those countries, along with increased imports from the rest of the world, and would raise aggregate demand in the world. In some periods—as now—that might be welcome. But if it generated inflationary pressures, those would be countered by more restrictive policy by the monetary authorities that openly or implicitly target inflation, a group that currently includes the euro area, the United Kingdom, and the United States. As long as inflation is targeted in important markets, SDR allocations will not be inflationary at the global level.

One possible objection to this modest proposal is that its focus on "reserves" covers only the foreign assets held by the monetary authorities of each country. Many governments have created sovereign wealth funds (SWFs) to invest abroad in a wider portfolio than those typically held by monetary authorities. SWFs raise their own concerns and have led the IMF to issue guidelines for appropriate behavior in managing them (see Truman 2010). Germany and Japan (not to mention Sweden, Switzerland, and several other countries) run large current account surpluses matched by private capital outflows that seek yield and diversification of risk by adding foreign investments to domestic investment. This is to be expected as the world's capital markets become more integrated. A country can reduce its reserves by allowing or even encouraging private capital outflow; it can also reduce its reserves by switching official funds to an SWF for the purpose of making longer-term, more risky investments abroad. There should be no objection to this process as long as the SWFs follow the guidelines (or, as Truman has suggested, stiffened guidelines) and as long as the flow is one way. That is, countries should not switch funds back and forth between reserves and SWFs, except in extreme situations. This dimension could be covered in the provisions for monitoring compliance.

To sum up: the proposal is to issue SDRs at five-year intervals (the allotments to be made annually) equal to internationally agreed-upon national target levels of reserves, and to enforce adjustment to those targets. This would accomplish three objectives with respect to the international monetary system. First, it would introduce a meaningful and operational indicator for balance of payments adjustment in a world with a globalized capital market that permits intertemporal trade—something that we do not have now. Second, it would introduce symmetry into the adjustment process, requiring countries with balance of payments surpluses to adjust along with those in deficit. Third, it would provide incremental liquidity to the world economy in the form of an internationally agreed-upon unit, thus reducing dependence on national currencies to play this role.

REFERENCES

Olivera, J. H. G. 1971. "The Square-Root Law of Precautionary Reserves." *Journal of Political Economy* 79 (5): 1095–104.

Solomon, Robert. 1982. *The International Monetary System, 1945–1981*. New York: Harper & Row.

Triffin, Robert. 1960. *Gold and the Dollar Shortage*. New Haven, CT: Yale University Press.

Truman, Edwin M. 2010. *Sovereign Wealth Funds: Threat or Salvation?* Washington, DC: Peterson Institute for International Economics.

Williamson, John. 1977. *The Failure of World Monetary Reform, 1971–1974*. New York: New York University Press.

———. 2004. "Current Account Objectives: Who Should Adjust?" In *Dollar Adjustment: How Far? Against What?*, edited by C. Fred Bergsten and John Williamson. Washington, DC: Institute for International Economics.

Williamson, John, and Molly Mahar. 1998. "Appendix A: Current Account Targets." In *Real Exchange Rates for the Year 2000*, edited by Simon Wren-Lewis and Rebecca Driver. Washington, DC: Institute for International Economics.

CHAPTER 10

Global Bond Market Spillovers from Monetary Policy and Reserve Management

ROBERT N. MCCAULEY

The idea that policy in one country affects other countries through exchange rates is a staple of international finance. Exchange rate policy in one country affects other countries because there is only one exchange rate in a two-country world, two in a three-country world, and so on. With floating exchange rates, domestic monetary policy affects other countries through the exchange rate, among other channels. In particular, monetary easing, in the conventional sense of a reduction of the short-term policy rate, induces exchange rate depreciation. This, of course, implies exchange rate appreciation and disinflation for the rest of the world.

Unconventional monetary policy in the form of large-scale bond purchases intended to reduce bond yields extends but does not alter the transmission of policy easing through the exchange rate. There is no reason to believe that a given decline in, say, two-year yields resulting from central bank purchases of bonds would have a different effect on the exchange rate than the same decline resulting from a lower short-term policy rate.[1] In this sense, those who expressed the view that unconventional monetary policy amounted to a "currency war" could have leveled the same charge, whatever its merit, at conventional monetary policy.

Large-scale bond purchases do, however, heighten strategic interactions in the global bond market. In particular, a policy to lower dollar bond yields makes investors more receptive to dollar debt issued by firms from around the world. The induced dollar borrowing allows firms outside the United States to sidestep

The author thanks participants in the symposium for discussion, especially Claudio Borio, Rex Ghosh, Peter Hördahl, Pat McGuire, Catherine Schenk, Hyun Song Shin, Vladyslav Sushko, Philip Turner, Goetz von Peter, and William White. The research assistance of Bilyana Bogdanova, José-Maria Vidal-Pastor, and Jhuvesh Sobrun is gratefully acknowledged. Views expressed are those of the author and not necessarily those of the Bank for International Settlements.

[1]Nevertheless, market participants may attach importance to the size, or the relative size, of central bank balance sheets. See the discussion in He and McCauley 2013.

domestic monetary policy. In addition, lower bond yields in a key currency such as the dollar tend to lower domestic currency bond yields around the world. Again, the influence of domestic monetary policy in the form of setting short-term interest rates is reduced.

Moreover, strategic interactions in global bond markets arise unintentionally as central banks act in their capacity as reserve managers. These operations may be considered incidental to the policy of managing the exchange rate but can nevertheless influence bond yields in the reserve currencies, even without any intention to do so. Thus, recent unconventional monetary policies to purchase bonds in large amounts in order to affect yields interact with long-standing and sizable reserve management operations in bond markets.

This chapter compares the narrow and unrealistic conditions under which conventional monetary policy entails no bond market interactions with actual conditions, in which large-scale bond purchases ease global financing conditions for bond issuance in the same currency and depress yields in bond markets in other currencies. It also analyzes episodes of central bank interactions in the global bond market, suggesting that they can either reinforce or offset each other. The chapter suggests that central banks should consider the implications of their operations in the global bond market.

MONETARY POLICY WITHOUT GLOBAL BOND MARKET EFFECTS

Obstfeld and Rogoff (2002) reach the conclusion that there is no useful role for monetary policy coordination in a model that does not have a bond market. If one seeks to understand central bank interactions in the global bond market, a richer framework is required.

One can imagine a world with bond markets but without bond market spillovers. Each bond market would price bonds strictly on the basis of the expectations hypothesis, so that 10-year bond yields would be nothing more than the expected short-term rates over the 10 years (possibly plus an exogenous term premium). In this world, if central banks set the short-term interest rate in response to, say, a Taylor rule, bond yields would be correlated only to the extent that inflation and employment deviations from targets were themselves correlated across economies. In other words, bond yields would co-move only to the extent that central banks responded to common disturbances to inflation or growth.

In this world, a central bank that bought bonds would have no effect on bond yields other than the signal value of the purchases for future short-term policy rate setting. There is thus scope for forward guidance (Filardo and Hofmann 2014), and asset purchases would at most add credibility to such guidance.

In this world, if central banks in some countries sought to restrain currency fluctuations by setting interest rates more in line with those set for key currencies, one would observe greater linkage of bond yields, even assuming that bond yields are set by expected short-term rates. Hofmann and Bogdanova (2012), Taylor (2013), and Hofmann and Takáts (2015) argue that one can in fact observe such

Figure 10.1. Policy and Taylor Rates[1]
(Percent)

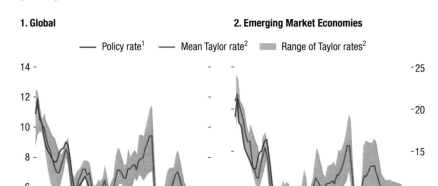

1. Global   2. Emerging Market Economies

—— Policy rate[1]   —— Mean Taylor rate[2]   ▨ Range of Taylor rates[2]

Sources: IMF, International Financial Statistics and World Economic Outlook databases; Bloomberg; CEIC database; Consensus Economics; Datastream; national data; BIS calculations.
[1]Weighted average based on 2005 GDP and purchasing power parity (PPP) exchange rates. "Global" comprises all economies listed here. Advanced economies: Australia, Canada, Denmark, the euro area, Japan, New Zealand, Norway, Sweden, Switzerland, the United Kingdom, and the United States. Emerging market economies: Argentina, Brazil, Chile, China, Chinese Taipei, Colombia, the Czech Republic, Hong Kong SAR, Hungary, India, Indonesia, Israel, Korea, Malaysia, Mexico, Peru, the Philippines, Poland, Singapore, South Africa, and Thailand.
[2]The Taylor rates are calculated as $i = r^{*} + \pi^{*} + 1.5(\pi - \pi^{*}) + 0.5y$, where π is a measure of inflation, y is a measure of the output gap, π^{*} is the inflation target, and r^{*} is the long-run real interest rate, here proxied by real trend output growth. The graph shows the mean and the range of the Taylor rates of different inflation/output gap combinations, obtained by combining four measures of inflation (headline, core, GDP deflator, and consensus headline forecasts) with four measures of the output gap (obtained using Hodrick-Prescott [HP] filter, segmented linear trend and unobserved components techniques, and IMF estimates). Π^{*} is set equal to the official inflation target/objective, and otherwise to the sample average or trend inflation estimated through a standard HP filter. See Hofmann and Bogdanova 2012.

follow-the-leader behavior. In Figure 10.1, panels 1 and 2 show that central banks systematically set policy rates below Taylor rule norms in the mid-2000s and since 2008, after having earlier tracked such norms.

Resistance to exchange rate appreciation has also largely driven the reserve accumulation shown in Figure 10.2. Peak reserves may have been reached in 2014, and the implications of emerging market central banks selling reserve currency bonds—dubbed "quantitative tightening" by Winkler, Sachdeva, and Saravelos (2015)—are discussed later.

Figure 10.2. Global Foreign Exchange Reserves

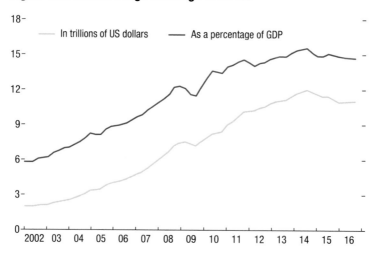

Sources: Datastream; IMF, International Financial Statistics and World Economic Outlook databases.

Thus, in this world, if policymakers set rates to avoid exchange rate appreciation, they choose to import the monetary policy of a key currency country (Bernanke 2012). By contrast, a fully independent monetary policy would tend to insulate the domestic bond market from external pressures, *if* bond yields simply reflected future short-term policy rates.

In the real world, a sizable and varying portion of bond yields cannot be explained by expected future short-term rates. This component, known as the "term premium," is discussed in the following section, along with evidence that it is subject to a strong global influence (Rey 2013). This means that central bank operations in bond markets can have effects that spill over through the global bond market. Neither the model of Obstfeld and Rogoff (2002) nor a model in which bond yields respond only to expected policy rates is adequate.

If central banks can influence these term premiums by large-scale bond purchases, there is much scope for bond market interactions. The following discussion covers spillover through the bond market in which the purchases take place, and spillover through bond markets in other currencies that are integrated with the target market.

LARGE-SCALE BOND PURCHASES AND DOLLAR BONDS OF NON-US BORROWERS

The Federal Reserve's large-scale asset (bond) purchase programs are intended to compress the term premium in the US Treasury bond market (Bernanke 2013). A policy that is often described as "quantitative easing" attempts to reduce the expected return from a fixed-rate bond relative to that of a short-term bill rolled over for the life of the bond. This interpretation of large bond purchases as compressing the term premium has received support from Gagnon and others (2011), Krishnamurthy and Vissing-Jorgensen (2011), and D'Amico and King (2013).

While intended to make it easier and cheaper for US firms and households to issue corporate bonds and fixed-rate mortgages, the Federal Reserve's large-scale bond purchases also eased and cheapened dollar bond issues by firms and governments outside the United States. And it was the stock of dollar bonds issued by nonfinancial borrowers outside the United States that proved most responsive to the Federal Reserve's compression of the term premium.

Despite the Federal Reserve's purchases, some stocks of dollar bonds have in fact not risen over the past eight years (Figure 10.3, panel 1).[2] The largest stock (other than US Treasury bonds) is that of agency bonds, mostly mortgage-backed securities supported by Fannie Mae and Freddie Mac. With the slow recovery of the housing market, agency bonds only in 2016 exceeded their 2008 outstanding value. The second largest stock in 2008 comprised private-label asset-backed securities. Dominated by mortgage-backed securities, this stock continues to run down, notwithstanding the revival of auto-loan-backed securities.

By contrast, two stocks of bonds have responded to the opportunity presented by the Federal Reserve. US nonfinancial firms have raised $2.3 trillion. To what extent these firms used the proceeds of bond issues to expand their operations or to make payouts to shareholders remains unclear (Van Rixtel and Villegas 2015). The fourth largest stock in 2008 was that of nonbank borrowers resident outside the United States; these borrowers ramped up their outstanding value from $2.3 trillion to $4.7 trillion.

Thus, if the Federal Reserve's buying of Treasury and agency bonds is seen as working through prices (compressing the term premium) to encourage investors to bid for riskier bonds, it succeeded most with bonds issued by nonbank borrowers outside the United States. Investors lined up not only for dollar bonds issued by US firms but also for those sold by non-US firms and governments.

This conclusion is backed by evidence that the compression of the term premium opened portfolios to dollar bond issues by borrowers resident outside the United States (Lo Duca, Nicoletti, and Martinez 2014; McCauley, McGuire, and Sushko 2015b). Figure 10.3, panel 2 shows that the coefficient obtained from a rolling 16-quarter regression of the growth rate of offshore dollar bonds on the (lagged) term premium change turned significantly negative after the Federal Reserve announced its large-scale bond purchases. This indicates that a lower term premium in the previous quarter was associated with faster growth in the

---

[2]Not shown in Figure 10.3, panel 1, are dollar bonds of US holding companies, US-chartered banks, US finance companies, US state and municipal governments, and non-US bank and nonbank financial borrowers.

Figure 10.3. Federal Reserve Spurs Dollar Bond Issuance by Non-US Borrowers

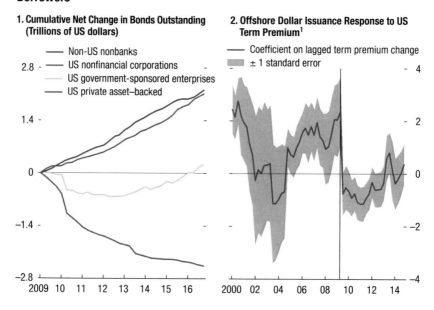

1. Cumulative Net Change in Bonds Outstanding (Trillions of US dollars)

- Non-US nonbanks
- US nonfinancial corporations
- US government-sponsored enterprises
- US private asset–backed

2. Offshore Dollar Issuance Response to US Term Premium[1]

- Coefficient on lagged term premium change
- ± 1 standard error

Sources: Bank for International Settlements (BIS), International Debt Securities Statistics; Bloomberg L.P., Board of Governors of the Federal Reserve, US Flow of Funds; McCauley, McGuire, and Sushko 2015b; and BIS staff calculations.
[1]In panel 2, response of the quarterly growth in the stock of US dollar bonds issued outside the United States to the (lagged) change in the real term premium, estimated from 16-quarter rolling regressions that also include the lagged Chicago Board Option Exchange Volatility Index to control for overall financial market conditions; see McCauley, McGuire, and Sushko 2015b. The vertical line indicates the end of quarter one, 2009. The 10-year real term premium is estimated using a joint macroeconomic and term structure model; see Hördahl and Tristani (2014).

stock of dollar bonds issued by non-US-resident nonfinancial borrowers in the present quarter. Thus, in the wake of the Federal Reserve's bond buying, we see not only strong dollar bond issuance by non-US borrowers but also a positive response of that issuance to (lagged) changes in the term premium.

In sum, the unconventional US monetary policy in the form of large-scale bond purchases may not have been intended to change the behavior of borrowers outside the United States; nevertheless, it induced them to build up their dollar liabilities.

SPILLOVERS FROM US BOND YIELDS TO GLOBAL BOND YIELDS

If the Federal Reserve's bond buying made global investors receptive to dollar bond issuance by non-US residents, it also affected pricing of bonds denominated in other currencies. In a globally integrated bond market, what starts in the dollar does not stay in the dollar (Rey 2013). Instead, lower yields for US Treasury bonds lead to lower yields on other governments' bonds, as long as global investors balance their bond portfolios across markets that are open to investment (IMF 2014). At the limit, if bonds in different currencies served as very close substitutes in private portfolios, it would not matter which bonds officials purchased.

Much analysis suggests that the Federal Reserve's large-scale purchases of US bonds, or announcements thereof, led to substantial changes in yields on other sovereign bonds (Table 10.1). Neely (2015), for example, finds that 20 percent to 70 percent of the announcement effects of Federal Reserve bond buying diffused to mature bond markets. Bauer and Neely (2014) find that the effect worked through shared term premium (that is, through channels other than correlated expectations of future short-term rates) in the larger German and Japanese markets. Rogers, Scotti, and Wright (2014) confirm Neely's findings using high frequency futures data. Following Bernanke, Reinhart, and Sack (2004), who analyze the Japanese exchange rate intervention of 2003–04, Gerlach-Kristen, McCauley, and Ueda (2016) find that investment of dollars purchased against the yen in US Treasury bonds lowers their yields but also that one-third to two-thirds of the effect passes through to other mature bond markets. This analysis includes not only sovereign bonds but also generic private rates (as represented by interest rate swaps). Obstfeld (2015) reports long-term level (cointegration) regressions that suggest that major government bond markets move in synch with the US Treasury market, with a median half-life of adjustment of about one year.

Several studies suggest that bond markets in emerging markets now respond more to changes in global bond markets than they did a decade ago, when local Asian bond markets (except for those of Hong Kong SAR and Singapore) showed low correlations with US Treasury bonds (McCauley and Jiang 2004). More recent work by Turner (2014), Miyajima, Mohanty, and Yetman (2014), and Chen and others (2015) shows a tighter linkage, including between India and the United States, although still excluding China (see Sobrun and Turner 2015).

The integration measured by Obstfeld (2015) can easily be read as the influence of the largest, deepest, and most liquid government market on other bond markets. This reading does not just draw on size but is also informed by persuasive episodes.

The global bond market strains of 1994 stand out (Borio and McCauley 1996). The Federal Reserve started a tightening cycle in February 1994, even as the Bundesbank, then the European anchor policymaker, extended a long easing (Figure 10.4, panel 1). In the bond market, US Treasury yields rose and, contrary to the direction of actual and expected policy rates in Europe, German bund yields and French treasury bond yields rose more or less in step. Adrian and Fleming (2013)—using Adrian, Crump, and Moensch (2013)—find that almost all the rise in US rates reflected expected future policy rates. By contrast, the German and French government bond markets' rise in yields could not be put down to expected policy rates but rather reflected a widening term premium.

Table 10.1. Estimates of Spillovers of US Bond Yields to Mature Bond Markets
(Basis points per 100 basis points on the US Treasury bond)

Bond Market	Gerlach-Kristen, McCauley, and Ueda 2015: Japanese Intervention, 2003–04		Neely 2015: LSAP1 Events	Bauer and Neely 2014: LSAP1 Events	Rogers, Scotti, and Wright 2014: Intra-Day Data	Obstfeld 2015: Monthly Levels, 1989–2013
	Government	Swap				
Australia	50	60	67	37		74
Canada	63	68	53	54		129
Switzerland	61	53				88
Germany	53	44	41	44	36	115
Spain	53	44				111
France	52	44				118
Italy	52	44			16	158
Japan	35	51	19	12	20	69
United Kingdom	65	49	46		48	137

Sources: Cited works; and author's calculations.
Note: LSAP1 = first Federal Reserve large-scale asset (bond) purchase.

In short, US and European monetary policy diverged, but US and European bond yields tracked each other higher, with the term premium widening in Europe. Central banks were not playing follow-the-leader, but bond market investors were.

Some of those engaged in constructing the euro anticipated (or at least hoped) that the larger euro-denominated bond market would have more ballast and thus would sail more steadily and prove less subject to being tossed about by waves moving east across the North Atlantic. Through 2013 (see Figure 10.4, panel 2), these hopes proved largely unfulfilled as euro bond yields tended to follow dollar bond yields closely.

Note that the 1994 episode (shown in Figure 10.4) did not feature unconventional monetary policy in the sense of large-scale interventions in the bond market. But the lesson learned from that episode was the asymmetric influence of conventional US monetary policy working only through bond markets dominated by private investors.

Central banks have since operated in the bond market, both incidentally and purposefully. First, reserve managers invested the proceeds of large-scale foreign exchange accumulation in key currency bonds, and second, unconventional monetary policy took the form of large-scale bond buying.

RECENT EPISODES OF CENTRAL BANK INTERACTIONS IN THE GLOBAL BOND MARKET

Once central banks begin to operate in size in the bond market, they add new channels of interaction to those that operate at one remove through short-term policy rate setting and its effect on bond markets dominated by private investors. The interaction can be reinforcing, even cooperative (at least implicitly), with

Figure 10.4. Policy Rates and Bond Yields
(Percent)

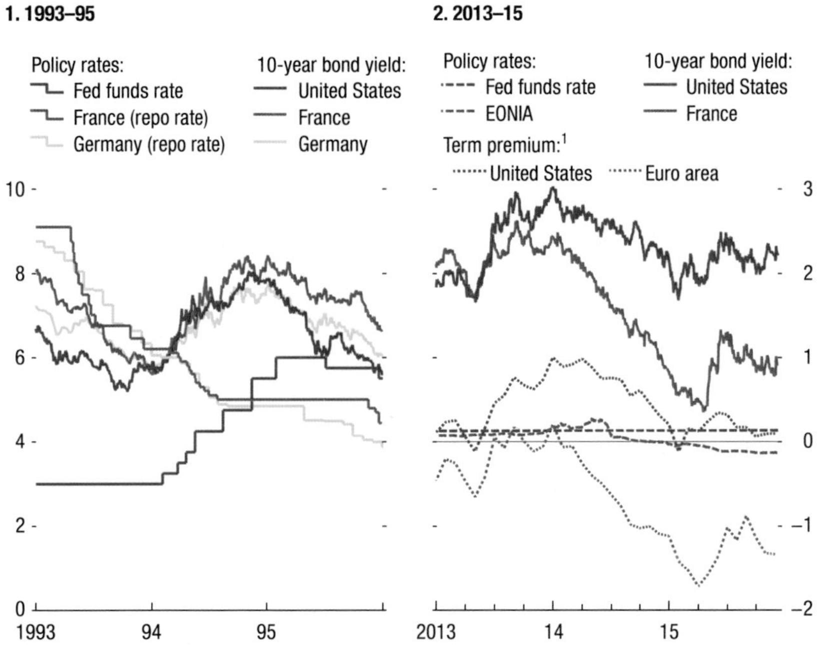

1. 1993–95

Policy rates:
⌐L Fed funds rate
⌐L France (repo rate)
⌐L Germany (repo rate)

10-year bond yield:
— United States
— France
— Germany

2. 2013–15

Policy rates:
---- Fed funds rate
---- EONIA

10-year bond yield:
— United States
— France

Term premium:[1]
······ United States ······ Euro area

Sources: Bloomberg L.P.; national statistics; and Bank for International Settlements staff calculations.
[1]Decomposition of the 10-year nominal yield according to an estimated joint macroeconomic and term structure model; see Hördahl and Tristani 2014. Yields are expressed in zero coupon terms; for the euro area, French government bond data are used.

central banks on the same side of the bond market. Or the interaction can involve action at cross-purposes, with central banks on opposite sides of the bond market. Policy friction can arise even when central banks are on the same buy side of the market, as the case of Brazil and the United States in 2010–11, discussed later in this chapter, suggests.

Table 10.2 reduces the number of players to two but allows the dramatis personae to vary.[3] Interactions are novel when both parties operate in the bond market, but the cases discussed include interactions between a central bank operating only on short-term policy rates and a central bank operating in the bond market.

---

[3]Debt managers are also important official players in bond markets, capable of responding to market developments (McCauley and Ueda 2009; Blommestein and Turner 2012; Greenwood and others 2014).

Table 10.2. Recent and Possible Central Bank Interactions in the Global Bond Market

| Other | Federal Reserve | |
	Ease	Hold
Tighten	Brazil[1]–United States, 2010–11	EMs sell US Treasuries, 2015
Hold		(Twin-taper China–United States, 2014)
Ease	Large-scale bond purchases (QE) and foreign exchange reserve managers' bond purchases, 2009–13	European Central Bank–United States, 2014

Source: Author.
[1] Central bank only raising policy rate. EM = emerging market; QE = quantitative easing.

Policy and Reserve Management Friction: The Conundrum, 2004–05

The so-called conundrum of US bond yields not responding to US policy rates provides a mixed case: bond market operations of reserve managers interacting with the Federal Reserve's conventional setting of short-term policy rates. Interpretations of this episode vary, and what follows emphasizes the international aspect.

Backus and Wright (2007), for instance, while emphasizing domestic factors, neatly summarize the conundrum in Figure 10.5. The Federal Reserve's experience of bond yield rates rising rapidly in 1994 led it to make strong efforts to communicate its intentions clearly in the early 2000s. The outcome, however, was a very calm market in which 10-year yields (blue line) and thus key fixed-rate mortgage rates barely moved. Indeed, calculated 10-year forward rates (yellow line) actually fell. Kim and Wright (2005) found that the term premium declined between mid-2004 and mid-2005. The sense was that the Federal Reserve's policy was not gaining traction in the bond market.

One reading of the evidence highlighted the strong buying of US Treasury and agency bonds by the foreign official sector (Bernanke 2005; Warnock and Warnock 2009). Even as the Federal Reserve raised its federal funds target from 1 percent in 2004 to 4.25 percent in 2006 and 5.25 percent in 2007, foreign central banks raised their holdings of US bonds from $1.2 trillion to $2.3 trillion between June 2004 and June 2007 (McCauley and Rigaudy 2011). Because most mortgages in the United States have fixed rates, the lack of response of bond yields to policy rates was problematic. Only in hindsight is it easy to suggest that the Federal Reserve could have responded by selling bonds out of its portfolio of $700 billion in Treasury securities (Turner 2013).

Reinforcing Bond Market Operations: Quantitative Easing and Emerging Market Reserve Investment, 2009–13

Bond market operations can be reinforcing, as during 2009–13. In Figure 10.6, panel 1, the widening of the blue area in 2009 marks the beginning of large-scale bond purchases by the major advanced economy central banks. Foreign exchange

Figure 10.5. US Bond Conundrum, 2004–05
(Percent)

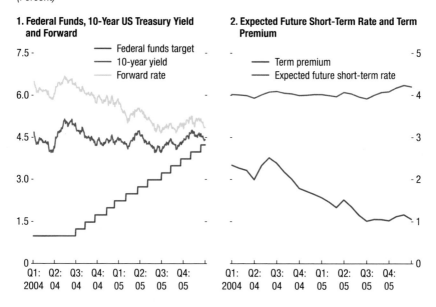

Source: Backus and Wright 2007, figures 2 and 9.

reserves invested in major government bond markets—mostly by emerging market economies (red area)—had already grown substantially in the 2000s and, after a drawdown in 2008, resumed growing in 2009. The share of reserves invested in government bonds is estimated from reported holdings for dollar and sterling and assumed to be 80 percent for euro and yen (see McCauley and Rigaudy 2011 on the investment of US dollar reserves). Whatever the accuracy of the estimation, major central banks surely joined emerging market central banks in buying bonds in quantity in 2009–13.

Thus, despite talk of currency wars (see next subsection below), central banks stood together on the bid side of the bond market. Official holdings reached 40 percent of the bonds of the US, euro area, Japanese, and U.K. governments. Of course, the intention of foreign exchange reserve managers differed from that of central banks engaged in quantitative easing; and reserve managers' bond purchases had none of the regular rhythm of the policy-driven bond purchases. That said, knowingly or not, emerging market reserve managers' purchases of bonds in reserve currencies could only have reinforced the effect of quantitative easing in lowering bond yields in the key currencies, especially the dollar.

The fact that the combination of quantitative easing and reserve management has led to a bond market dominated by official holders is most evident and most readily measured in the US bond market. At the end of the third quarter of 2015, official

Figure 10.6. Officials Hold a Big Share of SDR Currency Government Bonds[1]
(Trillions of US dollars)

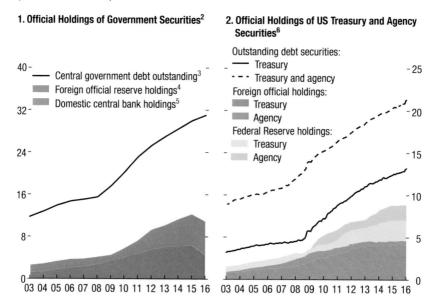

1. Official Holdings of Government Securities[2]

— Central government debt outstanding[3]
▨ Foreign official reserve holdings[4]
▨ Domestic central bank holdings[5]

2. Official Holdings of US Treasury and Agency Securities[6]

Outstanding debt securities:
— Treasury
--- Treasury and agency
Foreign official holdings:
▨ Treasury
▨ Agency
Federal Reserve holdings:
▨ Treasury
▨ Agency

Sources: Bank of Japan flow of funds accounts; Board of Governors of the Federal Reserve, flow of funds accounts; European Central Bank; IMF, Currency Composition of Official Foreign Exchange Reserves; Japan Ministry of Finance; national data; Thomson Reuters Datastream; U.K. Debt Management Office; U.K. Office for National Statistics; US Department of the Treasury; and Bank for International Settlements staff calculations.
[1]Different valuation methods based on source availability.
[2]Covers the euro area, Japan, the United Kingdom, and the United States; for the euro area, Japan, and the United Kingdom, converted into US dollars using Q2 2015 constant exchange rates.
[3]For the United States, total marketable Treasury securities, excluding agency debt.
[4]For euro- and yen-denominated reserves, 80 percent is assumed to be government debt securities; for dollar-denominated reserves, as reported by the US Treasury International Capital System; for sterling-denominated reserves, holdings by foreign central banks.
[5]For the euro area, national central bank holdings of general government debt and European Central Bank holdings under the Public Sector Purchase Programme and the Securities Market Programme.
[6]Agency debt includes mortgage pools backed by agencies and government-sponsored enterprises (GSEs) as well as issues by GSEs; total outstanding Treasury securities are total marketable Treasury securities.

holders—both foreign official institutions (Figure 10.6, panel 2, red area) and the Federal Reserve (gold area)—held more than half of all outstanding US Treasury bonds. If the US public debt stock is defined more broadly to include agency bonds, the official holding of this $20 trillion stock is still above 40 percent, which reflects a very heavy official footprint in the world's biggest sovereign bond market.

During this period of reinforcing bond market operations, however, some policies were at cross-purposes. A case in point is Brazil, where the corporate sector was increasing its dollar debt even as the central bank raised the policy rate (see discussion in next section).

Policy at Cross-Purposes: Brazil–United States, 2010–11

In 2010–11, authorities in Brazil, which had a booming economy, sought to restrain inflation by raising the short-term policy rate. In particular, the Central Bank of Brazil raised its SELIC policy rate (the short-term interest rate) from 8.75 percent in April 2010 to 12.5 percent in July 2012. This was a notable tightening in a world in which many central banks were avoiding widening the gap between their policy rates and the Federal Reserve's interest on excess reserves of 25 basis points (Figure 10.1). McCauley, McGuire, and Sushko (2015b) present econometric evidence that shows that dollar credit grew faster in this period where such interest rate gaps were wider. For its part, the Federal Reserve started its $600 billion large-scale asset (bond) purchase (LSAP2) program in November 2010 and Operation Twist (which bought long-term Treasury bonds with the proceeds of sales of short-term Treasury securities) in September 2011.

Brazilian firms tried to sidestep the tightening of monetary policy at home by increasing their dollar bond issuance (Figure 10.7; also see McCauley, McGuire, and Sushko 2015a). The stock of bonds sold through offshore financing subsidiaries (shown by the yellow area in Figure 10.7) grew faster than the stock of bonds sold by firms resident in Brazil (shown in blue; see also Avdjiev, Chui, and Shin 2014). The Brazilian authorities responded with taxes on offshore borrowing of short maturity and succeeded in increasing the maturity of dollar credit (Pereira da Silva 2013; Barroso, Pereira da Silva, and Soares 2013). Still, dollar credit, especially through the bond market, rose very quickly in the face of the tightening of Brazilian monetary policy.

Conundrum II? Euro Area–United States in 2014

Many observers, for instance El-Erian (2015),[4] read the evidence presented in Figure 10.4, panel 2 as pointing to the influence of the euro area bond market on the US bond market in 2014. While the nominal yield gap between German and US bonds has not been so wide in recent memory, the negative term premiums in the euro area bond market in 2014 seemed to have led their US dollar counterparts down. Mojon and Pegoraro (2014) present three-year term premiums for German bunds and US Treasuries and reach the same conclusion. Formal econometric work on this relationship is under way, but it is a plausible conjecture that 2014 saw "reverse causation" in trans-Atlantic bond markets; that is, the euro area bond market led and the US bond market followed. This conjecture raises the broader question of policy frictions in the global bond market.

Quantitative Tightening? Emerging Market Bond Sales in 2015

In 2015 policymakers lined up on opposite sides of the global bond market, with the euro area and Japan as bond buyers against emerging markets as bond sellers. The former were purchasing their own domestic bonds, whereas the latter

---

[4]*Financial Times*, March 9, 2015, "Outcome of Policy Tug-of-War Proving Hard to Predict."

Figure 10.7. Outstanding Dollar Credit to Brazilian Nonfinancial Borrowers
(Billions of US dollars)

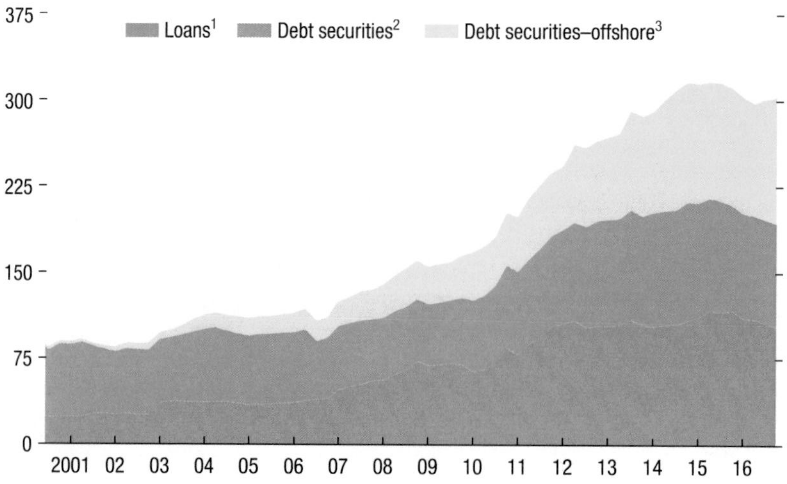

Source: McCauley, McGuire, and Sushko 2015a.
[1]US dollar loans to nonbank residents of Brazil.
[2]Outstanding US dollar international bonds issued by nonbank residents of Brazil.
[3]Outstanding US dollar international bonds issued by offshore affiliates of nonbanks with a parent entity headquartered in Brazil.

sold a diversified portfolio of key currency bonds, mostly dollar bonds but also euro and yen bonds.[5] Again, private investors' treatment of these bonds as close substitutes allows us to consider this scenario as one with officials on both the buy and sell sides of the global bond market.

Finer data than those in Figures 10.2 and 10.6, panel 1, suggest a drawdown of reserves in emerging markets. Moreover, this ongoing reserve drawdown looks broadly based. In 2008, the renminbi was temporarily stable against the dollar; recently, the renminbi, in tandem with other emerging market currencies, has been under downward pressure against the dollar. And while estimates vary, China's foreign exchange reserves are generally thought to have fallen in 2015.

Again, any bond sales by emerging market central banks would occur as a by-product of currency management. In particular, as the dollar appreciates, emerging market currencies tend to fall against it; indeed, they need to depreciate against the dollar just to keep the nominal effective exchange rate constant. But such

---

[5]Sales of euro area or Japanese government bonds by foreign official holders might make it easier for the respective central banks to hit their buying targets, but such sales would tend to reduce the impact of bond buying on yields. Note also that, to the extent that such euro and yen bond sales are matched by sales of dollar bonds, foreign official holders become one of the channels for spillovers.

Figure 10.8. Foreign Official US Treasury Holdings and 10-Year Interest Rate Swap Spreads[1]
(Billions of US dollars)

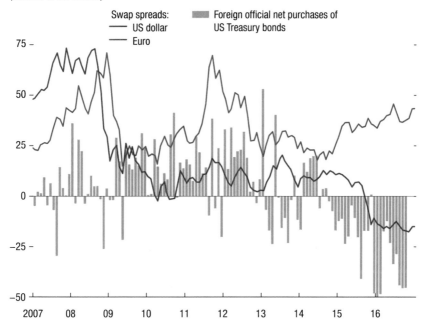

Sources: Bloomberg, Datastream, US Treasury International Capital transactions data; BIS calculations.
[1]Monthly average of daily observations.

depreciation against the dollar can induce hedging by firms that have borrowed dollars, and emerging market nonbanks have borrowed $3.3 trillion (McCauley, McGuire, and Sushko 2015a). Hedging puts further downward pressure on the domestic currency and, to the extent that the central bank counters this pressure, it sells reserves and eventually sells bonds (McCauley 2015; McCauley and Shu 2016).

Bond sales by foreign exchange reserve managers in 2015 are widely seen as having thrown the large US bond market out of kilter (Sundaresan and Sushko 2015). As emerging market central banks sold dollars to limit depreciation of their currencies, they seem to have sold US Treasury bonds to raise dollar cash. As they sold bonds, dealers were reluctant to increase their holdings in anticipation of selling them in turn to long-term investors. As a result, US Treasury yields at the key 10-year maturity have risen above the generic private sector yield represented by 10-year interest rate swaps (Figure 10.8).[6] Such a configuration of yields

---

[6]The US Treasury International Capital transactions data in Figure 10.8 show sales, while the holdings data do not (http://ticdata.treasury.gov/Publish/mfh.txt). Usually the holdings data are regarded as higher quality, but the transactions data seem to be consistent with market participants' perception of official selling.

is so anomalous that only a brave speculator would take the risk of betting on a return to normal: emerging market central bank sales of US Treasuries could accelerate and increase the dislocation of yields.

Note that the anomaly has not appeared in the euro bond market, where the central bank continues to buy government bonds apace. This dislocation may prove to be just the first symptom of divergent operations in the global bond market by major central banks.

Looming Transatlantic Divergence in Bond Market Operations?

More remote is the possibility that the Federal Reserve will sell bonds, or at least let them run off at maturity without replacement, even as the Eurosystem and the Bank of Japan continue to buy domestic bonds. This possibility does not seem imminent: the Federal Reserve has signaled that it will not stop rolling over its bond portfolio (which entails tens of billions in gross purchases per month) until sometime after its first hike in the short-term policy rate. And a backdrop of official purchases of euro and yen bonds could actually ease the market's response to the Federal Reserve's initial rate hikes. Outright sales from the bond portfolio could come later still. (Similarly, the Bank of England has said that it will begin to sell gilts well after the lift-off of its short-term policy rate.)

However, if the possibility of these major central banks finding themselves on opposite sides of the global bond market is considered, there is a case for central banks taking the view that this market is a sort of global commons. Central banks might well take into account their interactions in the global bond market, lest their own policies prove to be constrained by market dynamics to which their earlier actions may have contributed.

CONCLUSIONS

This chapter analyzes actual and prospective interactions among central banks operating in the global bond market. Both unconventional monetary policy and reserve management involve purchases (and potentially sales) of bonds. High substitutability of bonds in private portfolios means that the total purchases by central banks have an impact on global bond yields and, thereby, on global financial conditions.

Bond purchases compress the term premium in the target market and induce a shift of borrowing into it. Firms outside the United States have added to their dollar debt significantly in the aftermath of the global financial crisis, especially through the issuance of dollar-denominated bonds. Bond purchases in one market can also compress the term premium in other bond markets that are globally integrated.

Central bank operations in bond markets can be on the same side, reinforcing each other, or on opposite sides, at cross-purposes. After the global financial crisis, major central banks and major reserve managers stood shoulder to shoulder as buyers of bonds. Ironically, this was at times a symptom of policy friction: emerging market central banks intervened to limit currency appreciation—and incidentally bought reserve currency bonds, partly in response to behavior induced by quantitative easing.

At present, large bond purchases by the European Central Bank and the Bank of Japan may be countered to some extent by dollar bond sales by major reserve holders resisting domestic currency depreciation. With the Federal Reserve signaling higher policy rates followed at some point by a rundown of its holdings of bonds, policy frictions could arise in the global bond market. As a matter of enlightened self-interest, policymakers might well internalize the effects of their bond market operations on other policymakers.

Models that do not have bond markets and those that have bond markets that anchor yields solely on expected future policy rates cannot be used to analyze the potential gains from cooperation.

REFERENCES

Adrian, T., R. K. Crump, and E. Moensch. 2013. "Pricing the Term Structure with Linear Regressions." *Journal of Financial Economics* 110 (1, October): 110–38.

Adrian, T., and M. Fleming. 2013. "The Recent Bond Market Selloff in Historical Perspective." Federal Reserve Bank of New York, *Liberty Street Economics* (August 5).

Avdjiev, S., M. Chui, and H. S. Shin. 2014. "Non-financial Corporations from Emerging Market Economies and Capital Flows." *BIS Quarterly Review* (December): 67–77.

Backus, D. K., and J. H. Wright. 2007. "Cracking the Conundrum." *Brookings Papers on Economic Activity* 1: 293–329.

Bank for International Settlements (BIS). 2015. *85th Annual Report*. Basel: BIS.

Barroso, J. B., L. Pereira da Silva, and A. Soares. 2013. "Quantitative Easing and Related Capital Flows into Brazil: Measuring Its Effects and Transmission Channels through a Rigorous Counterfactual Evaluation." Working Paper 313 (July), Central Bank of Brazil, Brasilia.

Bauer, M., and C. Neely. 2014. "International Channels of the Fed's Unconventional Monetary Policy." *Journal of International Money and Finance* 44 (June): 24–46.

Bernanke, B. 2005. "The Global Saving Glut and the U.S. Current Account Deficit." Homer Jones Lecture, Federal Reserve Bank of St. Louis, St. Louis, Missouri, April 14.

———. 2012. "U.S. Monetary Policy and International Implications." Speech at "Challenges of the Global Financial System: Risks and Governance under Evolving Globalization," seminar sponsored by the Bank of Japan/International Monetary Fund, Tokyo, Japan, October 14.

———. 2013. "Long-Term Interest Rates." Speech at "Annual Monetary/Macroeconomics Conference: The Past and Future of Monetary Policy," Federal Reserve Bank of San Francisco, San Francisco, California, March 1.

Bernanke, B., V. Reinhart, and B. Sack. 2004. "Monetary Policy Alternatives at the Zero Bound: An Empirical Assessment." *Brookings Papers on Economic Activity* 2: 1–100.

Blommestein, H. J., and P. Turner. 2012. "Interactions between Sovereign Debt Management and Monetary Policy," in *Threat of Fiscal Dominance?* BIS Paper 65 (March): 213–37.

Borio, C., and R. McCauley. 1996. *The Economics of Recent Bond Market Volatility.* BIS Economic Paper 45 (July).

Chen, Q., A. Filardo, D. He, and F. Zhu. 2015. "Financial Crisis, Unconventional Monetary Policy and International Spillovers." BIS Working Paper 494 (March), Basel.

D'Amico, S., and T. B. King. 2013. "Flow and Stock Effects of Large-Scale Treasury Purchases: Evidence on the Importance of Local Supply." *Journal of Financial Economics* 108 (2, May): 425–48.

Filardo, A., and B. Hofmann. 2014. "Forward Guidance at the Zero Lower Bound." *BIS Quarterly Review* (September): 37–53.

Gagnon, J., M. Raskin, J. Remaché, and B. Sack. 2011. "The Financial Market Effects of the Federal Reserve's Large-Scale Asset Purchases." *International Journal of Central Banking* 7 (1): 3–43.

Gerlach-Kristen, P., R. McCauley, and K. Ueda. 2016. "Currency Intervention and the Global Portfolio Balance Effect: Japanese Lessons." *Journal of the Japanese and International Economies* 39: 1–16.

Greenwood, R., S. G. Hanson, J. S. Rudolph, and L. Summers. 2014. "Government Debt Management at the Zero Lower Bound." Working Paper 5, Hutchins Center for Fiscal and Monetary Policy, Brookings Institution, Washington, September 30.

He, D., and R. McCauley. 2013. "Transmitting Global Liquidity to East Asia: Policy Rates, Bond Yields, Currencies and Dollar Credit." BIS Working Paper 431 (October), Basel.

Hofmann, B., and B. Bogdanova. 2012. "Taylor Rules and Monetary Policy: A Global 'Great Deviation'?" *BIS Quarterly Review* (September): 37–49.

Hofmann, B., and E. Takáts. 2015. "International Monetary Spillovers." *BIS Quarterly Review* (September): 105–18.

Hördahl, P., and O. Tristani. 2014. "Inflation Risk Premia in the Euro Area and the United States." *International Journal of Central Banking* 10 (3, September): 1–47.

International Monetary Fund (IMF). 2014. *2014 Spillover Report.* International Monetary Fund, Washington, DC.

Kim, D. H., and J. H. Wright. 2005. "An Arbitrage-Free Three-Factor Term Structure Model and the Recent Behavior of Long-Term Yields and Distant-Horizon Forward Rates." Board of Governors of the Federal Reserve System, Finance and Economics Discussion Series 2005-33.

Krishnamurthy, A., and A. Vissing-Jorgensen. 2011. "The Effects of Quantitative Easing on Interest Rates: Channels and Implications for Policy." *Brookings Papers on Economic Activity* 2: 215–87.

Lo Duca, M., G. Nicoletti, and A. V. Martinez. 2014. "Global Corporate Bond Issuance: What Role for US Quantitative Easing?" European Central Bank Working Paper 1649 (March), Frankfurt-am-Main.

McCauley, R. 2015. "Capital Flowed Out of China through BIS Reporting Banks in Q1 2015." *BIS Quarterly Review* (September): 28–29.

McCauley, R., and G. Jiang. 2004. "Diversifying with Asian Local Currency Bonds." *BIS Quarterly Review* (September): 51–66.

McCauley, R., P. McGuire, and V. Sushko. 2015a. "Dollar Credit to Emerging Market Economies." *BIS Quarterly Review* (December): 27–41.

———. 2015b. "Global Dollar Credit: Links to US Monetary Policy and Leverage." *Economic Policy* 30 (82) (April): 187–229.

McCauley, R., and J.-F. Rigaudy. 2011. "Managing Foreign Exchange Reserves in the Crisis and After." In *Portfolio and Risk Management for Central Banks and Sovereign Wealth Funds.* *BIS Papers* 58 (October): 19–47.

McCauley, R., and C. Shu. 2016. "Dollars and Renminbi Flowed out of China." *BIS Quarterly Review* (March): 26–27.

McCauley, R., and K. Ueda. 2009. "Government Debt Management at Low Interest Rates." *BIS Quarterly Review* (June): 35–51.

Miyajima, K., M. Mohanty, and J. Yetman. 2014. "Spillovers of US Unconventional Monetary Policy to Asia: The Role of Long-Term Interest Rates." BIS Working Paper 478 (December), Basel.

Mojon, B., and F. Pegoraro. 2014. "Decoupling Euro Area and US Yield Curves." Banque de France, *Rue de la Banque* 1 (December).

Neely, C. 2015. "The Large-Scale Asset Purchases Had Large International Effects." *Journal of Banking and Finance* 52: 101–11.

Obstfeld, M. 2015. "Trilemmas and Tradeoffs: Living with Financial Globalization." BIS Working Paper 480 (January), Basel.

Obstfeld, M., and K. Rogoff. 2002. "Global Implications of Self-Oriented National Monetary Rules." *Quarterly Journal of Economics* 117 (2, May): 503–35.

Pereira da Silva, L. 2013. "Global Dimensions of Unconventional Monetary Policy—An EME Perspective." In *Federal Reserve Bank of Kansas City Jackson Hole Economic Policy Symposium Proceedings*, 373–85.

Rey, H. 2013. "Dilemma Not Trilemma: The Global Financial Cycle and Monetary Policy Independence." In *Federal Reserve Bank of Kansas City Jackson Hole Economic Policy Symposium Proceedings*, 285–333.

Rogers, J. H., C. Scotti, and J. H. Wright. 2014. "Evaluating Asset-Market Effects of Unconventional Monetary Policy: A Cross-Country Comparison." *Economic Policy* 29 (80, October): 749–99.

Sobrun, J., and P. Turner. 2015. "Bond Markets and Monetary Policy Dilemmas for the Emerging Markets." BIS Working Paper 508 (August), Basel.

Sundaresan, S., and V. Sushko. 2015. "Recent Dislocations in Fixed Income Derivatives Markets." *BIS Quarterly Review* (December): 8–9.

Taylor, J. 2013. "International Policy Coordination and the Great Deviation." Paper presented at the American Economic Association meeting in San Diego, California, January 4–6.

Turner, P. 2013. "Benign Neglect of the Long-Term Interest Rate." BIS Working Paper 403 (February), Basel.

———. 2014. "The Global Long-Term Interest Rate, Financial Risks and Policy Choices in EMEs." BIS Working Paper 441 (February), Basel.

Van Rixtel, A., and A. Villegas. 2015. "Equity Issuance and Share Buybacks." *BIS Quarterly Review* (March): 28–29.

Warnock, F. E., and S. C. Warnock. 2009. "International Capital Flows and U.S. Interest Rates." *Journal of International Money and Finance* 28: 903–19.

Winkler, R., M. Sachdeva, and G. Saravelos. 2015. "The 'Great Accumulation' Is Over: FX Reserves Have Peaked, Beware QT." Deutsche Bank Market Research, Special Report, September 1, London.

CHAPTER 11

International Liquidity and Governance

EDWIN M. TRUMAN

This chapter elaborates on some current problems with the international monetary system. At the time of writing, one of the pressing problems facing the International Monetary Fund—which threatened to undermine its legitimacy and therefore its effectiveness—was the failure by the US Congress to ratify the 2010 quota reforms. At the time, I delineated four options for how the IMF might proceed in the face of a recalcitrant Congress. Although Congress finally approved the quota change in December 2015, I have kept the description of the options in this chapter both because I believe the implicit threat that the rest of the IMF membership might find ways to proceed without Congress' consent helped spur that approval and because such options might prove necessary in the future—should the United States (or some other country) be unwilling to ratify quota changes that reflect changing economic realities.

The central problem with the international monetary system remains its asymmetric adjustment process. My preferred solution is a surveillance process with robust procedures and penalties; they might deal with currency wars but are less likely to be useful in dealing with secular stagnation in its various articulations. My views on surveillance were largely incorporated in the report of the Palais Royal Initiative (Truman 2010). That report was greeted with a huge yawn by both the official and broader policy community, so it is time to move on.

I do not agree that we have a problem with regulating global liquidity in the classic sense of harnessing the "exorbitant privilege" of the United States to finance its internal and external deficits at will. The international monetary system in this dimension is the shrinking tail on the growing dog of the international financial system. And the international financial system is increasingly a multicurrency system. Today not only most advanced countries but also a growing number of emerging market and developing countries share in the exorbitant privilege. They finance substantial amounts of their internal and external deficits via local currency bonds subject to their own laws. Credit Suisse estimates that, as of the end of November 2014, the average nonresident share of the local currency bonds of 10 emerging market and developing countries was 30.7 percent. The shares range from a high of 44.5 percent for Malaysia to a low of 18.3 percent for Thailand (Credit Suisse 2014).

The good news is that governments are taking on less direct currency risk; the bad news is that private borrowers are lagging behind and, more important, the international monetary and financial systems face a growing risk of disruption despite efforts to strengthen international cooperation in financial sector supervision and regulation. The disruption risks do not arise from global liquidity per se (net flows associated with the financing of current account deficits and surpluses) but from the exponential growth of gross financial flows regardless of the currency of denomination or issuing jurisdiction (global liquidity more broadly defined). This is where the IMF is relevant. The IMF is the central institution of the international monetary system. The first purpose of the IMF, stated in Article I of its Articles of Agreement, is "to promote international monetary cooperation." The institution's central role is now at risk. It faces two challenges: promoting further governance reform of the IMF, and ensuring the Fund has adequate financial resources.[1]

On the first challenge, one can debate whether the IMF has adequate financial resources to meet the immediate needs—disruption needs—of the global economy and financial system. Whether the IMF has adequate financial resources to support the international monetary and financial system in the future, in particular through the middle of the next decade, is less open to debate. Almost certainly it does not. Estimates of the IMF's future financial needs are controversial. That said, the following considerations are relevant.

In the past, the need for IMF's financial resources has been underestimated. The Thirteenth General Review of Quotas was completed in January 2008; it concluded that there was no need to increase IMF's financial resources. Following the outbreak of the virulent phase of the global financial crisis nine months later in September 2008, usable IMF financial resources from quotas and permanent borrowing arrangements more than tripled, from about $250 billion to slightly more than $750 billion via ad hoc bilateral borrowing and subsequently via the permanent expansion of the New Arrangements to Borrow (NAB).

Despite reforms put in place since the global financial crisis, the scale of financial crises and the need for international support in the interests of the global economy and financial system as a whole will likely grow faster than nominal GDP.

Many thought that the IMF's financial resources as of 2010 were sufficient to meet likely needs. But subsequent ad hoc borrowing totaling $461 billion has been arranged, and those lines are not permanent. IMF permanent resources (via quotas or the NAB) should at least be sufficient to replace these ad hoc borrowing arrangements.

The IMF conducts a regular review of its financial resources every five years. The Fourteenth General Review of Quotas was completed in December 2010.

---

[1] The bulk of the remainder of this piece draws upon Truman 2015.

However, an increase in quota resources agreed then was not fully ratified until February 2016, thus delaying the start of the Fifteenth Review, originally scheduled to be completed by December 15, 2015. Consequently, the next review would not be scheduled for completion until 2020 or five years from the completion of the Fifteenth Review. Given the delay in implementing increases in resources under the Fourteenth Review, it is reasonable to expect that any added resources approved under the Sixteenth Review will not be available until the mid-2020s.

It follows that deciding now on an increase in IMF quotas (or other permanent resources) of at least $500 billion to a total of $1.25 trillion, if not a doubling of such resources to $1.5 trillion, is a conservative estimate of what will be necessary to carry the IMF through the middle of the next decade. Without sufficient IMF financial resources, we are likely to see a continuation of globally inefficient and distortionary accumulations of international reserves by countries that have the ability to self-insure. Although I am skeptical of the force of the insurance motive for accumulating international reserves, as long as the IMF itself is starved for financial resources, the argument resonates.

The other challenge to the IMF's future involves its governance structure. Does that structure reflect the changing shape of the global economy? Clearly, the answer is no. A process of evolutionary reform of the IMF's governance was agreed to at the London Group of Twenty (G20) summit in April 2009. It was advanced in Pittsburgh in September 2009, and a breakthrough agreement was reached in Seoul in November 2010. The package of quota and governance reforms included the promise and prospect of further evolution that was expected to be agreed on at the end of 2012 and later at the end of 2014. However, the evolutionary process of IMF governance reform stalled because the US authorities—the executive and legislative branches of the government—were unable to pass the necessary legislation to permit implementation of the 2010 package until February 2016.

However, the failure of the United States to ratify the IMF reform is only a symptom of larger issues. The causes, in my view, are several. The United States—the hegemonic (if you like) creator, promoter, and protector of the IMF and of its role at the center of the international monetary system—is withdrawing from that role, and no other nation appears to be willing and able to step up and take its place.

The result is a fragmentation of global monetary cooperation in which different standards and amounts of external financial support are available to different groups of countries. We see this in many areas, but focusing on monetary cooperation broadly defined, we have the New Development Bank (established by Brazil, Russia, India, China, and South Africa) with its Contingent Reserve Arrangement; the Asian Infrastructure Investment Bank (led by China); the Chiang Mai Initiative Multilateralization (an Asian self-help financing arrangement); and the European Stability Mechanism (a European self-help financing arrangement). The emergence of these groups is symptomatic of the fragmentation of international monetary cooperation. Cooperation on a global level underlies everything the IMF does to promote economic growth and financial stability. Because the further evolution of IMF governance has been frozen, the legitimacy and effectiveness of the institution have been weakened. The weakening is not yet fatal, but it is debilitating.

The leadership of the IMF recognizes this challenge. In October 2014 the International Monetary and Financial Committee (IMFC) instructed the IMF to "build on its existing work and stand ready with options for next steps" if the 2010 reforms were not ratified by the end of 2014. On December 12, 2014, the IMF's managing director, Christine Lagarde, announced that the IMF would respond with a meeting of the Executive Board in January 2015. On January 28, the Executive Board proposed a resolution to the IMF Governors that would (1) move the date for completion of the Fifteenth General Review of Quotas to December 15, 2015, and (2) call upon the Executive Board "to work expeditiously and to complete its work as soon as possible on interim steps in the key areas covered by the 2010 quota and governance reforms, pending their full implementation, and thus to enable the Board of Governors to reach agreement on steps that represent meaningful progress toward the objectives of the 2010 Reforms by June 30, 2015." I would submit that the IMF needed more than "interim steps." The challenges to the IMF were fundamental: would the institution continue to grow and evolve, or would it be imprisoned in the world of 2010?

At the time, I saw four broad options, which I reproduce here:

OPTION ONE

First, the members of the IMF can continue to wring their collective hands and wait for the US Congress to pass the necessary legislation. In spite of the disappointment and anger at the US authorities for their repeated failure to deliver on the 2010 quota and governance reform package, other IMF members may fail to reach agreement on what to do in response. They may continue to give the United States a free ride. Of course, this option was no more than a punt, with the hope that the US authorities will come to their senses. It does not offer a path to the future.

OPTION TWO

The principal drawbacks associated with this first, more-of-the-same, option are that it would not address the longer-term financial needs of the IMF, nor would it promote the further governance reforms anticipated when the 2010 package was completed. Consequently, a second option is to restart the process anticipated in 2010 and review (and presumably revise) the IMF quota formula, using the new formula as a basis for a second package of IMF governance reforms linked to an increase in total quotas and a further redistribution of quota shares as part of the Fifteenth General Review of Quotas. It would be feasible to complete that review by the middle of December 2015, as the Governors' resolution specifies. A plausible minimum target for the size of this increase in IMF quotas is a further doubling relative to what the fourteenth review is expected to produce. This would imply an increase in the IMF's financial resources of about 75 percent.

The problem is that many IMF members would be reluctant to adopt another IMF Governors' resolution on this subject until the 2010 reform package has been approved. Nevertheless, adoption of a Governors' resolution on the fifteenth review that proposes further financial resources for the IMF and associated governance reforms might be viewed as being in the interests of the IMF as a whole and consequently in the interests of its individual members. It would signal intent to act to reform IMF governance further, even if its implementation would be delayed to an uncertain future date. It would also put in place the capacity to increase the IMF's quota resources if the need should arise, rather than having to rely on ad hoc borrowing or to mobilize from scratch an increase in IMF quotas. However, fundamental questions about the future of the IMF and US support for it would remain.

OPTION THREE

A more promising third option would involve US administration support for an augmented reform and financial package that could go into effect without the approval of the US Congress—risking a US veto over certain structural aspects of the IMF's operation.

The key procedural feature of this option, which I have previously described as "Plan B," is that it can be implemented without congressional action.[2] US law requires congressional approval to implement an increase in the US IMF quota, but congressional approval is not required for the United States to vote favorably on an IMF Governors' resolution to increase its quota, subject to congressional approval, or the quota of any other IMF member. Moreover, a Governors' resolution involving an increase in the US quota can be drafted in which formal US approval of an increase in its own quota can be delinked from implementation of the resolution. The US Treasury Secretary can vote in favor of a quota reform resolution that could be implemented even if Congress fails to approve US participation. Implementation might, for example, require acceptance of increases in IMF quotas by countries with only 70 percent of total votes.

This option has four basic elements, as follows:

- First, set aside the 2010 IMF reform package with its three interlinked components that, in effect, require congressional approval of the US quota increase before any of the components can be implemented.[3]

---

[2] I first outlined this proposal in Truman 2014.

[3] The three interlinked proposals were (1) the doubling of IMF quotas, with the funds in large part transferred from commitments to the New Arrangements to Borrow, (2) an amendment providing for an all-elected Executive Board, and (3) a commitment by European members to reduce by two the number of seats on the Executive Board occupied by representatives from advanced countries.

- Second, resubmit to the IMF membership the amendment of the IMF Articles on an all-elected IMF Executive Board as a stand-alone proposal.

- Third, combine the IMF quota reform component of the 2010 package with the Fifteenth General Review of Quotas, as discussed under option two.

- Fourth, assuming that the United States would risk losing its veto power, at least temporarily, if the new combined quota and governance reform package were implemented, the approach should include three elements to increase its attractiveness:

  ○ Revise the quota formula to increase the weight of the GDP blend variable (60 percent GDP at market and 40 percent GDP at purchasing power parity exchange rates) from its current 50 percent to 90 percent. This would be attractive to the United States because its calculated quota would increase.

  ○ Double total IMF quotas, again, relative to their size anticipated in the 2010 package. This would be attractive to the emerging market and developing countries because it would maximize the possibility of a shift in voting shares and their access to IMF financing.

  ○ Provide in the IMF Governors' resolution that changes in quotas will take effect when formal consents are received from members with less than 83.3 percent of the total voting power in the IMF—say, 75 percent or 80 percent. This would be attractive to every country except the United States.

This approach would further advance IMF governance reform and could preserve the existing US voting share in the IMF while also putting the United States on the spot to participate. On the other hand, the United States might balk, and the IMF would have to look for other ways to get around US intransigence.

OPTION FOUR

Faced with US unwillingness to risk losing its veto in the IMF by embracing the third option and unwilling to allow a dysfunctional US political system to continue holding the IMF hostage but wanting to preserve the institution's central position in the international monetary and financial system, the other members of the IMF could put in place an augmented reform and financing package without the consent (or, potentially, the participation) of the United States. The objectives of this option would be to permanently eliminate the US veto, promote governance reform, and provide the IMF with added financial resources for the future.

This option would establish a "SupraFund," separate from but linked to the current IMF with almost all the same features. The SupraFund would be empowered to lend to the current IMF. The members of the SupraFund would commit themselves to all the obligations and procedures associated with the current IMF with one exception: that the 85 percent majority required for some decisions in the IMF would be reduced at least to 80 percent, and the 70 percent majority required for other decisions might be reduced commensurately.[4]

For its part, the current IMF would establish a borrowing arrangement with the SupraFund. Such an arrangement—like the New Arrangements to Borrow, General Arrangements to Borrow, and ad hoc bilateral borrowing by the IMF—would require only a simple majority of votes of the members under IMF Article VII, section 1. In other words, the United States alone could not block this decision.

The current membership of the IMF could establish a SupraFund with the same membership as the IMF. The management, Executive Board, and staff would be identical to those of the current institution, and the resources of the SupraFund would be the addition to the IMF quotas from the Fifteenth General Review. Over time, the SupraFund would expand relative to the current IMF, as there would be no need to grow the old IMF.

The temptation to make changes to the IMF Articles of Agreement (in addition to the voting majorities) when they are incorporated into the articles of the SupraFund would be strong, but this temptation should be resisted. Otherwise, the negotiations would be prolonged, and the risk would increase that a large number of members of the current IMF would not participate in the SupraFund, which would weaken its authority and legitimacy. This challenge illustrates just how difficult it would be today to reconstruct from scratch the institution that was founded 70 years ago. Since IMF members are free to withdraw, it also illustrates the continuing value of that construction, no matter how imperfect it is perceived to be, in binding countries together for a common purpose.

* * *

In the event, the US Congress was persuaded to ratify the quota reforms without these more drastic options being implemented. It seems plausible, however, that the risk that the rest of the IMF membership might proceed without the United States (as it was, for instance, with the creation of the Asian Infrastructure Investment Bank), helped spur Congress' approval. The 2010 quota reform was an important step in recognizing economic realities, but it is surely not the last word on this matter. If, one day, it proves necessary to put forward a SupraFund option, I would hope that the United States would join the SupraFund and accept the hastening of the inevitable day when its capacity to block certain decisions in the IMF is eliminated because its size relative to the global economy has shrunk. This would be a complex way of implementing that reality, but at least the United States would get out of the way of progress on IMF governance reform and on increasing its resources.

---

[4]To avoid a continuation of the European Union veto in the IMF, the 85 percent voting majorities might be reduced to 70 percent.

However distasteful such a step would be for Washington, a credible option for moving forward without the United States would put much-needed, meaningful pressure on US politicians and policymakers. The IMF should be prepared to go it alone without Congress or even without Washington. Option three is preferable, because it provides for a more orderly evolution of the IMF, but if the US administration refuses to cooperate, option four should be ready to go next time.

REFERENCES

Credit Suisse. 2014. "Emerging Markets: Non-Residents' Holdings in Local Currency Government Bonds" (November).

Truman, Edwin M. 2010. "Strengthening IMF Surveillance: A Comprehensive Proposal." Policy Brief 10-29, Peterson Institute for International Economics, Washington, DC, December.

———. 2014. "Time for the United States to Risk Its IMF Veto." *Real Time Economic Issues Watch* (April 11), Peterson Institute for International Economics, Washington, DC.

———. 2015. "What Next for the IMF?" Policy Brief 15-1, Peterson Institute for International Economics, Washington, DC, January.

PART IV

Prospects for the Future: Toward a More Cooperative System

CHAPTER 12

Three Myths about International Policy Coordination

Atish R. Ghosh

The strange thing about international policy coordination, as David Lipton remarks in the foreword to this volume, is the unanimity about it: economists are unanimous that policy coordination is welfare enhancing, while policymakers are equally unanimous that whatever the merits of others coordinating with *their* policies, they have no desire to coordinate their own policies with those of others. Catherine Schenk, in Chapter 4 of this volume, gives several examples of failures to coordinate macroeconomic policies internationally. Why this lack of enthusiasm for macroeconomic policy coordination? This chapter analyzes the arguments typically made against the feasibility of coordination and seeks to debunk three myths or misperceptions about why international policy coordination is impossible in practice:

1. The mandate of national authorities is to look after their own economy, not those of foreign countries, so it is not possible to alter policies even if this would benefit the rest of the world.

2. The gains from coordination are too small to make policy coordination worthwhile.

3. Uncertainty about the effects of policies—especially cross-border transmission effects—is too great to make coordination feasible.

Like all good myths, each of these may have a grain of truth. A careful look at the analytics, however, shows why they are not (necessarily) correct.

THE ANALYTICS OF POLICY COORDINATION

The case for policy coordination is based on the welfare economics of public goods. To the extent that national policies have both domestic and cross-border effects, and since there is no global "market" in macroeconomic policies in which these externalities can be priced, achieving Pareto-efficient outcomes requires international policy coordination (Hamada 1974, 1976; Canzoneri and Henderson

---

This chapter draws heavily on the analysis in Ghosh and Masson 1994.

1991; Ghosh and Masson 1994).[1] When a policy's spillovers are positive (meaning it has a beneficial impact on the foreign country), it represents a global public good and hence will be undersupplied in the uncoordinated equilibrium; when the spillovers are negative, it represents a public bad and will thus be oversupplied from the global perspective. The essence of coordination is getting policymakers to recognize—and to internalize—these spillovers when setting policies.

It is generally assumed that, in the absence of coordination, policies will be at a Nash equilibrium: authorities set policies to maximize their own country's welfare, ignoring the impact on other countries and taking their policies as given. (As discussed in the next section, the assumption that the authorities are in fact maximizing their own country's welfare is not innocuous, and has important bearing on the estimated gains from policy coordination.) The resulting equilibrium will not be Pareto-efficient in the sense that, starting at the Nash equilibrium, there exists a perturbation of the foreign country's policies that will result in a first-order gain to the home country but only a second-order loss for the foreign country. By symmetry, there exists a perturbation of the home country's policies (relative to their Nash setting) that will result in a first-order gain for the foreign country at the cost of a second-order loss to the home country. The fact that there are first-order gains and only second-order losses means that both countries can be made better off relative to the Nash equilibrium. But since achieving those first-order gains inflicts second-order losses, both parties will have to make policy adjustments relative to their Nash settings. One country acting unilaterally to do the other a favor will make itself worse off. The essence of policy coordination is identifying and implementing this mutually beneficial "trade" of policy adjustments.

A Trade Theory Analogy

The analytics can be understood in terms of the gains from (Ricardian) trade. Suppose policymakers in two symmetric countries have an objective function defined over two targets, $v(y_1, y_2)$, which are affected by domestic and foreign policies, m, m^*:

$$y_1 = \alpha_1 m + \beta_1 m^* + \xi_1 + \varepsilon_1$$

$$y_2 = \alpha_2 m + \beta_2 m^* + \xi_2 + \varepsilon_2$$

where α and β are domestic and cross-border transmission multipliers, respectively; ξ represents shocks that can be observed or estimated before policies are

---

[1] This is essentially a "revealed preference" argument: since the parties to a cooperative agreement could choose the same policies they would have chosen in the noncooperative equilibrium, coordination should not make them worse off and in general should be welfare enhancing. The only exception is when the constraints facing the policymakers change when they coordinate; Rogoff (1985) constructs such an example, in which coordination exacerbates policymakers' time consistency problems and therefore reduces welfare. The compendium by Buiter and Marston (1984) includes several studies of policy coordination in the 1980s; Jeanne (2014) examines possible gains from coordination in the current global conjuncture.

chosen, and ε are shocks that occur after policies have been chosen. In the foreign country, analogously, policymakers have an objective function defined over two targets, $v^*(y_1^*, y_2^*)$, which, in turn, are affected by domestic and transmitted policies $y_1^* = \alpha_1^* m^* + \beta_1^* m + \xi_1^* + \varepsilon_1^*$, $y_2^* = \alpha_2^* m^* + \beta_2^* m + \xi_2^* + \varepsilon_2^*$; the objectives and the relationship between policies and targets in the foreign country may be completely different from those in the home country, though for algebraic simplicity, we follow most studies in assuming fully symmetric countries.

In the Nash (or noncooperative) equilibrium, the home policymaker sets his instrument to maximize his own utility, taking as given the foreign country's instrument setting:

$$\partial v / \partial m \big|_{m^*} = 0 \Rightarrow \alpha_1 \left(\partial v / \partial y_1 \right) + \alpha_2 \left(\partial v / \partial y_2 \right) = 0$$

Hence:

$$\left[\left(\partial v / \partial y_1 \right) / \left(\partial v / \partial y_2 \right) \right] = -\left(\alpha_2 / \alpha_1 \right)$$

In other words, as illustrated in Figure 12.1, the marginal rate of substitution (MRS) between the two targets should be set equal to the marginal rate of transformation (MRT) achievable by the use of the home country's instrument. The foreign policymaker will likewise set the MRS between his two targets equal to the MRT achievable with his own policy instrument.

Starting at this Nash equilibrium, suppose there is a perturbation in the foreign country's policy (the home policymaker will do likewise). The impact on the home country's welfare is

$$\partial v / \partial m^* = \beta_1 \left(\partial v / \partial y_1 \right) + \beta_2 \left(\partial v / \partial y_2 \right) = \left(1 / \alpha_1 \right) \left(\partial v / \partial y_2 \right) \left[\alpha_1 \beta_2 - \beta_1 \alpha_2 \right]$$

This expression will be nonzero except in the degenerate cases where policymakers have as many instruments as targets (here, one, so this would mean $\partial v / \partial y_2 = 0$), or the trade-off across targets achievable by the domestic effects of policies $\left(\alpha_1 / \alpha_2 \right)$ is identical to that achievable through the transmission effects $\left(\beta_1 / \beta_2 \right)$. Hence, at the Nash equilibrium, there exists a perturbation in the foreign country's policy settings that would raise the welfare of the home country (the direction of the perturbation—an increase or a decrease in the use of the policy—would be determined by the sign of the spillover). As shown in Figure 12.1, this perturbation of the foreign policy instrument allows the home country to trade off between its two objectives at the rate $\left(\beta_2 / \beta_1 \right)$, thus achieving a higher indifference curve. Analogously, starting at the Nash equilibrium, there exists a perturbation of the home country's policy that makes the foreign country better off (the first-order impact of this perturbation on the home country itself is zero since, at the Nash equilibrium, $\partial v / \partial m = 0$). Pareto-improving moves from the Nash equilibrium are therefore always possible.

To obtain the coordinated equilibrium, consider a global social planner who sets both the home and foreign country's policies in order to maximize a weighted average of the two countries' objective functions:

$$\omega \partial v / \partial m + (1-\omega) \omega \partial v^{*} / \partial m = 0$$

$$\omega \partial v / \partial m^{*} + (1-\omega) \omega \partial v^{*} / \partial m^{*} = 0$$

If the problem is symmetric (which it need not be, but it makes the exposition simpler), this is equivalent to maximizing the home country's objective function subject to the constraint that $m = m^{*}$:

$$\partial v / \partial m = \left(\partial v / \partial y_1 \right) \left(\alpha_1 + \beta_1 \right) + \left(\partial v / \partial y_2 \right) \left(\alpha_2 + \beta_2 \right) = 0$$

Hence:

$$\left(\partial v / \partial y_1 \right) / \left(\partial v / \partial y_2 \right) = -\left(\alpha_2 + \beta_2 \right) / \left(\alpha_1 + \beta_1 \right)$$

That is, the marginal rate of substitution between the targets is set equal to the marginal rate of transformation achievable through the *combination* of the domestic and foreign policies, attaining a higher level of welfare than in the Nash equilibrium.

An Example

An example helps clarify. Suppose policymakers have two objectives: minimizing the output gap and maintaining financial stability:

Figure 12.1. A Trade-Theoretic Interpretation of Policy Coordination

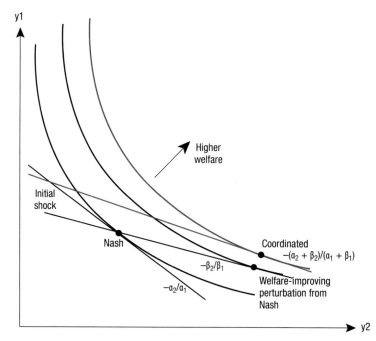

Source: Author's illustration.

$$v = Max -\frac{1}{2}\{y^2 + \lambda \psi^2\}$$

where y is the output gap, ψ is a measure of excessive credit growth, and λ is the relative welfare weight on financial stability. Output is a function of domestic and foreign monetary policies:

$$y = \alpha_1 m + \beta_1 m^* - \xi$$

where $\xi > 0$ is a negative shock to aggregate demand, and where $\alpha_1 > 0$, $\beta_1 > (<)$ 0, and $\alpha_1 + \beta_1 > 0$. Credit growth is assumed to be a function of domestic monetary policy alone:

$$\psi = \alpha_2 m$$

For simplicity, and without loss of generality, the foreign country is assumed to be identical.

In the Nash equilibrium, each policymaker sets its monetary policy without regard to the impact on the foreign country and takes as given the other's monetary policy. The resulting policy settings are given by:

$$m^N = m^{*N} = \frac{\alpha_1 \xi}{\alpha_1(\alpha_1 + \beta_1) + \lambda \alpha_2^2} > 0$$

In the coordinated equilibrium, a global social planner chooses both countries' monetary policies, subject to the symmetry constraint:

$$m^C = m^{*C} = \frac{(\alpha_1 + \beta_1)\xi}{(\alpha_1 + \beta_1)^2 + \lambda \alpha_2^2} > 0$$

Under both the Nash and coordinated equilibriums, therefore, monetary policy will be expansionary. Which will be more expansionary? Comparing policies in the two regimes:

$$m^C > m^N \Leftrightarrow \alpha_1(\alpha_1 + \beta_1)^2 + \lambda \alpha_2^2(\alpha_1 + \beta_1) > \alpha_1(\alpha_1 + \beta_1)^2 + \lambda \alpha_2^2 \alpha_1$$

which simplifies to:

$$m^C > m^N \Leftrightarrow \lambda \alpha_2^2 \beta_1 > 0$$

This example illustrates the two general results obtained above. First, if policymakers do not care about financial stability ($\lambda = 0$), then they have one target (the output gap) and one instrument (their own monetary policy), so there are no gains from coordination ($m^C = m^N$). Second, whether coordinated policies are more or less expansionary depends on the sign of the transmission multiplier, β_1. In the face of a negative demand shock, if foreign monetary policy is positively transmitted to the home country, it represents a positive externality or a public good; in the Nash equilibrium, therefore, monetary policy is insufficiently expansionary. Conversely, if monetary policy is negatively transmitted, it represents a public bad for the rest of the world, and the Nash policy setting, which ignores this spillover, will be excessively expansionary.

Although coordination is welfare superior to the Nash equilibrium (for both countries), notice that the home country can make itself even better off by deviating from the agreed-upon coordinated package, because at the cooperative equilibrium, $\partial v/\partial m\big|_{m'=m^{*C}} \neq 0$. For instance, in this example, it is readily verified that:

$$\partial v(m^C, m^{*C})/\partial m\big|_{m'=m^{*C}} = -\frac{\beta_1\xi\lambda\alpha_2^2}{(\alpha_1+\beta_1)^2+\lambda\alpha_2^2}$$

Therefore, $\partial v(m^C, m^{*C})/\partial m > 0\,(<0)$ if $\beta_1 < 0\,(>0)$. Recall that if $\beta_1 < 0$, the Nash equilibrium is overly expansionary and in this case the home country can improve welfare (relative to the coordinated equilibrium) by expanding monetary policy (relative to its coordinated equilibrium setting). In other words, starting from the coordinated equilibrium, provided the foreign country sticks to the agreement, the home country can make itself (even) better off by defecting toward the Nash policy setting. Of course, each country has the same incentive, and if both defect, the agreement breaks down and both countries are worse off.

Effect of Multiplier Uncertainty

Beyond additive shocks, there may be (and generally is) uncertainty about the effects of policies on targets. Rather than being known constants, suppose that the multipliers have given means and variances: $\mu_{\alpha_1}, \sigma_{\alpha_1}^2; \mu_{\alpha_2}, \sigma_{\alpha_2}^2; \mu_{\beta_1}, \sigma_{\beta_1}^2$. For simplicity, we begin with the case in which policymakers have only one objective:

$$v = Max-\frac{1}{2}E(y_1)^2$$

The resulting Nash policies are given by:

$$m^N = m^{*N} = \frac{\mu_{\alpha_1}\xi}{\mu_{\alpha_1}^2 + \sigma_{\alpha_1}^2 + \mu_{\alpha_1}\mu_{\beta_1}}$$

Under coordination, policies are:

$$m^C = m^{*C} = \frac{(\mu_{\alpha_1}+\mu_{\beta_1})\xi}{\mu_{\alpha_1}^2 + \sigma_{\alpha_1}^2 + \mu_{\beta_1}^2 + \sigma_{\beta_1}^2}$$

When there is no multiplier uncertainty, $\sigma_{\alpha_1}^2 = \sigma_{\beta_1}^2 = 0$, the Nash and coordinated policies become identical, $m^C = m^N$, so—as above—there are no gains from coordination because policymakers have as many instruments as targets. But when multiplier uncertainty exists, policies under the two regimes differ, so there are gains from coordination. Thus, uncertainty itself provides an incentive to coordinate.

What are the effects of multiplier uncertainty if there are already gains from coordination? In general, the effects are complex, but a basic principle is that uncertainty about domestic multipliers will tend to reduce the gains from coordination, whereas uncertainty about transmission multipliers will tend to raise them. This can be seen from the above expressions. Taking the limit $\sigma_{\alpha_1}^2 \to \infty$,

$m^C = m^N = 0$, the coordinated and Nash policies converge (toward zero, as the use of an instrument should become more conservative when its effects are uncertain; see Brainard 1967), so the gains from coordination diminish. Increased uncertainty about transmission effects, by contrast, leads to greater divergence between coordinated and uncoordinated policies: whereas the former converge to zero $\sigma^2_{\alpha_1} \to \infty, m^C = 0$, the latter are unaltered by transmission uncertainty. Therefore, as transmission uncertainty increases, so do the gains from coordination. Since the transmission effects of policies are generally more uncertain than their domestic impact, multiplier uncertainty typically raises the gains from policy coordination.

Sustaining Coordination

While the cooperative equilibrium achieves a higher level of welfare for both countries, it is fragile in the sense that, starting at the cooperative equilibrium, and assuming the foreign country does not respond, the home country can make itself even better off by deviating its policy from the agreed-upon cooperative setting: $\partial v(m^C, m^{*C})/\partial m \neq 0$. Any such deviation, however, will necessarily be at the expense of the foreign country, and vice versa:

$$\partial v(m^C, m^{*C})/\partial m = -[(1-\omega)/\omega]\partial v^*(m^C, m^{*C})/\partial m$$

Hence, after arriving at a cooperative agreement, both countries have the incentive to deviate (to "cheat") by pursuing different policies than those agreed upon. (This may seem implausible, as the policies pursued are public knowledge; in reality, however, policies need to be set on the basis of forecasts of the state of the economy, so governments can cheat by deliberately biasing or misrepresenting their true beliefs about the model or the state of the economy.) Unless there is some penalty for cheating, the coordinated equilibrium breaks down. In the absence of an international sanction, the only penalty would be a refusal to coordinate in the future—at least for some period (the "reversion" or "punishment" period). Cheating is detected ex post when outcomes are so different from those forecast that it would be implausible to attribute the outcome to stochastic shocks, ε. Hence, there is a trigger value (say, for y_1) such that if the observed outcome is sufficiently different from its forecasted value, $\bar{y}_1$, the authorities will be deemed to have cheated: in other words, to have implemented policies different from those agreed upon or deliberately misrepresented their forecasts of the shocks, ξ). For a given trigger level, $\bar{y}$, the probability that the reversionary period is triggered is then $Pr(y > \bar{y}) = Pr(\alpha_1 m^C + \beta_1 m^C + \xi + \varepsilon > \bar{y}) = Pr(\varepsilon > \bar{\varepsilon})$ for some corresponding $\bar{\varepsilon}$.

If the trigger is too tight (the value of $\bar{\varepsilon}$ is too low), the reversion to noncooperation will be imposed too often; if it is too loose, there will be ample scope for cheating. The trick is to calibrate the trigger so that, in weighing the costs and benefits, neither party has an incentive to cheat. In particular, the benefit of cheating needs to be weighed against the increased probability of getting caught (that is, triggering the punishment period).[2] But the increase in the probability is simply the derivative of the distribution function—the density function of ε. Therefore, ensuring incentive compatibility amounts to setting the trigger, $\bar{\varepsilon}_A$, to achieve a certain height of the density function ($\bar{\phi}$ in Figure 12.2). With such a trigger, in equilibrium, neither party will cheat. However, there will be random realizations of ε so that cooperation breaks down, and the parties must punish each other by refusing to cooperate, even though neither party cheated. The probability that the punishment period is triggered is given by the area under the density function to the right of $\bar{\varepsilon}_A$.

What is the effect of increasing uncertainty about domestic or transmission multipliers of such a trigger mechanism? It can be shown that the greater uncertainty flattens and widens the distribution function of ε, as depicted by density function B. To achieve $\bar{\phi}$ requires setting the trigger at $\bar{\varepsilon}_B$. As is clear from the diagram, however, the area under the curve (and thus the likelihood that the reversionary period is triggered due to stochastic shocks) is greater under trigger $\bar{\varepsilon}_B$ and density B than it is under $\bar{\varepsilon}_A$ and density A. Hence, greater uncertainty about the effects of policies (or the state of the economy) makes it more likely that a coordinated equilibrium will break down endogenously, even though, by construction, neither party cheats.

Finally, most theoretical studies of policy coordination assume symmetric countries for ease of exposition, but in reality, of course, countries have different economic and political weights—and correspondingly differing bargaining power. The beauty of the symmetric case is that each country's relative weight in the global social planner's objective function will naturally be one-half. But what happens when countries have to bargain over their (implicit) relative weight in the coordinated equilibrium? A key result from formal bargaining models is that when there is model uncertainty (and therefore scope for shifting the gains from coordination by misrepresenting beliefs over what is the true model describing the economy), it may be impossible to arrive at a cooperative agreement even though there would be positive gains for both parties under each possible model (see Ghosh and Masson 1994, Chapter 9).

Insights from the Analytics

The analytical framework presented here affords several insights. First, it makes clear that coordination does not involve one country acting altruistically toward the

---

[2]A marginal defection from the coordinated equilibrium will be worthwhile if

$$\partial v(m^C, m^{*C})/\partial m > (\partial \Phi/\partial m)\left\{\sum_{t=1}^{T} \delta^t(v^C - v^N)\right\}$$

where the punishment period (during which the countries will not coordinate) lasts for T years, Φ is the probability distribution function of ε, and δ is the policymaker's discount rate. Put differently, to prevent cheating, the trigger level should be set to ensure that

$$(\partial \Phi/\partial m) > \left\{\partial v(m^C, m^{*C})/\partial m\right\}\left\{\sum_{t=1}^{T} \delta^t(v^C - v^N)\right\}^{-1} \equiv \bar{\phi}.$$

Since the derivative of the distribution function is the density function, this means the trigger, $\bar{\varepsilon}$, must be set such that the density at $\bar{\varepsilon}$ is at least $\bar{\phi}$.

Figure 12.2. Uncertainty and Probability of Triggering Noncooperation

Φ

Φ̄ — Required height of density function to prevent cheating

Density function under high uncertainty

A   B

ε̄$_A$ ε̄$_B$ ε

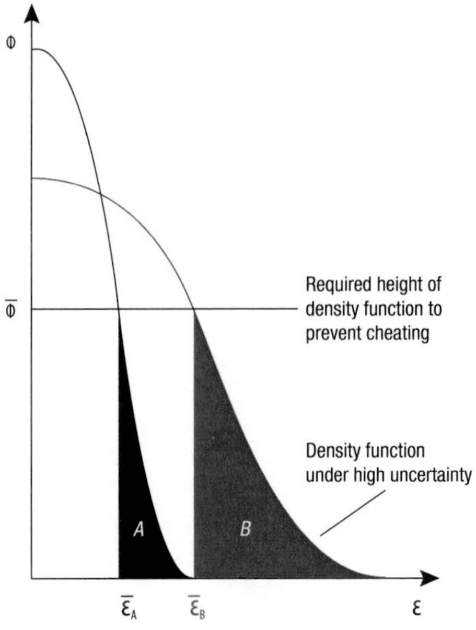

Source: Author's illustration.
Note: The area under the curve is the probability of triggering noncooperation. There is greater probability under high uncertainty (B) than under low uncertainty (A).

other: coordination is simply a mutually beneficial trade between countries, each of which seeks to maximize its own welfare. Nor does coordination imply aligning objectives across countries. On the contrary: for there to be gains from coordination, there must be some conflict between them, and each policymaker must have fewer instruments than targets. Second, as Figure 12.1 shows, policy coordination involves each policymaker achieving a more efficient trade-off between his objectives. As with most such efficiency arguments, this one implies that the gains from coordination will be in the order of "Harberger triangles." Third, uncertainty about the effects of policies, especially transmission effects, actually increases the welfare gains from coordination. At the same time, such uncertainty makes it more difficult to negotiate coordinated agreements and to sustain them in the face of shocks.

THREE MYTHS

With these analytical insights, we are ready to tackle the three myths about policy coordination.

1. *The mandate of national authorities is to look after their own economy, not those of foreign countries, so it is not possible to alter policies even if this would benefit the rest of the world.*

This claim is clearly wrong. Coordination involves *each* party achieving a higher level of welfare, so coordination is perfectly compatible with a purely national mandate. Notice, however, that coordination works when each national policymaker achieves a more efficient trade-off between his own objectives. If the policymaker negotiating the agreement has only one objective (for example, a central bank whose only mandate is price stability), coordination is not possible, as the policymaker does not face any trade-offs. More often, policymakers (whether central banks or ministries of finance) focus on one objective at a time (for example, unemployment during recessions or inflation when the economy is overheating) without recognizing that they face trade-offs between various objectives over time. Thus, during a recession, they may favor monetary expansion without taking account of potential financial stability risks down the road. But if that is the case, they are back to the one-instrument one-target world, in which there are no gains from coordination. Thus, the difficulty in coordinating policies does not stem from authorities having purely national mandates, it stems from policymakers acting as though they have as many instruments as targets.

2. *The gains from coordination are too small to make policy coordination worthwhile.*

As noted earlier, the gains from coordination will be in the order of Harberger triangles; in fact, empirically they are often estimated to be similar in magnitude to the gains from multilateral trade liberalization (Sachs and McKibbin 1985). The gains from coordination will also depend on the circumstances, increasing according to the extent to which countries' objectives are in conflict. When the world economy is enjoying sustained noninflationary growth, there will be few conflicts between countries' macroeconomic policies—and hence few gains from policy coordination. But in times of stress (such as the sharp disinflation programs in advanced economies during the early 1980s, the 1987 stock market crash, or the aftermath of the global financial crisis), individual countries' attempts at macroeconomic stabilization may be at odds with each other, with correspondingly *greater* gains from coordination.

One reason that the gains from coordination—even in times of stress—are usually estimated to be quite small is that policies are assumed to be at their Nash equilibrium; that is, they are assumed to be the best that the country can achieve on its own. In reality, however, policies are seldom set optimally, even within the national context: uncertainty, political constraints, and competing interests complicate domestic policymaking. There may be larger gains from coordination if the international agreement helps overcome domestic political constraints and helps achieve policies that are at least as good as the Nash equilibrium.

3. *Uncertainty about the effects of policies—especially cross-border transmission effects—is too great to make coordination feasible.*

This claim is half-true. Uncertainty about the effects of policies—especially about transmission effects—actually raises the gains from coordination. But, as discussed earlier, such uncertainty also makes it more likely that any coordinated package will break down in the face of unexpected shocks and makes it less likely that countries will be able to agree on policy coordination in the first place.

CONCLUSIONS

There are many obstacles to successful international policy coordination, including ignorance (sometimes perhaps willful) about what it means and what it entails. This chapter sought to dispel three oft-heard myths about why coordination is impossible by carefully looking at the analytics. Yet political and practical difficulties remain in achieving greater coordination; how to address them is the topic of the next three chapters.

REFERENCES

Brainard, W. 1967. "Uncertainty and the Effectiveness of Policy." *American Economic Review* 57: 411–25.

Buiter, W., and R. Marston. 1984. *International Economic Policy Coordination*. Cambridge, U.K.: Cambridge University Press.

Canzoneri, M., and D. Henderson. 1991. *Monetary Policy in Interdependent Economies: A Game Theoretic Approach*. Cambridge, MA: MIT Press.

Ghosh, A., and P. Masson. 1994. *Economic Cooperation in an Uncertain World*. Oxford, U.K.: Blackwell Publishers.

Hamada, K. 1974. "Alternative Exchange Rate Systems and the Interdependence of Monetary Policies." In *National Monetary Policies and the International Financial System*, edited by Robert Z. Aliber. Chicago, IL: University of Chicago Press.

———. 1976. "A Strategic Analysis of Monetary Interdependence." *Journal of Political Economy* 84 (August): 677–700.

Jeanne, O. 2014. "Macroprudential Policies in a Global Perspective." NBER Working Paper 19967, National Bureau of Economic Research, Cambridge, MA.

Rogoff, K. 1985. "Can International Monetary Policy Coordination Be Counterproductive?" *Journal of International Economics* 18 (May): 199–217.

Sachs, J., and W. McKibbin. 1985. "Macroeconomic Policies in the OECD and LDC External Adjustment." NBER Working Paper 1534, National Bureau of Economic Research, Cambridge, MA.

CHAPTER 13

Moving Toward a More Cooperative International Monetary System

Maurice Obstfeld

Discussion of the international monetary system covers many aspects, but three seem to come up again and again: exchange rates, international liquidity, and external adjustment.

For the most part, we live in a world of floating or managed floating exchange rates. One source of liquidity is private capital, which has reached a much higher level of mobility than at any time in history. But financial capital that flows in easily can also flow out easily, and this has resulted in high official demand for safe reserve assets. However, what is safe one day may be quite unsafe the next. Countries that fear a cutoff of foreign lending have accumulated large volumes of international reserves as a ready stockpile of unconditional international liquidity, assuming that these financial resources will remain easily usable even in crisis situations.

The nature of international adjustment is very different in today's world than it was in the past because of the evolution of international financial linkages. Broadly speaking, effective international adjustment implies that the national intertemporal budget constraint is met without the need for sharp compressions of spending. A relatively new aspect of international adjustment comes through international risk sharing, which results from extensive asset swapping and from large gross external positions and the effects thereon of asset price changes, including exchange rate changes.

Exchange rates are driven by capital movements that promote current account adjustment only with a very long lag, if at all. Thus the growth in capital mobility has accentuated a disconnect between the current account and the exchange rate's movement, at least over the medium term. Capital seems to flow in a single direction for a very long time—perhaps too long—and that can result in financial crises, which are one (unfortunate) form of adjustment. As in previous international monetary regimes throughout history, there is little or no pressure on surplus countries or creditor countries to adjust; the adjustment pressure remains on the borrowers and debtors.

In the current system, policy coordination problems inevitably arise. The exchange rate is always shared by two economies, so the resolution of any problem requires cooperation; however, cooperation very rarely occurs. Thus we have "currency wars" (which used to be known as competitive depreciation). After a brief respite, the currency war problem is very much back in our sights in the face of monetary policy and growth divergence between the United States and much of the rest of the world, and evidence of tension is quite evident in the area of trade. The current US administration faces congressional pressure to embed provisions in its ambitious trade agenda to address currency manipulation. Various segments of the US Congress support proposed legislation authorizing countervailing duties against trading partners with undervalued currencies; if such legislation is implemented, it is sure to draw challenges in the World Trade Organization. These initiatives are a reaction to the simple fact that exchange rates move. They move a lot, especially when international growth and payment patterns are unbalanced. When the home currency depreciates, home exporters like it; when the home currency gains in the foreign exchange market, they do not like it. The converse holds for the currencies of trading partners. If countries are to be dissuaded from taking matters into their own hands, more effective means of international macro coordination are required.

In addition to the standard, classic problems of the international monetary system, novel ones emerge from the widespread cross-border lending and borrowing in foreign currencies that the Bank for International Settlements (BIS), among others, has highlighted. The "original sin" problem has been a topic of discussion for a long time. The BIS has drawn attention to offshore dollar borrowing by firms in emerging markets, and we have recently witnessed another consequence of cross-border foreign currency borrowing: the spillover from Switzerland's sudden abandonment of the franc's cap against the euro in January 2015. The dramatic and sudden currency appreciation that followed washed across global financial markets in various ways, not the least of which was to Polish and Hungarian households that had financed mortgages with Swiss franc instruments.

To return to the topic of liquidity: large-scale reserve holdings by emerging market economies have been one of the answers that countries have found, and we have been discussing the reasons for the size and nature of reserve buildups for years. Gross reserve accumulation entails many negative externalities: for example, distortions in exchange and interest rates for the reserve center. In addition (analogous to some of the problems that arose under the gold standard), deflationary pressures may emerge when countries engineer unwarranted current account surpluses in order to accumulate reserves that do not have liabilities as counterparts. Moreover, a new form of the old Triffin paradox, discussed in Chapter 1, has arisen. Are there enough safe assets around to satisfy the global demand for reserve assets, especially now, as they are being bought up in the course of quantitative easing operations?

Recent attempts to address the systemic drawbacks of gross reserve accumulation include the IMF's expanded credit facilities and central bank swap lines, but these are at best a partial solution to the issue. Richard Cooper's proposal for Special Drawing Rights (SDRs) (see Chapter 9) could be a constructive element in solving this particular coordination problem.

Some of the most novel challenges arise in the area of adjustment, because adjustment is mediated so extensively by financial markets and asset prices. The global financial crisis showed the world how many global coordination problems can result from the extent of financial markets and from the political power of the actors in these markets.

As mentioned earlier, financial markets generally allow borrowing in quantities that are too big and for periods of time that are too long, until a financial crisis brings the exuberance to an end; afterward, credit may be too limited. Many countries still exhibit the aftereffects of the global liquidity surge of the 2000s. Much of the blame lies with micro-coordination problems in these markets. For example, the illusion exists that if a country lends short term, it can get out first— that its debt is effectively senior. Herding and the myopic competition over short-term returns also play roles. Such micro-coordination problems, if they occur widely and on a large scale, give rise to macro-coordination problems.

Fortunately, the need for cooperation in this area was recognized in the mid-1970s with the initiation of the Basel Committee. That group was a response to the realization that in a world of big exchange rate movements, financial stability could easily be in peril and that regulators should be exchanging information, coordinating on global best practices, and clarifying jurisdictional responsibilities. Over the ensuing four decades, the process of improving the world's financial policy coordination infrastructure has moved forward through successive Basel agreements, the Financial Stability Board, and the evolution of the IMF into a debt crisis lender and a monitor of world financial conditions. The comparison between what the IMF does now and what it did in the early 1970s is really quite remarkable. At one time people asked, "Without the Bretton Woods system, what will the IMF do?" Well, the IMF has found plenty to do as global markets have evolved, and it remains a remarkable provider of international public goods.

The global financial stability infrastructure is all the more necessary in a world of potentially big exchange rate changes. Monetary and financial forces are propagated across borders in a very powerful way, not just in the standard ways that we think about in the older-style macro models but through international banking activity and other credit extension, where loans and instruments traded in any country can be denominated in any currency.

Global standards as negotiated in the Basel agreements are critical for another reason, which centers on political externalities. Financial regulators can be buffeted by the political process and dominated by domestic actors, and they certainly have inadequate incentives to take account of negative externalities of lax regulation abroad. In this respect, the Basel rules provide an indispensable tool for coordination.

In addition to the wide acceptance of the macroprudential outlook, another development since the global financial crisis is a more flexible attitude toward capital controls. In the spring of 1985, capital controls were still present in

Europe in support of the European Monetary System of adjustable pegs, and of course they prevailed in many developing countries, especially after the 1980s debt crisis broke out. In a paper for the Brookings Institution, I took the view that controls ultimately would do more harm than good (Obstfeld 1985). Europe would soon move beyond them, and they seemed like a tool of the past. Richard Cooper, as a discussant of my paper, argued in his comments that we should take capital controls more seriously, and events have borne out his instincts. Since the global financial crisis, we have recognized capital controls more widely as an admissible and useful part of the toolkit in some circumstances.

The World Trade Organization includes safeguards against import surges under some conditions. Shouldn't countries that are facing a surge of capital inflows—which cause appreciation, dislocation, and unemployment, and possibly feed financial instability—have some tools to use, at least in some cases? But the ability to deploy capital account measures creates new coordination problems, including (as the IMF has long recognized) the possibility of manipulating currency.

Thus, capital controls also need some rules of the road, and the IMF seems likely to be a leader in this effort. Think about the difficulties of trade negotiations. Once you deal with tariffs and quotas, which are relatively transparent as barriers, there remains an array of other nontariff barriers and the inevitable disputes about regulatory standards and how those are applied to possibly disadvantage imports. The capital controls discussion involves many of the same issues. What are capital controls? What is macroprudential policy? What sorts of measures are labeled macroprudential but are actually meant to affect goods and services trade via the exchange rate or some other channel? What are acceptable departures from Basel or other norms in the regulatory sphere? Resolving these ambiguities is a big challenge for coordination, but because of the spectacular growth of international banking and finance, and the potential for good or for ill, this is a key area in which we badly need to move forward.

REFERENCE

Obstfeld, Maurice. 1985. "Floating Exchange Rates: Experience and Prospects." *Brookings Papers on Economic Activity* 16 (2): 369–464.

CHAPTER 14

Reforming the Global Reserve System

José Antonio Ocampo

The current global reserve system evolved out of the unilateral decision by the United States in 1971 to abandon the gold-dollar parity and convertibility of dollars for gold that was established at Bretton Woods in 1944. Although other currencies can compete with the US dollar as international means of payments and potential foreign exchange reserve assets, this competition has been weak owing to the "network externalities" in the use of currencies (whereby the value of a currency to a user depends on how widely it is used by others) and the fact that the United States has by far the largest market for liquid Treasury securities. According to IMF data on the composition of allocated foreign exchange reserves, in the fourth quarter of 2014, 62.9 percent of global reserves were held in US dollars, 22.2 percent in euros, and 14.9 percent in other currencies. Moreover, at least 80 percent of foreign exchange transactions are managed in US dollars. The current system can thus undoubtedly be called a *fiduciary* dollar standard—an important feature of which is that alternative reserve currencies float against each other. This chapter lays out the problems associated with the current international monetary system and discusses proposals for reform.

THE PROBLEMS OF THE CURRENT SYSTEM

The current global monetary system can be characterized as facing three distinct problems, which can be identified in a historical sequence (Ocampo 2010b, 2010c). The first is the problem emphasized by John Maynard Keynes (1942–43) in his proposals for a global monetary system in the years leading up to the 1944 Bretton Woods Conference. Keynes noted that this problem had been a feature of all international monetary systems: the asymmetric adjustment pressures on deficit versus surplus countries. The former are forced to adjust, and the latter are

A previous version of this paper was presented at the conference organized by the Central Bank of Austria and published in its Workshop Series No. 18. It draws in part from a World Institute for Development Economic Research (WIDER) Annual Lecture given by the author (Ocampo 2010a) and is part of a book on the international monetary system being prepared for WIDER.

Figure 14.1. Current Account Balance of Euro Area Countries
(Percent of GDP)

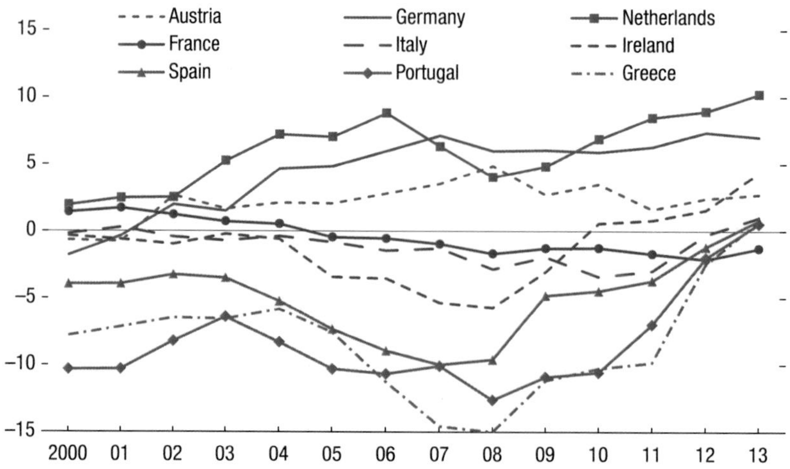

Source: IMF, World Economic Outlook database.

not, which creates a recessionary pressure on the world economy. The asymmetric adjustment problem is, of course, felt with particular severity during global recessions, when deficit financing dries up.[1]

There is perhaps no better example of this problem than the experience of the euro area countries during the global financial crisis. As Figure 14.1 shows, since 2007 Greece, Ireland, Portugal, and Spain have experienced massive current account adjustments of 9 to 16 percentage points of GDP. Italy, the third largest economy in the euro area, has also experienced a significant adjustment of about 4 percentage points. By contrast, surplus countries—Germany, the Netherlands, and, to a lesser extent, Austria—have not reduced their surpluses by any significant amount; in fact, some surplus countries have even increased them.

The second problem is generated by the use of a *national* currency (the US dollar) as the major *international* currency. This problem was formulated in the 1960s by the Belgian economist Robert Triffin and came to be known as the "Triffin dilemma" (Triffin 1961, 1968; for a recent formulation, see Padoa-Schioppa 2011). As discussed in Chapter 1 of this volume, the essential issue is that provision of international liquidity requires the reserve-issuing country or countries to run a balance of payments deficit, in either the current or the capital account, even though this could eventually lead to a loss of confidence in that currency. In the 1960s, this dilemma was reflected in the tendency of the United States to gradually lose gold reserves, but if the United States had tried to correct

---

[1] I have also referred to this problem as the "anti-Keynesian bias" of the system.

Figure 14.2. US Current Account and Real Exchange Rate

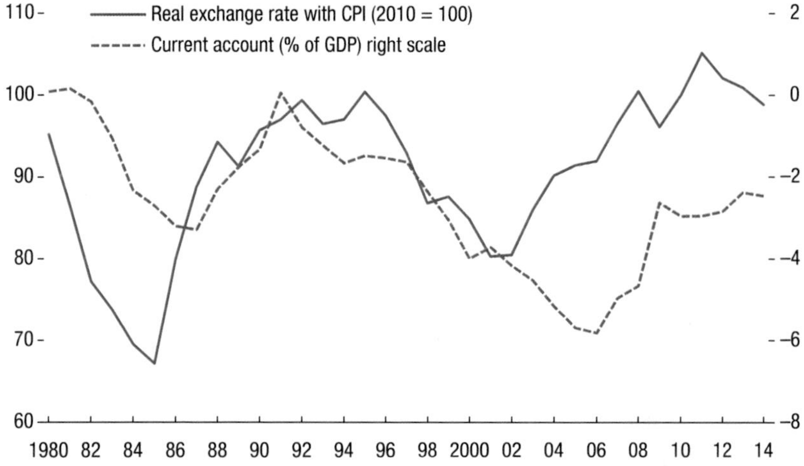

Source: IMF, International Financial Statistics database.
Note: An increase in the real exchange rate is a real depreciation. CPI = consumer price index.

its deficit to avoid the loss, the action would have squeezed international liquidity. After failing to manage the loss of gold reserves through the Gold Pool (Eichengreen 2007, Chapter 2), the United States finally decided to abandon convertibility of dollars for gold in 1971.

This decision changed the nature of the Triffin dilemma. The United States was essentially left with no effective constraint to run balance of payments deficits, which generated both a long-term trend of rising current account deficits and strong fluctuations in the exchange rate of the dollar against other currencies (Figure 14.2). The former could be said to generate expansionary (and, under some conditions, inflationary) pressures on the global economy during the periods when the United States is running deficits; in turn, reductions of the US current account deficit have always been associated with global slowdowns or recessions (1980–82, 1990–91, 2008–09, and to some extent 2001). Thus, the system can be said to alternate between expansionary and recessionary biases. The instability of the US dollar exchange rate can be understood, in Triffin's terms, as cycles of confidence in the US dollar as a reserve currency. The instability also implies that, since the early 1970s, the dollar has lacked an essential feature of the currency that is at the center of the global monetary system: a stable value.

Being at the center of the system generates several advantages for the United States; among them are the appropriation of seigniorage from the use of the dollar as a global currency, the ability to borrow at low interest rates, and an increased demand for the services provided by its financial industry. But its position also has costs for the United States, particularly if (as has been the norm in recent decades) it involves current account deficits, which represent leakages in aggregate demand. This means, in turn, that the effectiveness of US expansionary policies is reduced by the spillovers these policies generate on the rest of the world during periods of dollar appreciation. This is what happened in the aftermath of the Lehman Brothers collapse in September 2008, so that part of the stimulus of US expansionary policies was exported to the rest of the world.[2]

The third problem with the current international monetary system is the inequities generated by the need of developing countries to accumulate foreign exchange reserves to manage the strong procyclical swings in capital flows, which are transfers of resources to reserve-issuing countries. This *inequity bias* became very visible in the 1990s, especially in the aftermath of the sequence of crises in emerging market economies that started in east Asia in the late 1990s. As Figure 14.3 indicates, until the 1980s the foreign exchange reserves of low- and middle-income countries were similar to those of high-income countries: 3 percent to 5 percent of GDP. Since then, however, they have diverged—sharply since the Asian crisis. Before the recent North Atlantic financial crisis (end-2007),[3] high-income and low-middle-income countries, excluding China, held average reserves equivalent to 17.7 percent and 26.9 percent of GDP, respectively, while low-income countries held reserves of about 17.4 percent of GDP. With the exception of Japan, high-income Organisation for Economic Co-operation and Development (OECD) countries continued to hold reserves of less than 2 percent of GDP. Since the beginning of the financial crisis, however, low-income countries have lost reserves, while the OECD countries have increased their reserve holdings, but only to about 3.6 percent of GDP.

This phenomenon, which has come to be known as "self-insurance," involves not only accumulating reserves to face an eventual sudden stop in external financing but also absorbing through reserve accumulation a large part of what countries consider excess capital inflows. The basic rationale for this policy is to avoid appreciation pressures and growing current account deficits during periods of booming capital inflows, which (as past experience amply demonstrates) are strong predictors of crises during the downswing of the capital account cycle that follows. There is increasing evidence that strong reserve positions and avoidance of overvaluation and current account deficits significantly contributed to the relatively good performance of developing countries during the North Atlantic financial crisis.[4] In a broad sense, self-insurance is a prudential or countercyclical macroeconomic policy aimed at moderating the domestic effects of procyclical

---

[2]This problem for the reserve-issuing country has been highlighted by Stiglitz (2006, Chapter 9) and can be seen as a lack of control by the reserve-issuing country over its balance of payments, as underscored by Greenwald and Stiglitz (2010).

[3]Following other authors, I will use this term rather than "global financial crisis." The crisis did have global effects, but it was concentrated in the United States and western Europe.

[4]See, among others, Frankel and Saravelos 2010, and Llaudes, Salman, and Chivakul 2010.

Figure 14.3. Total Reserves (Excluding Gold), by Level of Development
(Percent of GDP)

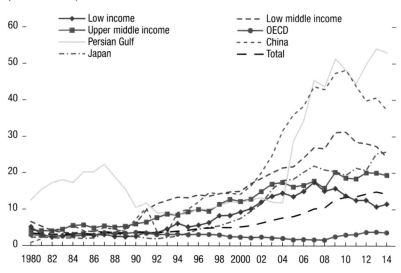

Source: IMF, International Financial Statistics database for total reserves excluding gold series.
Note: Categorization by level of development according to World Bank for the year 2000. Organisation for Economic Co-operation and Development (OECD) excludes Japan. China and the Persian Gulf countries (Bahrain, Iran, Iraq, Kuwait, Oman, Qatar, Saudi Arabia, and the United Arab Emirates) are not included in any other category.

capital flows. Despite this positive effect, the policy generates a "fallacy of composition" effect: if many countries adopt a policy aimed at generating surplus or small current account deficits, they contribute to the generation of global imbalances.

REFORMING THE SYSTEM

These deficiencies in the global monetary system are, in different ways, at the center of the reform proposals formulated at the beginning of the 2007 crisis. They included the proposal by the central bank governor of China to gradually eliminate the role of the dollar at the center of the system (Zhou 2009). In turn, the Stiglitz Commission, convened by the president of the United Nations General Assembly, proposed that reforms of the global reserve system should be at the center of the global reform agenda (UN 2009). The Palais Royal Initiative (2011), convened by former IMF managing director Michel Camdessus together with Alexandre Lamfalussy and Tommaso Padoa-Schioppa, also presented a series of reform proposals. However, actions have been limited, and the reforms of the international monetary system did not fully enter into either Group of Twenty (G20) or IMF debates.

There are essentially two paths forward, and they can be combined in a complementary way.[5] The first—in a sense the inertial solution—is to enhance the multicurrency features of the current system. The increasing use of the euro for global transactions and as a global reserve asset is one of the possibilities, although the recent crisis has shown that there may be limits to this approach in the current setup, as the euro is backed by a heterogeneous group of countries with uneven strength, and there is in fact no homogeneous euro bond market. The internationalization of the renminbi is a complementary possibility. This process is being pushed by market forces and facilitated by Chinese authorities, but it is being constrained by the limited domestic financial development in China and by the inconvertibility of the renminbi (Yu 2014). However, full convertibility may not be necessary for the renminbi to play the role of a reserve asset if full convertibility is guaranteed for central banks that hold renminbi as reserves. This approach may be inconvenient for the Asian giant, as it can expose the country to destabilizing external shocks (Gallagher and others 2014). In addition to the euro and the renminbi, other currencies can play secondary roles, and local currencies can be used on a broader scale for intraregional trade.

The basic advantage of a multicurrency arrangement is that it allows reserve holders—especially emerging economies—to diversify the composition of their foreign exchange reserve assets and thus counteract the instability that characterizes all individual currencies under the current system. However, exchange rate flexibility among alternative reserve currencies would be not only an advantage but also a potential risk. Flexibility would make the system more resilient than the fixed gold-dollar parity that led to the collapse of the original Bretton Woods arrangement, but if central banks around the world actively substitute among currencies to enjoy the benefits of diversification, this could increase exchange rate volatility among major reserve currencies. For this reason, a multicurrency arrangement might need an IMF "substitution account" to serve as a stabilizing mechanism, which means that it might have to rely on at least some elements of the second alternative.

Also, this reform would not address any of the other deficiencies of the current system. The benefits from the reserve currency status would still be captured by industrialized countries and eventually by China, so the system would continue to be inequitable. This reform would not solve the asymmetric adjustment bias of the current system either, nor would it reduce emerging market and developing economies' demand for self-insurance. Finally, in the light of the growing demand for reserves, the dominance of the US dollar could worsen the net external liability position of the United States and other problems associated with the Triffin dilemma.

---

[5]There are, of course, other alternatives. One would be going back to some form of gold standard or at least to a greater use of gold as a reserve asset. But this goes against long-term trends toward moving away from this "barbarous relic" (to use Keynes's terminology), which includes the growing demonetization of gold since the 1970s. It would also go against the "embedded liberalism" of the post-WWII arrangements, as emphasized by Eichengreen (2008).

The second alternative is to move toward a global currency, initially perhaps only as a reserve asset. Although other routes are possible,[6] the best would be the use of Special Drawing Rights (SDRs) issued by the IMF; indeed, this would fulfill the aspiration written into the IMF's Articles of Agreement when this instrument was created of "making the special drawing right the principle reserve asset in the international monetary system" (Article VIII, Section 7, and Article XXII).[7] As Triffin (1968) envisioned, this would complete the transition that began in the nineteenth century of placing fiduciary currencies at the center of modern monetary systems.

Proposals for periodic SDR allocations follow two models. The first is countercyclical allocations—concentrating them in periods of global financial stress and possibly partially destroying them once financial conditions normalize (UN 1999; Camdessus 2000; Ocampo 2002; Akyüz 2005). This approach would develop a countercyclical element in world liquidity management. The second model proposes regular allocations in proportion to the additional global demand for reserves. Most estimates indicate that annual allocations of $200–$300 billion would be reasonable.[8] These allocations would increase the share of SDRs in non-gold reserves only to somewhat above 10 percent in the 2020s, indicating that they would still largely complement other reserve assets.

Under current rules, the IMF makes SDR allocations on the basis of long-term global need and with the purpose of supplementing existing reserve assets. As mentioned in Chapter 1, so far there have been three general SDR allocations: the original in 1970–72 for SDR 9.3 billion; the second in 1979–81 for SDR 12.1 billion; and the third, proposed in 1997 partly to allocate SDRs to members that had joined after 1981 (not effective until the Fourth Amendment of the IMF Articles of Agreement, of which it was a part, was approved by the US Congress in 2009) for SDR 161.2 billion. In addition, the Fourth Amendment to the Articles of Agreement provided for a special one-time allocation of SDR 21.5 billion in 2009 as one of the measures to boost international liquidity during the North Atlantic financial crisis.

SDR allocations are based on IMF quotas and therefore are much larger for high-income countries. Table 14.1 shows that the share of high-income countries in the allocation has gradually declined over time, although it was still close to 70 percent in 2009, with the falling share of OECD countries partly compensated by the rise of high-income non-OECD (mainly Persian Gulf) countries. Middle-income countries have increased their share of allocations by 6 percentage points since the early 1970s, with China constituting over half of that. By

---

[6]The reform could also be implemented by creating a new institution (a Global Reserve Bank) or a network of regional arrangements. See, in this regard, UN 2009, Chapter 5. But creating new institutional frameworks would be time-consuming and may not be politically viable.

[7]See Solomon 1982, Chapters 4–8, for a history of the debates on global monetary issues that led to the creation of SDRs.

[8]For a survey of different estimates, see Erten and Ocampo 2014, Chapter 9.

Table 14.1. SDR Allocation, by Income Level

	Allocations (Millions of SDRs)			Allocation to Each Group (Percent of Total Allocations)		
	1970–72	1979–81	2009	1970–72	1979–81	2009
High-Income Countries: OECD	6,818	7,956	114,905	73.8	66.2	62.9
Japan	377	514	11,393	4.1	4.3	6.2
Excluding Japan	6,441	7,442	103,512	69.8	61.9	56.7
United States	2,294	2,606	30,416	24.8	21.7	16.7
High-Income Countries: Non-OECD	41	363	10,797	0.4	3.0	5.9
Gulf Countries	1	286	8,835	0.0	2.4	4.8
Excluding Gulf Countries	40	77	1,962	0.4	0.6	1.1
Middle-Income Countries	2,144	3,359	53,347	23.2	28.0	29.2
China	0	237	6,753	0.0	2.0	3.7
Excluding China	2,144	3,122	46,594	23.2	26.0	25.5
Low-Income Countries	230	338	3,604	2.5	2.8	2.0
Total Allocation	9,234	12,016	182,653	100.0	100.0	100.0

Source: IMF International Financial Statistics database.

Note: OECD = Organisation for Economic Co-operation and Development; SDR = Special Drawing Right.

contrast, low-income countries have seen their share reduced from already marginal levels.

SDRs are defined by the IMF as an "international reserve asset."[9] However, under the current rules, countries pay interest on allocations of SDRs and receive interest on holdings. In this sense, SDRs are both an asset and a liability. Moreover, since countries that use them make net interest payments to the IMF, they should also be considered as a credit line that can be used unconditionally by the holder, that is, an unconditional overdraft facility. However, the fact that all central banks accept SDRs makes them effectively an international reserve currency. Use of SDR allocations is widespread and works rather smoothly; developing countries use them frequently, but they have also been used by industrialized countries at critical junctures (Erten and Ocampo 2014, Chapter 9).

Perhaps the most important and simplest reform would be to finance all IMF lending and conduct all IMF operations with SDRs, thus making global monetary creation similar to domestic money creation by central banks. This idea was suggested by the IMF economist Jacques Polak in 1979. According to his proposal, IMF lending during crises would create new SDRs, but these SDRs would be automatically destroyed once the loans were repaid. The alternative I have suggested would be to treat the countries' unused SDRs as deposits with (or lending to) the IMF that could then be used by the institution to lend to other countries in need (Ocampo 2010b). Either of these proposals would involve eliminating the distinction between the IMF's General Resources and SDR accounts (which are offshoots of the debates of the 1960s) and make SDRs a relatively limited instrument of global monetary cooperation (Polak 2005, part II).

---

[9]See, for example, http://www.imf.org/external/np/exr/facts/sdr.htm.

Using SDRs to finance IMF programs would also help correct the significant lags in increasing the size of the Fund in relation to that of the world economy, and especially in relation to the size of international capital flows (IMF 2010). An additional problem is that despite the agreed-upon reallocation of quotas in 2006 and 2010, the existing quotas do not reflect various countries' shares of the world economy today. The underrepresentation of developing countries in the quota allocation increases the inequities associated with the fact that the largest demand for reserves comes from the developing world.

These inequities mean that efforts to reform quota allocations must continue. The inequities can be partially corrected with a mix of two types of reforms. The first is an asymmetric issuance of SDRs, in which all or a larger proportion of allocations would be given to countries with the highest demand for reserves; essentially, developing countries. One simple formula proposed by John Williamson (2010) is to give 80 percent of allocations to emerging market and developing economies and 20 percent to industrial countries, with allocations within each group determined according to IMF quotas. The second kind of reform would be to create a "development link" in SDR allocations. In this approach, the IMF could employ SDRs that are not used by member states to provide development financing or, better yet, leverage development financing by, for example, allowing unused SDRs to be used to buy bonds from multilateral development banks or institutions that contribute to the provision of global public goods, such as climate change mitigation and adaptation (UN 2009).[10]

Reforms such as this would go a long way to correct some major problems of the current system, particularly the Triffin dilemma and the inequity bias, but they would not solve the asymmetric adjustment bias. This problem could be partly solved by two further complementary reforms: (1) the creation of at least a moderate version of Keynes's overdraft facility,[11] and (2) withdrawing allocations of SDRs to countries with excessive reserves, using a definition of "excessive" that takes into account the high demand for reserves by emerging market and developing economies.

As noted earlier, SDRs should also be used to create a substitution account similar to that proposed in the debates of the late 1970s, which would allow countries to transform their dollar reserves (or those denominated in other currencies) for SDR-denominated assets issued by the IMF).[12] This instrument

---

[10]There is also the possibility of using the allocations to industrial countries to directly finance additional official development assistance and the provision of global public goods (Stiglitz 2006, Chapter 9). In the same line of reasoning, former IMF managing director Dominique Strauss-Kahn raised during his tenure the possibility of using them to finance programs to combat climate change. These proposals have many virtues but pose the problem that such transfers are fiscal in character and may thus require in every case approval by national parliaments.

[11]As already indicated, a possible interpretation is that SDRs, as currently designed, are in fact such a facility (Erten and Ocampo 2014, Chapter 9).

[12]*Financial Times*, December 11, 2007. "How to Solve the Problem of the Dollar," http://www.iie.com/publications/opeds/oped.cfm?ResearchID=854.

would provide stability to the current system and, as already pointed out, might prove essential to manage some of the instabilities generated by the multicurrency arrangements. It would also be a transition mechanism for an ambitious reform effort (Kenen 2010b). Of course, it would be essential to negotiate how to distribute the potential costs of this mechanism. The literature contains conflicting estimates of the costs if a substitution account had been adopted in the past: Kenen (2010a) provides a positive view, while McCauley and Schenk (2014) provide a negative view.

The reform could also add more currencies to the SDR basket, as was already done with the renminbi in 2016, and could allow the broader use of SDRs in private transactions (as, for example, suggested by Kenen 1983; Eichengreen 2007; and Padoa-Schioppa 2011). One simple reform could be to allow deposits by financial institutions in central banks (either reserve requirements or excess reserves) to be held in SDRs. However, the system could also work if SDRs are used only as a reserve asset and a means of financing IMF lending, as long as central banks fulfill the basic commitment to convert SDRs into convertible currencies when needed, which is what makes SDRs an effective monetary instrument for transactions among central banks. Allowing the broader use of SDRs would make the reform costly for the United States and therefore is likely to elicit resistance, which could make SDRs subject to the instability that characterizes private markets. In any case, it might be necessary to embed the reforms in rules that make holding SDRs attractive for central banks (an adequate return) or other rules that guarantee an active demand for SDRs: for example, commitments to not reduce SDRs held by individual central banks below certain limits relative to the allocations they have received (obviously if they are not borrowing from the IMF).

CONCLUSIONS

The most desirable reform of the current global reserve system involves moving to a fully SDR-based IMF with a clear countercyclical focus. This would include countercyclical *allocations* of SDRs and countercyclical IMF *financing* entirely in SDRs. In the former case, it could include criteria for SDR allocations that take into account the very different demand for reserves by emerging and developing countries relative to industrial countries. The use of SDRs to finance IMF programs would help consolidate the reforms of the credit lines that were introduced during the North Atlantic financial crisis, particularly the creation of contingency credit lines and the much larger levels of financing relative to quotas. The introduction of a substitution account by which central banks could exchange SDRs for the reserves in currencies they no longer wish to hold would make SDRs a complement to the multicurrency arrangement that may be emerging; this approach could make the reforms more attractive to the United States. A combination of reforms is probably the best practical option for a stable international monetary system.

REFERENCES

Akyüz, Yilmaz. 2005. *Reforming the IMF: Back to the Drawing Board.* Global Economy Series, No. 7. Penang, Malaysia: Third World Network.

Camdessus, Michel. 2000. "An Agenda for the IMF at the Start of the 21st Century." Remarks at the Council on Foreign Relations, New York, February 1.

Eichengreen, Barry. 2007. *Global Imbalances and the Lessons of Bretton Woods.* Cambridge, MA: MIT Press.

———. 2008. *Globalizing Capital: A History of the International Monetary System.* 2nd ed. Princeton, NJ: Princeton University Press.

———. 2011. *Exorbitant Privilege: The Rise and Fall of the Dollar and the Future of the International Monetary System.* New York: Oxford University Press.

Erten, Bilge, and José Antonio Ocampo. 2014. "Building a Stable and Equitable Global Monetary System." In *Alternative Development Strategies for the Post-2015 Era,* edited by José Antonio Alonso, Giovanni Andrea Cornia, and Rob Vos, Chapter 9. United Nations Series on Development. New York: Bloomsbury.

Frankel, Jeffrey, and George Saravelos. 2010. "Are Leading Indicators of Financial Crises Useful for Assessing Country Vulnerability? Evidence from the 2008–2009 Global Crisis." NBER Working Paper 16047, National Bureau of Economic Research, Cambridge, MA.

Gallagher, Kevin, José Antonio Ocampo, Ming Zhang. and Yu Yongding, eds. 2014. *Capital Account Liberalization in China: The Need for a Balanced Approach.* Boston: Pardee Center, Boston University.

Greenwald, Bruce, and Joseph E. Stiglitz. 2010. "A Modest Proposal for International Financial Reform." In *Time for a Visible Hand: Lessons from the 2008 World Financial Crisis,* edited by Stephany Griffith-Jones, José Antonio Ocampo, and Joseph E. Stiglitz. New York: Oxford University Press.

International Monetary Fund (IMF). 2010. "Fourteenth General Review of Quotas: The Size of the Fund: Initial Considerations." International Monetary Fund, Washington, DC, March 12.

Kenen, Peter B. 1983. "Use of SDR to Supplement or Substitute for Other Means of Finance." In *International Money and Credit: The Policy Roles,* edited by G. M. von Furstenberg, Chapter 7. Washington, DC: International Monetary Fund.

———. 2010a. "Reforming the Global Reserve Regime: The Role of a Substitution Account." *International Finance* 13 (1): 1–23.

———. 2010b. "An SDR-based Reserve System." *Journal of Globalization and Development* 1 (2): Article 13.

Keynes, John M. 1942–43. "The Keynes Plan." Reproduced in *The International Monetary Fund 1945–1965: Twenty Years of International Monetary Cooperation* (1969, vol. III, 3–36), edited by J. Keith Horsefield. Washington, DC: International Monetary Fund.

Llaudes, Ricardo, Ferhan Salman, and Mali Chivakul. 2010. "The Impact of the Great Recession on Emerging Markets." Working Paper 10/237, International Monetary Fund, Washington, DC.

McCauley, Robert N., and Catherine R. Schenk. 2014. "Reforming the International Monetary System in the 1970s: Would an SDR Substitution Account Have Worked?" Working Paper 444, Bank for International Settlements, Basel, Switzerland, March.

Ocampo, José Antonio. 2002. "Recasting the International Financial Agenda." In *International Capital Markets: Systems in Transition,* edited by John Eatwell and Lance Taylor, 41–73. New York: Oxford University Press.

———. 2010a. "Reforming the International Monetary System." 14th Annual Lecture, United Nations University World Institute for Development Economics Research (UNU-WIDER), Helsinki, Finland, December 9.

———. 2010b. "Reforming the Global Reserve System." In *Time for a Visible Hand: Lessons from the 2008 World Financial Crisis,* edited by Stephany Griffith-Jones, José Antonio Ocampo, and Joseph E. Stiglitz, Chapter 16. New York: Oxford University Press.

————. 2010c. "Special Drawing Rights and the Reform of the Global Reserve System." In *Reforming the International Financial System for Development*, edited by Jomo Kwame Sundaram, Chapter 13. New York: Columbia University Press.

Padoa-Schioppa, Tomasso. 2011. "The Ghost of Bancor: The Economic Crisis and Global Monetary Disorder." In *Reform of the International Monetary System: The Palais Royal Initiative,* edited by Jack T. Boorman and André Icard, Chapter 6. New Delhi, India: SAGE Publications.

Palais Royal Initiative. 2011. "Reform of the International Monetary System: A Cooperative Approach for the 21st Century." In *Reform of the International Monetary System: The Palais Royal Initiative,* edited by Jack T. Boorman and André Icard, 7–26. New Delhi, India: SAGE Publications.

Polak, Jacques J. 1979. "Thoughts on an International Monetary Fund Based Fully on SDR." Pamphlet Series 28, International Monetary Fund, Washington, DC.

————. 2005. *Economic Theory and Financial Policy: Selected Essays of Jacques J. Polak 1994–2004*, edited by James M. Boughton. Armonk, New York: M.E. Sharpe.

Solomon, Robert. 1982. *The International Monetary System 1945–1981.* New York: Harper & Row.

Stiglitz, Joseph E. 2006. *Making Globalization Work.* New York: W.W. Norton.

Triffin, Robert. 1961. *Gold and the Dollar Crisis.* Revised ed. New Haven, CT: Yale University Press.

————. 1968. *Our International Monetary System: Yesterday, Today and Tomorrow,* New York: Random House.

United Nations (UN). 1999. "Towards a New International Financial Architecture." Report of the Task Force of the Executive Committee on Economic and Social Affairs of the United Nations. New York, January 21.

————. 2009. Report of the Commission of Experts of the President of the UN General Assembly on Reforms of the International Monetary and Financial System (Stiglitz Commission). New York, September. http://www.un.org/ga/econcrisissummit/docs/FinalReport_CoE.pdf.

Williamson, John. 2010. "The Future of the Reserve System." *Journal of Globalization and Development* 1 (2): Article 15.

Yu, Yongding. 2014. "How Far Can Renminbi Internationalization Go?" Working Paper No. 461, Asian Development Bank Institute, Tokyo, February.

Zhou, Xiaochuan. 2009. "Reform the International Monetary System." People's Bank of China, Beijing. http://www.pbc.gov.cn/english//detail.asp?col=6500&ID=178.

CHAPTER 15

Macroeconomic Policy: What and How to Coordinate Internationally

ALEXANDER K. SWOBODA

In an IMF blog post, Olivier Blanchard, Jonathan Ostry, and Atish Ghosh (2013) compare international policy coordination to the Loch Ness monster: much discussed but rarely seen. In view of its potential benefits—theoretical, real, or envisaged—why is the international coordination of macroeconomic policies so rarely practiced, and what can be done to improve the process?

Game theory provides one set of answers, and political considerations provide another. Historical attempts to coordinate, as well as missed opportunities to do so, help explain why macroeconomic policy coordination is so rare. These instances also provide an insight into the requirements for effective policy coordination and the role of coordinating mechanisms. For example, the exchange rate regime plays a major role in the coordination of monetary policies. When monetary policy is burdened with too many tasks, exchange rate regimes tend to become unstable, and currency wars threaten. These issues are taken up in turn in this chapter.

POLICY COORDINATION IN THEORY

As discussed in Chapter 12 of this volume, the standard analytical case for policy coordination is simple: if all the objectives of policymakers cannot be satisfied simultaneously, they will have to trade off the achievement of at least one objective with that of at least one other. In a Pareto analysis, to do so efficiently (to be on the contract curve), it must be impossible in equilibrium to gain in terms of one objective without losing in terms of another. Policy coordination should make it possible to reach such an efficient outcome. But if coordination in principle can lead to a welfare gain, why is there so little of it in practice? One answer, from a game theory perspective, is that the incentives policymakers face resemble the payoffs of a prisoner's dilemma. The best uncoordinated strategies from each player's perspective will typically lead to a Nash equilibrium—an inefficient outcome off the contract curve—even though coordination of policies would make it possible to reap the gains from moving from this inefficient point to a cooperative Pareto-efficient equilibrium.

An example from Meyer and others (2002) illustrates the prisoner's dilemma well in an international context.[1] Suppose that two identical countries, A and B, are hit by a symmetric negative productivity shock that increases inflation above target in both countries. The central bank in each country wants to tighten monetary policy, but—assuming floating exchange rates—when A tightens, its currency appreciates, putting further inflationary pressure on B and reducing the latter's welfare. B in turn will want to tighten more than it otherwise would have, producing an additional negative spillover. The result is a Nash equilibrium, in which both countries end up with excessively tight monetary policy.

Why do we end up in a prisoner's dilemma? The information conditions and commitment mechanisms required in a game theory perspective to lead to the cooperative Pareto-efficient solution are unlikely to be met in practice. Information asymmetries, disagreements about the true model of the economy, and the absence of credible commitment mechanisms all contribute. Ostry and Ghosh (2013) provide a lucid assessment of such obstacles in the context of international policy coordination. Among the many possible reasons for the episodic nature of policy coordination exercises, they emphasize three: disagreement about the cross-border transmission effects of policies and about the prevailing economic situation; policymakers' lack of recognition of trade-offs across objectives (single-target-mindedness); and lack of incentives for large countries, as the gains from coordination (like the gains from trade) are likely to be greater for smaller countries.

TWO MISSED OPPORTUNITIES FOR COORDINATION

Still, one may wonder why, in "obvious" cases, more coordination did not take place. Consider, for instance, the mid-1980s. The focus of coordination efforts within the Group of Seven (G7) was to reduce current account imbalances—the deficit of the United States and the surpluses of Germany and Japan, among others—while maintaining or reestablishing internal balance in the coordinating countries. These efforts culminated in the Plaza Agreement of 1985 and the Louvre Accord of 1987, in which participating countries pledged to undertake a number of macroeconomic and structural policies to bring about the desired outcome (Meyer and others 2002). Major countries—notably France, Germany, Japan, and the United States—pledged to undertake specific fiscal and monetary measures, structural reforms of various types, and commitments to resist protectionist measures.

An important element of both agreements was the exchange rate: Plaza called for a depreciation of the US dollar vis-à-vis the currencies of its main trading partners; the Louvre Accord sought to stabilize the dollar close to the depreciated level it had reached at the beginning of 1987. These currency movements were

---

[1]Meyer and others (2002) provide a very good survey of the theoretical literature on international macroeconomic policy coordination and its practical relevance.

deemed necessary to bring the market exchange rate toward the equilibrium level consistent with the various measures to which parties to the agreements had committed themselves and to rebalance their current accounts. Concerted intervention and talking the US dollar down or up were among the means to ensure that outcome.

Reaching these agreements was in one sense a no-brainer. The obvious way to reduce the current account imbalances was to reduce domestic demand in the United States and increase it in the surplus countries, with fiscal policies as the instrument of choice. At the same time, the increased net exports of the United States would have helped maintain full employment there, while increased domestic demand would have substituted for diminished net exports in the surplus countries. Thus, the international coordination effort called for measures that were in the narrow national interests of the countries themselves. Indeed, there were national pressures for adoption of some of those policies quite independent of international considerations. In addition, at least formally, there was no shortage of potential instruments to reach the desired targets; there was apparently no prisoner's dilemma or difficult international trade-off.[2]

Although the agreements were reached, they were only partly honored. The fiscal measures, in particular, were mostly not honored. As Meyer and others (2002) indicate, the monetary commitments were fulfilled for a short while, but the "fiscal commitments largely were not achieved, particularly French promises to reduce taxes, Japanese promises on fiscal stimulus, and US pledges on deficit reduction" (20).

Another example, in similar circumstances, of a missed policy coordination opportunity occurred in the mid-2000s. Imbalances, particularly in the current accounts of East Asia (mainly China), Europe, and the United States were again an overriding concern. The situation required the United States to reduce its budget deficit or to take structural fiscal measures to raise national saving relative to investment, and for China to increase consumption to raise domestic expenditure relative to output. These measures would have had to be taken simultaneously to stabilize world aggregate demand and help maintain internal balance in both countries. As for Europe, it needed to make its output more responsive to aggregate demand changes through structural (particularly labor market) reforms. Turning to exchange rate implications, the floating rate policies of the euro area and the United States freed their monetary policies to deal with internal balance concerns, while the renminbi needed to appreciate in real terms in tandem with the reduction of China's current account surplus. How that real appreciation would occur—whether through nominal appreciation or domestic inflation—depended on China's choice of an exchange rate regime.

The following questions are relevant: Why was this policy package not adopted, even though it reflected a broad consensus among economists (except for the

---

[2]For a general analysis of international macroeconomic policy coordination and an application to the mid-1980s, see Genberg and Swoboda 1991.

issue of renminbi appreciation) and even though the proposed policies would have been in the national interest of the countries concerned?[3] Why were the measures agreed to under the Plaza Agreement and the Louvre Accord for the most part not carried through?

A primary issue concerns the nature of the policies that are to be coordinated: monetary, fiscal (both level and structure), macroprudential, debt management, and structural (supply side). First, as economists, we tend to devise packages that assume or propose specific and significant changes in taxes, government spending, or interest rates. But these changes would have to take place at the center of national political processes that make them extremely difficult to implement (except perhaps monetary policy, about which more later). Second, prevailing uncertainty and doubts about the nature of the relevant model of the economy or of the size (and sometimes even the sign) of the impact of some policies (for example, fiscal) make it difficult to reach an agreement on policy packages or on the specific quantitative adjustment required of individual national policies. Third, there is the first mover or collective action problem: in the cases mentioned above, for example, achieving the desired current account rebalancing while maintaining output and employment requires that all players move simultaneously.

INSTRUMENTS, TARGETS, ASSIGNMENTS, AND SOME IMPLICATIONS

In addition to the game theory perspective, some practical lessons for policy coordination can be drawn from the targets and instruments approach.[4] The first basic element of that approach that is relevant here is the Tinbergen principle: if you want to reach n independent targets of policy simultaneously, you need n independent policy instruments. The second relevant basic element is Mundell's principle of effective market classification, which suggests that the instruments be assigned to the targets according to their comparative advantage to ensure convergence rather than (possibly explosive) divergence of the targeted variables from their target value.[5] These considerations, as well as some of the preceding arguments, help motivate the following six principles for effective international policy coordination:

1. Try to free some instruments that are constrained for political or other reasons, so they can be applied to their main economic goals. This is valid at both the national and international levels. Inability to coordinate policies at the national level—be it failure to free instruments, failure to reach an efficient internal trade-off, or any other reason—explains part of the difficulty of international policy coordination. How can a credible commitment to change domestic

---

[3]For a detailed analysis of this case, see Swoboda 2007.

[4]Meade 1951, Tinbergen 1952, and Mundell 1962 are the prominent early authors who applied this approach.

[5]See Mundell 1962 and Mundell 1968, Chapter 14.

policies be made for the sake of international coordination if coordination between different domestic policies (for example, monetary and fiscal) is not achieved at the national level? Several studies indicate that the welfare gains from moving from inefficient domestic Nash equilibria to an "international Nash equilibrium" may significantly outweigh those to be reaped from moving to the international cooperative equilibrium. And there would be additional (just as significant) gains from moving from historical domestic equilibria to the domestic Nash equilibria.[6] That said, international pressure or constraints are sometimes used by governments to free the instruments needed to achieve internal goals and secure a better domestic outcome.

2. In a decentralized or uncertain policy setting, the instruments used to achieve the target matter. That is the point of Mundell's assignment (or effective market classification) principle of pairing instruments with targets in a way that will ensure convergence toward those targets. This leads to Mundell's proposal that under fixed exchange rates, monetary policy should be assigned to maintain balance of payments equilibrium (to maintain exchange rate parity) and fiscal policy assigned to maintain internal balance. Under flexible exchange rates, monetary policy and fiscal policy can both be used for internal balance. Alternatively, Genberg and Swoboda (1991) point out that, under flexible exchange rates, if the current account is a policy target, the stable assignment is to use fiscal policy to achieve this target while monetary policy should be aimed at internal balance. The point here is that in a dynamic setting in which each instrument is adjusted in response to the discrepancy between the actual and the desired value of a specific target variable, it is crucial to assign instruments to targets in a way that allows the economic system to converge on its desired state rather than to move away from it. For instance, under floating rates, trying to achieve a particular current account position through monetary policy's impact on the exchange rate while aiming fiscal policy at the internal balance is likely to be destabilizing.

3. It is more important to move instruments in the right direction (the direction suggested by the assignment principles) than to change them by the estimated amount required to attain the final equilibrium. This follows from the preceding point, from Brainard 1967 on the optimal approach to targets under uncertainty, and from standard arguments concerning fine tuning and the various lags in the transmission of policy.

4. Policy actions should be stated in terms of available policy instruments and not in terms of endogenous variables. Policy commitments are all too often expressed in terms of reaching particular values or ranges of endogenous variables, such as real exchange rates, rather than in terms of the actual instruments that will be used to reach the target.

---

[6]See Meyer and others 2002 for references to some of these studies.

5. Focus coordination on target variables that are relevant in terms of welfare (for example, growth, inflation, and unemployment) rather than on intermediate targets, such as current account balances or real exchange rates.

6. Keep it simple. Pursuing too many independent goals makes a shortage of instruments almost a certainty. Proposing too many measures at the same time dilutes accountability. The motto here is "focus on essentials."

COORDINATING MECHANISMS

In addition to respecting certain principles, effective coordination requires a mechanism if the goal is to move toward a more cooperative system. Mechanisms can be discretionary (as, for instance, the G7 or G20 efforts) or based on rules (like the World Trade Organization's most favored nation clause). The mechanism can be centralized (for example, delegated to an international agency or enforced by a hegemon) or decentralized (for example, the market as an information aggregator and sanction mechanism). Fixed exchange rates under the Bretton Woods system can be considered a coordinating mechanism, with the United States as the nth country playing the dominant role in setting the overall monetary/macroeconomic tone in the world economy. Under floating exchange rates, attempts at macroeconomic coordination have been mostly discretionary and have taken place under the aegis of the various G-groups or under the umbrella of government organizations such as the Organisation for Economic Co-operation and Development and, principally, the IMF.

Various suggestions have been made to strengthen and add to the available coordinating mechanisms, both in discretionary and rule-based fashions. For instance, for the discretionary approach, Ostry and Ghosh (2013) emphasize the role of a "neutral assessor" in "helping to bridge the divergent views of national policymakers—with the key requirement that the assessor be perceived as impartial in its assessment" (6). The idea is that this assessor should be able to provide a neutral best estimate of various channels of transmission of policy, identify alternative policy strategies, and evaluate the costs and benefits of the options, thus providing assessments on the basis of which participants in the exercise can agree on policy packages that result in net welfare gains for all. The IMF is obviously best suited to play this role in the present context, even if the participants in the coordination exercise are a subset of the membership, such as the G20 countries. Identifying an assessor seems to be a most important first step in improving the odds for successful coordination; to be credible, the assessor must be able to tell the truth ruthlessly and relentlessly.

In addition to discretionary modes of coordination, some rules of behavior apply across the board and obviate or supplement the need for emergency coordination or for specific agreements among the Group of Three (G3) or others. Such rules should ensure that the system as a whole has self-stabilizing properties and does not generate excessive negative spillovers. For instance, one rule of behavior for a system of fixed exchange rates to function properly and for payments adjustment to take place is that participating countries may not completely sterilize reserve flows. Simple rules of behavior are more difficult to formulate when currencies are floating, though the assignment rules mentioned previously are a possible example. Another example is safeguards to limit negative spillovers or "guideposts for conduct in the international monetary system" that constitute Ostry and Ghosh's (2013) second set of proposals. They suggest two such guideposts: one for the current account, the other for the capital account.

To control for negative spillovers through the current account, their first guidepost "would seek to prevent currency misalignments—the notion being that policy agendas need to add up to a multilaterally consistent whole with multilaterally desirable external balances and exchange rates" (26). This proposal is not without its dangers. It threatens to violate the fourth and fifth principles listed above; namely, do not treat an endogenous variable as an instrument and choose a variable directly relevant for welfare as your target. One can certainly agree that estimates of discrepancies between current and equilibrium real exchange rates based on some vision of target current accounts (as in the IMF's External Balance Assessment approach) are useful indicators of policy inconsistencies and misalignments—but this does not provide guideposts for appropriate conduct in any systematic way. Rather it could be a useful tool for the independent and neutral assessor.

The second guidepost Ostry and Ghosh propose "is the mirror of the first, centering on financial flows instead of trade" (2013, 26). To moderate boom and bust cycles associated with capital flows, macroprudential and capital control measures could be useful at the country level, but as the capital exports of one country are another's capital imports, some international coordination of such measures would seem appropriate. And some dos and don'ts would be useful. In this context, a few proposals exist to coordinate monetary policies to avoid large capital flows and their attendant exchange rate fluctuations (see the next section).

MONETARY POLICY COORDINATION AND CURRENCY WARS

Calls for the coordination of national monetary policies—notably to avoid currency wars—contain a deep irony. One of the main points of the adoption of floating exchange rates is to free monetary policy for domestic purposes. The Bretton Woods system broke down in large part because countries were not willing or not able to "coordinate" their monetary policies, that is, to pursue monetary policies consistent with the maintenance of fixed exchange rates. Thus, floating exchange rates were expected to obviate the need to coordinate monetary policies and make the pursuit of monetary independence possible. There are at least two reasons why this does not work.

First, money is not neutral, at least not in the short run. Nonneutrality of money implies spillovers from national monetary policy to domestic output, the real exchange rate, the current account, foreign income, and real interest rates in the short run.[7] Those spillovers could, in an ideal world, be taken care of by other policies (fiscal, structural, and so on), leaving each country free to concentrate its monetary policy on a single target, as in price level or inflation targeting. However, in the real world, such policies are not available, for political or other reasons.

Second, national monetary policy is increasingly being asked to pursue multiple objectives (for example, employment, growth, and financial stability), as well as to target the exchange rate and the current account, even where price stability is its main stated objective. This overburdening of monetary policy is bound to produce policy conflicts (and perhaps central banker schizophrenia) within and across borders. One consequence is that very little is being done, or can effectively be done, to mitigate the spillovers from divergent (conventional or unconventional) monetary policies, resulting in excessively volatile capital flows and currency wars.

This suggests a final question: Why is the international coordination of monetary policies so much more difficult than cooperation in trade through the World Trade Organization or cooperation in financial regulation through, among others, the Bank for International Settlements and the Financial Stability Board? I believe it is precisely because of the inability or unwillingness to coordinate policy instruments other than monetary policies: as a consequence, monetary policies cannot be freely devoted to domestic price stability goals, as should be the case under flexible exchange rates. It is the very nature of macroeconomic policies that makes them so difficult to coordinate, nationally but even more so internationally. For example, national fiscal instruments—at the center of national political processes—are not easily moved for purely economic reasons, and are the subject of substantial inertia. We are coming back full circle to the importance of the coordination of fiscal policies for the stability of the international monetary and financial system. Perhaps the saying that IMF stands for "It's mainly fiscal" is worth remembering—not only in national settings but also in the context of international macroeconomic policy coordination.

REFERENCES

Blanchard, O., J. Ostry, and A. Ghosh. 2013. "International Policy Coordination: The Loch Ness Monster." iMFdirect–The IMF Blog, December 15. https://blog-imfdirect.imf .org/2013/12/15/international-policy-coordination-the-loch-ness-monster/.

Brainard, W. 1967. "Uncertainty and the Effectiveness of Policy." *American Economic Review Papers and Proceedings* 57 (2): 411–25.

Genberg, H., and A. Swoboda. 1991. "The Current Account and the Policy Mix under Flexible Exchange Rates." In *International Financial Policy: Essays in Honor of Jacques J. Polak,* edited by J. A. Frenkel and M. Goldstein, 420–54. Washington, DC: International Monetary Fund.

---

[7]These spillovers tend to be stronger the more integrated the world economy, the more differentiated national policies, and the greater the concentration of output and wealth in a few countries.

Meade, J. 1951. *The Balance of Payments: The Theory of International Economic Policy I*. Oxford, U.K.: Oxford University Press.

Meyer, L., B. M. Doyle, J. E. Gagnon, and D. W. Henderson. 2002. "International Coordination of Macroeconomic Policies: Still Alive in the New Millennium?" International Finance Discussion Paper 723, Board of Governors of the Federal Reserve System, Washington, DC, April.

Mundell, R. A. 1962. "The Appropriate Use of Monetary and Fiscal Policy under Fixed Exchange Rates." *IMF Staff Papers* 9 (1): 70–79.

———. 1968. *International Economics*. New York: Macmillan.

Ostry, J. D., and A. Ghosh. 2013. "Obstacles to International Policy Coordination, and How to Overcome Them." Staff Discussion Note 13/11, International Monetary Fund, Washington, DC.

Swoboda, A. K. 2007. "International Monetary and Financial Architecture in an Integrating World Economy." In *The Swiss National Bank, 1907–2007*, 781–814. Zürich, Switzerland: Neue Zürcher Zeitung Publishing.

Tinbergen, J. 1952. *On the Theory of Economic Policy*. Amsterdam: North-Holland.

CHAPTER 16

Toward a More Cooperative International Monetary System: Some Remarks

PAUL A. VOLCKER

When I saw the impressive poster for this symposium—"From Great Depression to Great Recession: The Elusive Quest for International Policy Cooperation"—it occurred to me that I was probably the only participant who was alive during the Great Depression. Admittedly I was a bit young, and I didn't have very well-conceived views on the monetary system back then. But by the time the IMF came along after World War II, I was an adult and aware of what was going on. What characterized that period was a rule book, a limited but quite precise rule book: you maintained a fixed exchange rate, and you only changed the parity if your balance of payments was in "fundamental disequilibrium," which was hard to ascertain, but it sounded good as a principle. The other rules were that countries should not devalue to gain competitive advantage, and they should not restrict current account transactions. Initially, there seemed to be a lot of promise to those rules, but in reality the Bretton Woods system came into effect only in the late 1950s, and by the late 1960s it was breaking down. It is fair to say that in the 45 years since then, the IMF has not been able to write a new rulebook and get agreement on it. Perhaps the symposium should have been called "From Great Depression to Great Recession: The Elusive Quest for a New Rulebook."

What is interesting is that there has been much more adherence to the rulebook in the trade field. We monetary economists always thought that trade was on a lower level of intellectual interest and imagination, but trade policies have been better than monetary policies at following the rules. The IMF has become sort of a firehouse—a very fancy firehouse, but a firehouse nonetheless. You call upon it when there is an emergency, and it has been very convenient to call upon.

When it comes to giving policy advice and encouraging policy coordination, the IMF has not been a great success. And I can give you some insights into the reasons why. I used to have some responsibility in the United States government, and when the IMF was telling other governments what to do, I often had some sympathy for what it was saying. When it was telling me what to do, I would respond, "I know more about the United States than you do. I know more about what I can do, and what is politically possible, and what is not possible. Go away." Of course, the United States is in a better position to say that than some other countries, but I think it is inherently difficult for an international organization—regardless of how well designed—to enforce discipline on sovereign countries that have their own problems, their own political constraints, and their own economic judgments.

Let me make a simple declaration: you are not going to get coordination by discretionary persuasion. You cannot expect an international organization to successfully impose its own judgment on countries unless they are desperate for help, in which case it can. (And that has been done constructively in many cases.) But you are not going to get coordination unless you have some known rules of the road to which there is some political commitment on the part of the member countries. What is needed, in my view, is to develop some simple, sensible rules that countries are willing to follow in today's highly complex—and ever more complex—evolving financial system.

Exacerbating the problems of the international monetary system are free financial markets, which are prone to excesses (even Adam Smith warned about this) that have become worse as a result of technological and other changes. The question is whether you can deal with these potential excesses before they become catastrophic. We had a problem in the United States with subprime mortgages, which went from nothing to a trillion and a half dollars in three years. That is a pretty big change—big enough to bring down the whole economy. The counterpart in the international sphere was the growing current account imbalances. The United States was running deficits of a size that it had never run before, fed (or matched) by surpluses in China and elsewhere. We loved borrowing all that money at 2 percent per year, and they loved lending it to us and exporting to us. It was all great—until it all came crashing down.

These excesses are happening all the time. I am told that at the onset of the global financial crisis, emerging market and developing countries had some $6 trillion of dollar-denominated debt. Today the figure is closer to $9 trillion. This is because you can borrow from the United States for nothing and lend it abroad to somebody in an emerging market for something, and something is better than nothing—until the borrower cannot pay it back. If the borrowers' currency goes down, they will have a hard time repaying. I don't know whether these countries will run into trouble, but it would be good to have someone—the IMF?—watching, and maybe doing something before it all explodes.

We spend a lot of time worrying about leverage in the banking system. Maybe the next problem will be in the so-called shadow banking system, or maybe in the corporate sector. Even as we speak, someone, somewhere is inventing ways to leverage themselves; the ability of people in the market to think up new financial wizardry is astonishing. As the financial system becomes more and more international, with ever larger cross-border capital flows, it becomes potentially more prone to excesses. National regulation can go some way to prevent these excesses, but the cross-border nature of the transactions means that, inevitably, there needs to be an international policy dimension to limit imbalances and address vulnerabilities.

One—though not the only—problem with trying to coordinate policies internationally is the strong and continuing disagreements about the impact of policies and their cross-border effects. That is why I believe we need some relatively simple rules. Let me suggest a few worth thinking about. One (described by Richard Cooper in Chapter 9) is based on large accumulation or decumulation of reserves, which would serve as a signal that at least some discussion is required. Another rule would be on exchange rates—not a formal, fixed exchange rate, but some reasonable margin of fluctuation beyond which international discussion and perhaps policy action would be triggered. A third possibility would be rules to better manage cross-border capital flows.

Formulating such rules is the essential challenge for the current generation of policymakers. We had a narrow escape with the global financial crisis, in which we avoided catastrophe by a lot of ad hoc measures. I do not know how long it will take to develop some rules or whether I will be around for it, but it is something that I would very much like to see in my lifetime—because I certainly hope never to see another Great Depression, or even another near miss.

CHAPTER 17

Toward a More Stable International Monetary System: Key Takeaways

Atish R. Ghosh and Mahvash S. Qureshi

As with previous crises, the global financial crisis has prompted greater calls for international policy cooperation and for enhancing the IMF's surveillance and lending roles to prevent and mitigate future crises. What does this imply in practice? This chapter summarizes the key takeaways from the lively discussions during the symposium on the impediments to international policy cooperation and on the IMF's role in helping to address some of the challenges.

INTERNATIONAL POLICY COOPERATION

International policy cooperation is very much like Nessie, the lovable Loch Ness monster: oft-discussed, seldom seen. The first question that arises in talking about cooperation is, what does it mean in an international policy context? The answer is not straightforward, because cooperation is an ill-defined concept that means different things to different people. At its most basic level, cooperation might simply mean explaining the logic of domestic policy actions to others. In this sense, policy cooperation has happened in the past and is on an upward trend—not least with central banks being more transparent domestically.[1]

Cooperation could also refer to the creation of multilateral institutions and arrangements. If so, we have made progress on that front as well. Examples include the provision of liquidity through central bank swap lines and IMF liquidity provision facilities set up after the global financial crisis.

However, if cooperation refers to setting, and following, some well-defined rules of the road, we have not done that since the breakdown of the Bretton

---

[1] An interesting historical example of cooperation at this basic level *not* happening is the Bank of Japan's continuing to purchase US dollars following the suspension of dollar convertibility in 1971. This was intended as a sign of solidarity with the United States but was interpreted by US officials as a deliberate attempt to keep down the value of the yen (Volcker and Gyohten 1992).

Woods system in the early 1970s. And the principles that we do have are generally too vague and too hobbled by conceptual disagreements to be of much practical use. For instance, we all agree that exchange rates should not stray too far from equilibrium values; but determining "equilibrium values" and how far is too far is, in practice, fraught with difficulties.

When economists refer to cooperation, they generally have the highest degree of cooperation in mind; that is, moving from the Nash to the coordinated equilibrium. This is a more ambitious—and arguably more useful—definition, but if that is the definition, then Nessie has indeed rarely been seen, with just a handful of sightings in the past 40 years: Bonn, Plaza, Louvre, and the Group of Twenty (G20) fiscal stimulus.

Analyzing these various facets of cooperation, some key insights emerge from historical experience:

- Constants in a changing world. The core challenges to the international monetary system—facilitating external adjustment, ensuring an equitable burden of adjustment between surplus and deficit countries, and regulating the supply of global liquidity—have been constant through the decades. But their importance has grown with increased financial integration, the growing volume of private capital flows, and the emergence of complex financial systems prone to excesses. Rising gross flows have also meant that deficit and capital-recipient (and surplus and capital-source) are not necessarily synonymous: capital-recipient countries may face payment difficulties when there are liability outflows (analogous to the adjustment difficulties of deficit countries), calling for shared responsibility between source and recipient countries in managing capital flows (analogous to the equitable burden of adjustment between surplus and deficit countries).

- Misaligned incentives. Countries act together when they are scared together; but step away from the abyss and the incentive to coordinate seems to melt away. Even central bank swap lines—often touted as a prime example of international cooperation—are seldom provided for purely altruistic reasons. Coordination is thus most likely to be possible when it involves countries moving policies in a direction that would be in their individual self-interest but whose benefit may be greater if they agree to act together. However, coordination is much harder when it requires governments to implement quite different policies from those they would have chosen on their own, policies that make sense only if all parties deliver on their respective commitments. (As a practical matter, it simplifies explaining the case for coordination domestically when coordination implies countries committing to the same policies or moving them in the same direction.) That is why the Group of 20 countries were able to coordinate their fiscal expansions during the global financial crisis and why it has been possible to reach agreement on financial sector regulation, such as the Basel agreements on financial stability. But other examples of coordination have been few and far between.

- Net *and* gross. Attempts at coordination are rare enough, but the few times that they have occurred have been when imbalances in net flows (and, therefore, exchange rate misalignments) have been apparent. But whether in the 1920s or in the 2000s, important vulnerabilities may be building up from gross positions long before the crisis, through cross-border bank flows and oversized banking systems. This implies that the gap between the desirable level of coordination and what actually takes place is even greater than we thought, because policymakers do not take much notice of problems with gross flows until they are manifested in net imbalances.

- Stretching the truth. Beyond genuine uncertainty, a major obstacle to coordination has often been deliberate disagreements about cross-border multipliers, with each party understating the negative spillovers of its policies and exaggerating the positive ones in order to shift the gains from coordination in its favor (Ghosh and Masson 1994; Ostry and Ghosh 2013). Unbiased analysis of domestic and cross-border effects of policies by a respected third party (a neutral assessor) might help build consensus and achieve more cooperative outcomes.

- Keeping it simple. Given the obstacles to coordination, simple rules of the road—indicators based on reserves accumulation or current account balances (specifying rules for the capital account would be trickier)—may be more effective than trying to achieve the theoretically optimal cooperative solution through tailor-made polices. In the financial sector, the Volcker Rule seeks to make deposit-taking institutions safer by prohibiting proprietary trading. Of course, as with any rules, there are many questions about how simple they should be and—especially in the sovereign context—how easily they can be enforced.

ENHANCING THE IMF'S ROLE

The IMF has played important—at times critical—roles in the international monetary system over the past 70 years. To meet current challenges, however, it may need to adapt further. Several possible actions and reforms merit consideration for (1) helping deficit (or capital-recipient) countries adjust without resorting to measures that are destructive to national or international prosperity; (2) promoting an equitable burden of adjustment between surplus and deficit countries, as well as a shared responsibility for management of capital flows between source and recipient countries; and (3) regulating global liquidity to foster noninflationary growth of world trade and incomes. These are discussed in turn below.

Helping Deficit (or Capital-Recipient) Countries Adjust

- Expand the global financial safety net. A basic question regarding the IMF's precautionary instruments, like the Flexible Credit Line (FCL), is whether these are intended to be permanent facilities in the sense that countries would renew them repeatedly—which would likely be required if they are to substitute for reserve accumulation—or only available during times of stress. In the former case, questions arise about the adequacy of the IMF's own resources, especially given the current practice of scoring commitments at 100 percent against its forward commitment capacity.[2] In the latter case, issues relate to the signal sent to markets when countries request an FCL or when there is ambiguity about why the arrangement was not renewed. A coordinated global financing mechanism, under which the IMF would automatically extend credit lines to eligible countries upon some event exogenous to the recipient countries, might address some of these issues (as well as the political stigma of requesting IMF support), while also saving on the aggregate use of IMF resources.

- Establish a sovereign debt restructuring mechanism. Collective actions clauses (CACs) are now more common, but recent legal decisions have thrown into question whether they suffice to ensure orderly restructurings. Whether the answer is an explicit sovereign debt restructuring body (as proposed by IMF's former first deputy managing director Anne Krueger in the early 2000s) or some other mechanism, this is potentially a live issue for sovereigns in advanced, emerging market, and developing countries alike. More generally, the international community needs to develop procedures to deal with situations in which clear-cut judgments about debt sustainability cannot be made and to ensure equitable burden sharing by and among private creditors that also minimizes the "value destruction" associated with debt default or restructuring.

- Sharpen policy advice on managing capital flows and exchange rate policy. Analytic work undertaken at the IMF over the past few years has recognized that regardless of any theoretical optimality, a free-floating exchange rate and full liberalization of the capital account (with no prudential or residency-based impediments to cross-border capital flows) may not to be optimal for many emerging market and developing countries. Still lacking, however, is guidance for policymakers who are coping with volatile capital flows on how the various elements of the policy response fit together: whether inflation targeters should intervene in foreign exchange markets and how to choose between prudential measures and capital controls. Given the volatility of capital flows, this is a salient issue for a large segment of the IMF membership.

---

[2]The switch to quota resources following the 2016 quota increase (under the Fourteenth General Review of Quotas) may give scope for scoring at less than 100 percent, with the New Arrangements to Borrow (NAB) as a backstop.

Promoting an Equitable Burden of Adjustment and Shared Responsibility

- Ensure evenhandedness in the assessment of exchange rate and monetary policies. Although IMF members have hard obligations regarding exchange rate policies (level of parity and intervention), no such obligations exist with respect to domestic policies, notably monetary and fiscal policies. Yet under a floating exchange rate, there is no meaningful distinction between monetary and exchange rate policies: inflation is the change of the price of the domestic money measured in terms of goods; currency depreciation is the change of the price of the domestic money measured in terms of the foreign currency. Although the issue has been brought to the fore in the context of unconventional monetary policies in advanced economies (with emerging markets questioning the difference between quantitative easing and foreign exchange intervention policies), there is a strong case for bringing greater evenhandedness in surveillance to exchange rate and monetary policies of all kinds. With regard to fiscal policy, while the cross-border spillovers are less direct, advice to surplus countries with ample fiscal space should be to avoid austerity or paying down public debt, thus easing the burden on deficit countries that have no choice but to adjust.

- Manage capital flows at both source and recipient country ends. The IMF's institutional view recognizes that management of capital flows may need to be a shared responsibility between source and recipient countries, but modalities for such cooperation need to be fleshed out and developed; for instance, "reciprocity," whereby home regulators impose the same macro-prudential regulations on their banks operating in foreign markets as the host regulator is imposing on its own banks. Since the global financial crisis, there may also be a need for fundamental rethinking of the role played by the financial sector within domestic economies and by global financial institutions in cross-border capital flows. This role may have become larger than is necessary, or healthy, for efficient intermediation of resources between savers and investors within or across national boundaries. Although *gross* capital flows are supposed to promote greater risk-sharing while *net* capital flows are supposed to promote intertemporal consumption-smoothing, this is not always the case. Moreover, as the experience of several small open economies has shown in recent years, oversized banking sectors can overwhelm the government's balance sheet in the event of a crisis, creating a feedback loop between sovereigns and banks that can amplify negative shocks.

Regulating Global Liquidity

- Provide global liquidity through regular Special Drawing Right (SDR) allocations. Expanding the private use of SDRs seems unrealistic, but there may be scope for greater regularity or automaticity (perhaps indexed to the growth in world trade or capital flows) in making SDR allocations, especially if there is the possibility of canceling SDRs or making the reconstitution requirement operational.[3] Greater use of designation (whereby member countries with sufficiently strong external positions are designated by the IMF to buy SDRs with freely usable currencies up to certain amounts from member countries with weak external positions) could also make a dent in surplus countries' reserve holdings.

Such measures would help strengthen the resilience and improve the functioning of the international monetary system. However, there will be occasions when at least the major economies need to coordinate policies—and take account of spillovers—more explicitly. The IMF could play an important role in this regard and foster greater international policy coordination by:

- Acting as a "neutral assessor" in identifying spillovers and scope for policy coordination. A major obstacle to negotiating macroeconomic policy coordination is (sometimes deliberate) disagreements about the model of the world economy and the signs and magnitude of cross-border spillovers. While countries may not always view the IMF as fully neutral, it is probably the only institution with sufficiently universal membership, analytical rigor, and relevant mandate to fulfill the role of neutral assessor.

- Formulating "rules of the road" to address spillovers through both the current and capital account. Rules exist on the conduct of exchange rate policies (namely, Article IV of the IMF's Articles of Agreement), but these rules are difficult to enforce. They should be extended to cover spillovers from domestic policies—monetary, fiscal, and financial measures—and to encompass both current and capital account transactions. Such rules would enhance the smooth functioning of the international monetary system in normal times, when episodic, explicit policy coordination is not required.

CONCLUSION

Where do we go from here? When it comes to the IMF, the experience of the past seven decades shows that the institution has adapted to meet the evolving needs of its member countries—and it can be hoped that the process will continue. The recent quota and governance reform will help strengthen the IMF's legitimacy in a changing global landscape and will boost its financial resources and credibility as an institution, and allow it to tackle the current challenges.

The goal of international policy cooperation faces formidable obstacles. Even within the national domain, cooperation between monetary and fiscal

---

[3] The IMF's SDR Department participants were subject to a "reconstitution requirement" before 1981 under which each participant was required to maintain its average daily holdings of SDRs at no less than a specified percentage of its net cumulative allocation over a five-year period ending each quarter. The initial specified percentage was 30, but it was reduced to 15 percent two years before the requirement was abrogated (IMF 2014).

authorities—not to mention the macroprudential regulator—is not always a straightforward task. Global cooperation in the spheres of international health and trade (now much more advanced than cooperation in macro policy, though still far from perfect) required decades of building both technical and political consensus. Rather than a piecemeal, episodic approach à la the Plaza or the Louvre, we need to be persistent in our efforts to build on existing institutions and modalities such as the Integrated Surveillance Decision (which allows the IMF to identify and propose Pareto-improving policies in response to spillovers) and multilateral surveillance products to help craft some simple rules of the road. Otherwise, we fear, it will be yet another case of "When all is said and done, more will have been said than done."

REFERENCES

Ghosh, A., and P. Masson. 1994. *Economic Cooperation in an Uncertain World*. Oxford, U.K.: Blackwell Press.

International Monetary Fund (IMF). 2014. *IMF Financial Operations 2014*. Washington, DC: IMF.

Ostry, J., and A. Ghosh. 2013. "International Policy Coordination." Staff Discussion Note 13/11, International Monetary Fund, Washington, DC.

Volcker, P., and T. Gyohten. 1992. *Changing Fortunes: The World's Money and the Threat to American Leadership*. New York: Times Books.

Index